SECOND LIFE

Published by Melbourne Books
Level 9, 100 Collins Street,
Melbourne, VIC 3000
Australia
www.melbournebooks.com.au
info@melbournebooks.com.au

Title: Second Life: A Story of Love, Loss and Hope
Author: David Hoysted
ISBN: 978-1-925556-88-9

A catalogue record for this
book is available from the
National Library of Australia

Front cover artwork, 'Lush Life'and
back cover artwork, 'untitled' by Nanette Hoysted

SECOND LIFE

A STORY OF LOVE, LOSS AND HOPE

DAVID HOYSTED

M
MELBOURNE BOOKS

PART
ONE

THE STROKE

Cherilyn rang. She and her husband Tam are long-term friends of mine. They live in Melbourne as I do now and they are in Albury on their way through to a week in Sydney. They are at the cemetery looking for Nanette's grave. I sent a map and the plot number to them and wondered if they'd found it.

I tell her to look to the top of the hill. There is a rotunda there next to a park bench where I often sit to eat my lunch when I visit.

'Can you see those Cherilyn?'

'Ah, yes I think I can now.'

'OK, Nan's plot is immediately to the right of the carpark. Just in front of the park bench.'

'Alright, what do you want us to say to her when we get there?' she asks.

I am a little surprised that Cherilyn asked such a touching and personal question. She's a scientist by trade and I didn't expect it.

'Tell her I love her, I constantly miss her, and I will be up to visit soon.' I hear Cherilyn in turn a little surprised by my response.

We say goodbye and only a few minutes later, Cherilyn texts: 'Found her. We told her how much you miss her.'

'Thank you so much!! It means a lot to know you're there with her,' I reply.

'Was important to us to visit her. Told her we miss her and the lovely dinners, but she is always with us through her art.'

'Thanks so much Cherilyn. I always love seeing her art at your place, and here at mine I'm surrounded by it.'

I sit in my lounge reflecting and the tears come. It's been two and a half years since she passed. Six years and three months since that first devastating stroke hit, changing both our lives forever. I've lost two Nanettes. Nanette number one: pre-stroke. The woman I loved and married. 'Love of my life, my wife, best friend and soul mate,' I concluded her eulogy with. Nanette number two: post-stroke. An innocent, childlike, beautiful blue-eyed angel who gave me some experience at being a father even though technically I am not. I still weep for both Nanettes now, but I am grateful to have had them both. My feelings are torn between which one I loved the most. It's a dead heat. Both Nanettes, but at different stages. Different in every way, even physically. But still the one.

I look to the corner of my room. To the arts and crafts table she found in a junk shop and on which the picture taken on Mother's Day 2014 sits. Only three months before the stroke. Those beautiful blue eyes shining. Dark hair to her shoulders. A cheeky half smile. Dimples in her cheeks. Her right hand raised holding her sunglasses. On her right wrist is the bracelet made of wooden beads. She was notoriously superstitious. Strange for someone so intelligent. She wore the bracelet so she was always touching wood, to withstand some lightning strike of fate. On her right ring finger, the Suzanne Felsen ring I bought her when travelling to America for work. She loved it. She's wearing a light blue scarf and jumper. The colour matches perfectly with her eyes. She looks well.

* * *

It is 25 August 2014, and before 6am. I make my way down the stairs, gathering my briefcase and overcoat. The taxi is outside waiting to take me to the airport. Nan sits at the top of the stairs in her dressing gown watching me leave, with Hester our Labrador just behind her.

'Look at Hester,' I say to Nan. She looks to be pulling a face, moving her eyes from side to side and raising her eyebrows alternately in a woebegone way. I think Hester is sad I'm heading off for another week. She is a sensitive dog. Nan knows what I mean and starts pulling the same face.

Nanette wanted me to retire and was unhappy when I took another contract in Melbourne, meaning I was away Monday to Friday, and back with her at our home in Albury on weekends. She was making the best of it though, coming down and spending every second week with me.

I wanted to work. I'd had a senior IT position and then lost it in my prime when the jobs were sent offshore to China. The company offered me a position in the U.S. – Chicago in fact. I was keen but Nan wouldn't go. She is close to her blind and widowed mother, and over the fourteen years since her father's death, has become her primary carer. They are best friends, and Nan wouldn't leave her. We had even been offered two properties together, one for Joan and one for us, but I couldn't get Nan and her mother to agree.

In the end, I took a redundancy package and left. I assumed I'd find alternative work and new opportunities to sink my teeth into. That was at the end of 2011.

I picked up an eight-month contract in Melbourne mid 2012–2013. It meant spending the weekdays away from Nan and weekends at home in Albury with her. I had hoped she would spend more time with me in Melbourne, but in the early days of that contract she didn't come down very much. I know she was disappointed that I chose to keep working and therefore keep travelling.

'I hope you know what you are doing,' she said a few weeks before this new contract began.

'What do you mean?' I asked.

'You and I get on better than any other couple that I know, we hate being away from each other, and … I don't think we will have that long.'

'What, is something wrong? Are you ill?'

'No.'

'Then why did you say that?'

She didn't answer satisfactorily. Mustn't have had anything more than an inkling, but it was concerning. She was a very intuitive person. Smart. Some people might say something like this to get attention. That wasn't Nan though. Only two weeks ago, she said she had a headache so severe she thought she was going to have a stroke. She had said things like this in the past, but not for some time.

'Do you need to go to the doctor, even for a check-up? Have your blood pressure taken?'

'No, I am absolutely fine. What's the point in having your blood pressure taken? It can be fine when you are in there and high when you leave.'

'I wish you would go to the doctor more often. I am concerned that if you had something seriously wrong with you, you wouldn't even go then.'

'I can assure you that if I thought there was something seriously wrong, I would go to the doctor.'

'Would you? Promise me on my life?'

'Yes, I promise you on your life!'

I wish I knew then what I know now about blood pressure. I would have sat her down and taken a reading. I don't know if it would have shown anything unusual nor whether I could have convinced her to act if it did. She could be stubbornly sure that she knew better. In this case she didn't.

I make my way to the door. She comes down the stairs, gives me a hug and kiss and I get into the taxi. The flight leaves on time and forty-five minutes later the SAAB is touching down at Tullamarine. I decide to ring Nan to let her know I've arrived. I had done so much flying over so many years, and she worried every time. She was a terrible flyer herself and was fearful I was going to drop out of the sky. I made around a hundred international trips, most of them very long haul, and there was nothing significant to report on other than the stress it gave my little wife, waiting every time for me to report in on arrival.

'I'm here,' I say when she answers the phone.

'Good, how was the flight?'

'It was smooth, no problem.' She mentions she is just getting dressed to walk the dog and would then start gardening.

'Ok, I'll call you later. Bye.'

'Have a good day. Bye,' she says.

I was employed to lead the merger of two Technical and Further Education Institutes (TAFEs). When I started, Nan had planned to come with me every second week, spending time at our apartment and amusing herself in Melbourne while I was at work. She had come down in weeks one and three, and this was week five. One of those earlier weeks coincided with her fifty-fourth birthday and we had dinner at Bacash, a highly rated fish restaurant near our apartment in South Yarra.

When it came time to plan this trip to Melbourne, she decided to stay home to garden and keep an eye on her mother Joan. I was disappointed because I was always happier when she was with me, but I decided not to rock the boat, still feeling a little guilty about working and leaving her alone for another week.

I have some meetings in Essendon for the afternoon so set out in the car for there, ringing Nan on the way.

'Hello there,' I say, 'How is the gardening?'

'I got a fair bit done this morning,' she replies. I notice she sounds tired and so I ask her if she has been overdoing it.

'Probably,' she says. After further comparing our mornings, we say goodbye and I drive on to Essendon. At the end of the day, I leave for our apartment in South Yarra. I stick to the freeways. Being from the country I hate city traffic jams and can't accept sitting still and going nowhere. It is approaching 6pm and as I drive towards home, I ring Nan again.

'I'm just about to sit down to my dinner,' she quickly says when she answers.

'OK then. I'll call again after I've had mine too. I'm nearly home anyway.'

We took possession of our apartment only three months earlier. We are very proud of it. Truthfully, we can't believe we own it. Located 400 metres from the botanical gardens and less than three kilometres from Bourke Street, it is our city pad. I can't get Nan to move, but I want to work. She is learning to enjoy time in Melbourne as a nice change from home in Albury.

I pour a gin and turn on the TV news. Nothing interesting there. As the gin starts to take effect, I become lazier about my eating options and settle on McDonald's from around the corner. Nan is a brilliant cook and loves doing it. We split our responsibilities in what is now an old-fashioned and almost frowned-upon way. I make the cash and she runs the household. It works well for us. I like working. She focuses on her art and looks after her mum. And she looks after me. I have no interest in cooking or gardening.

Recently she told me how she cooks vegetables for our everyday meals. Douse them in olive oil and into the oven on 200 degrees. No need to even peel them. She had strangely prefaced this instruction with 'if anything ever happens to me, this is how you do it. It's simple.' On that occasion I chose to ignore it, thinking she didn't sound at all serious or predictive as she said it. It seemed like such a remote possibility; almost ridiculous.

Around 7pm I decide to ring Nan again. It won't be long before she and Hester start heading to bed. They are getting earlier by the day. If it isn't one, it's the other taking the initiative. They have an understanding.

Dinner, a brief look at the TV and then up to bed. Maybe a bath for Nan beforehand or some reading perhaps. I told her if she continued the trend she would be going to bed before she even got up.

I dial the number and the phone rings out. Probably taking Hester out for a pee before bed I assume. I try again ten minutes later, and then five or ten minutes again after that. Same result. In the bath I decide, starting to get a little annoyed. When I try again shortly after I become angry, thinking she has left the phone off the hook. How am I going to speak with her? She might think I hadn't bothered to call.

I try again every five or ten minutes getting angrier until I start to wonder whether there is something wrong with our ageing dog. She is a Labrador approaching fourteen with various health issues and special dietary needs. Nan is cooking rice and vegetables for her every day. As a childless couple, we love our pets. I become concerned that something has gone wrong there. It is an inkling, but it is taking hold of me. There is no point trying Nan's mobile phone. She leaves it turned off unless she wants to make a call. She is saving the battery she would say. It was an old pre-smartphone Nokia, and the battery would last for a week! Mad!

I keep calling frequently but still no Nan. Ringing out. Thinking it through, I start to think that she would ring me if something had gone wrong with Hester. So, I begin thinking that is less likely too. Already feeling uneasy, my concern shifts to Nan. Is something wrong with her? She was fine over the weekend. She is rarely ill and although she sounded tired on the phone at lunch there is nothing further to go on. I don't like things standing undone. Don't like not knowing. I am uneasy. After an hour plus of unsuccessfully trying to call, I decide to ring Nan's sister, Jill.

'Hi Jill, it's David,' I say when she answers. It is after 8pm and unusual for me to ring at this time on a weeknight, especially when I am in Melbourne. 'I'm sure I am worrying unnecessarily, but I've been trying to ring Nan for over an hour. I spoke to her around six, but the phone just keeps ringing out now. Would it be possible that you do a check to make sure she's OK? She's probably left the bloody phone off the hook.'

'Oh, that's unusual,' Jill replies. 'We'll try her as well and go and check on her if we can't get through.'

'Thanks Jill. I'll talk to you later. Apologies if I'm being like Nanette and panicking unnecessarily.'

I quickly hang up to let her get on with it. I feel relieved that I'd been able to get onto Jill and start to settle, waiting for Nanette to call me and tell me she is OK. Twenty or thirty minutes elapse and still no call. I become anxious again and decide to ring Jill's husband, Frank. I know he will have his mobile and be with Jill.

'Hi David,' Frank answers in what remains of his American accent after forty-odd years in Australia. 'We are at your place. Everything is OK. It looks like Nan has fainted. We have the ambulance here and they are going to take her to the hospital. We had to break in via the glass door at the back.'

'I'm coming home,' I quickly respond.

'No, don't panic and rush home. It's late and a long drive. It will be OK. We will let you know what's happening.'

'I am on my way.'

I hang up and grab a suitcase and start throwing comfortable clothes in. I am in an anxious hurry but keep telling myself she has only fainted, and she must be OK. Anyway, I am going back. It is late but I'm a seasoned insomniac. I know I won't fall asleep on the road. It is a drag that I can't get there any quicker. There are no flights back to a regional town like Albury at this time and I wasn't going to wait until the next day.

I lock my apartment, double-checking things, not sure when I will be back. I throw the suitcase and my things into the BMW, and at right on 9pm, drive off. It is only a short distance before I will be on freeway the entire 300 kilometres, but it is frustrating to be dealing with traffic lights and city traffic blissfully unaware of the urgency. Every minor delay feels like a lifetime.

I calculate at least thirty minutes, even with a clear run, to be on Melbourne's outskirts. I plough ahead. 'I said you should go to the doctor,' I will lecture her when I see her. At least now she is in the hands of medical professionals, and she will be OK. I again remind myself, she has only fainted.

I am finally outside Melbourne. It is dark and cold. The traffic lightens off. Only me and semi-trailers at that hour. I know they have a job to do but I don't like being near them on the road. I push my Beemer beyond the speed limit to around 130 kph. I know it can fly well beyond that, but I want to get there safely. As I approach Seymour, an hour out of Melbourne, my phone suddenly rings. I grab it expecting it to be Frank or Jill with an update, but it is a private number calling.

'Is that David Hoysted?' a male voice on the other end asks.

'Yes, speaking,' I respond.

He identifies himself as a doctor in the emergency department at Albury Base Hospital where they have taken Nan. He asks where I am. I tell him I am somewhere near Seymour.

'You might have to turn around. We are trying to get her a bed in one of the city hospitals and if that comes up, we will be flying her down.'

'What?' I ask. 'What's happened?'

'We think she has suffered a stroke. A brain haemorrhage.'

This can't be right. I must have misheard. I know I haven't. Frank thought she had only fainted. What would Albury doctors know? I feel myself shrinking. Every part of me contracting inwards. My eyelids, my mouth, my shoulders. Contracting and tensing.

'Is this serious?' I ask, not really believing it could be.

'It's very serious. We are doing what we can.'

'What? I thought she had only fainted. Can you tell me, is she conscious? Has she been conscious?'

'No. She's unconscious. She hasn't been conscious since she was brought in. We've put her in an induced coma to let her body and brain rest as much as possible.'

'Oh God. I can't believe this. I'll be there as soon as I can. You'll ring me if I need to turn around? In the meantime, I'll keep coming to her. OK?'

'Yes David. We will ring you. Now listen to me. Be very careful. It's late. You are driving and you've had upsetting news. Will you do that?'

'Yes. I will be careful.'

We hang up. I am not crying as I am numbed by shock. It doesn't feel real. It can't be. I love her so much. She is everything to me. I can't lose her. My closest friend. My wife. I grip the steering wheel strongly, tensing my arms and torso, and pull myself towards it.

'NOT MY NANNY,' I scream.

ALBURY

Back when she was well and we lived in Albury, Nan sometimes made martinis, and we sat at home on a Saturday night sipping them and feeling like sophisticates. I've been a daily gin and tonic drinker for years, but gin martinis would be a nice variation for when friends come over.

I set out for Dan Murphy's to buy some vermouth and a shot glass. My gin apportionment is rough to say the least and I have a suspicion that my daily shot is well more than a standard drink, probably a double. Maybe more.

I cross Toorak Road and head through Fawkner Park towards Prahran. As I approach the other side, I notice a wheelchair approaching. I look down and then tell myself not to look away. Look at him and acknowledge if he looks up, but don't stare. Not like those hurtful twits who used to leer at Nan as though they'd luckily happened upon free admission to a freak show.

'Don't stare,' I'd exclaim in exasperation and embarrassment as they passed us. Or 'Would you like to take a photo as a keepsake?' It always got the right reaction: they'd correct themselves, hopefully full of remorse and resolve to never do it again. Nan seemed oblivious to all this, or at least didn't show anything.

The guy approaching me is middle-aged with dark but greying hair. He is leaning forward in his powered chair. As we near, we look at each other. I nod and he does too, but his nod is a forward lurch of his entire torso. ALS or maybe Parkinson's, I estimate. He is in control of his chair though. Nan didn't have that luxury of operating her own chair. Or making decisions to even get into her chair or initiate going somewhere.

Control. When we think we have it, it's at best fleeting. It's never complete and perhaps never real. Only our own perception. Once I had a great wife and marriage and a big job. Now I don't.

As I speed down the Hume Highway towards Albury that night, I have no control of my life nor my future anymore. I'm like an astronaut or cosmonaut lost in space with failed navigational equipment and no idea what to do next. It's dark, it's cold, it's late and I can't talk to anyone. I'm frightened. Frightened for Nan, frightened for me.

I can't even talk to Nan like I did when troubled at any other time in my life. All I know is she's unconscious in Albury Base Hospital and the situation is dire. She was always my first port of call. My 'one stop shop' as Caren my psychologist calls her.

I leave the orbit of Melbourne into the void of the unknown. It feels like a giant leap of faith. Venturing into an oblivion. Is that where Nan is? Has she already passed? Could it have happened and they haven't rung me yet? I'm on edge the whole time. Frightened the phone will ring. Frightened when it doesn't.

Trucks and small towns pass me like satellites in space. Signs of life, but not really. Those people and those places are unknown to me. They may as well not exist. No comfort there. I want my Nanny. I want to be with her. I want to see her, and hold her.

I've driven this road hundreds of times. For pleasure mostly but sometimes work as well. Returning from football matches or weekends away with Nan where we shopped, ate at a nice restaurant and stayed at a good hotel. Normally feeling the gentle, relaxed fatigue of some well-spent time and then returning to the comfort of home. Now all I feel is fear.

The towns slowly tick by. Kilmore, Seymour, Euroa, Benalla, Wangaratta. I pass the outskirts of Wodonga and the factory where I worked for twenty years. That was a second home as well. Made redundant two years earlier by a program to offshore all our IT capability to China. If that didn't happen, I might have been at home this evening with Nan. Not four hours away. Then again, with all the travel I did, I might have been on another continent. If only, might have, should have, what if?

My drive and impetus seem to drain as I pass the front of the hospital knowing I am finally here. I've driven the 330 kilometres non-stop. The tiredness sets in as soon as I stop the car, but I won't be able to sleep a wink. As I walk over to the emergency department, I see the usual assortment of dickheads that have caused themselves harm: through drunkenness, drugs, idleness or just good old-fashioned stupidity. There are elderly people and unwell kids as well.

I ring Jill and tell her I've arrived. Moments later a door to the left opens and Jill and Frank walk out. They look dishevelled and wide-eyed. Just like I feel. They lead me back through the same doors and down several corridors. I don't want to go any further. I want to be with her, but I don't want to see her. How can this be true?

We walk into a room and there she is. Splayed out on a bed. Flat on her back. Her hair is a mess. Ventilator tubes down her throat. She looks like she's already gone. The sight of her makes me double over in shock, pain, and anguish.

I look at Jill. She says something. I don't know what. I can't think. I can't process. I touch Nan. I speak to her. Trying to wake her. Thinking I can, thinking she will. There is no response. Nothing. Just the sound of the ventilator as it forces breath into her body.

* * *

I have a shot glass, some martini glasses, and several varieties of gin as I leave Prahran and make my way back home through Fawkner Park. I need to be home for a phone call with a consumer advocacy group for The Alfred Hospital. Nan spent a lot of time in their care, and I feel a debt of gratitude to them. The call will be a short discussion on the delivery of therapy for stroke victims in the immediate period after their admission to hospital.

Perhaps it's the forthcoming call sending my mind back to those days, but I'm struck by another sight on my way home. A mother is pushing a pram near me. Sitting forward in the pram is a baby girl, old enough to sit up. She has a splash of brown hair. It's not so much a matter of physical resemblance to Nan as it is her expression of childish innocence. Placid and content, completely and utterly dependent on her mother. A dependence that can be counted on. Wheeling through these same paths in the park where I walked Nan so many times for a break from our room at the nursing home. Wanting to feel fresh air and survey different scenery. I'm so struck by the demeanour of the child I don't even notice the mother. I'm staring at them. Lost in a reverie to a time now four years past. I can't quite get over the look on the child's face and how it resembled my darling.

I'm back in my kitchen unpacking my supplies. I gather myself and set up my laptop to start the Zoom session on stroke therapy. As the session starts, an attractive dark-haired young woman named Alana greets me with an unmistakable Kiwi accent. She expresses her gratitude for my involvement while we wait for the other attendee. His name is Paul, and soon after he arrives, it becomes clear he has suffered a stroke himself. His thinking is slowed and his speech a little slurred. He is laboured but doing his best and we listen patiently and supportively while he gives his answers to Alana's questions. She wants to know about the value of therapy, the value of timetabling therapy, how best to involve families in care, and then the one that pushes my buttons: the importance and timing of family meetings.

Six years on, the recollections associated with that topic still raise my blood pressure. The meetings involved a family member, the therapists and medical specialists treating the patient. I expected to feel outnumbered and ganged up on. The weight of numbers having the advantage as they planned to evict my precious darling from the hospital setting she so desperately needed. The collective belief was there was nothing more they could do for Nan, and it was time to move her to her new home in Aged Care. I rejected the idea and said I would argue it out with the medicos.

I'm recounting this to Alana and Paul and my anger is building as I relive it. The urge to fight for Nan is still there even though she's been gone for two-and-a-half years. I remember where I am and turn down the heat. I apologise to Alana, admitting that the topic still incenses me. I tell her I had to fight so much. She understands, as does Paul who tells me his wife has fought hard for him too.

The session comes to an end and I decide to go and visit Dianne at the Austin. I was seeing her for a few months but ended it. After that, she was told she had a brain tumour that needed to come out. Her brain surgery was four days ago, and it had gone well. She rang me that evening after the operation. I couldn't believe I was talking to her. I fired off questions to see how coherent she was. 'What is your full name? What is mine? What is your date of birth? What is your address?' She sounded wiped out but answered every one of them perfectly. She was right on the ball. It was amazing given what she'd been through. I was relieved. I was worried about her.

As I drive to the Austin, my blood is still pumping from that discussion about family meetings. I'm speeding out the Eastern Freeway, this time with my sound system blaring. Realising I'm over the speed limit and a bit wound up, I slow both myself and the car. I take a few deep breaths and concentrate on safe and steady driving.

Dianne is happy to see me when I arrive. Her hair is a mess and she's wearing no makeup. Excusable in a neurosurgery ward post-op I would say. I'm surprised they haven't shaved her head very much.

I had jokingly warned her that neurosurgeons might be good with a scalpel, but they are shit hairstylists. We were both expecting her to be half-bald. Her daughter is there and immersed in reading her texts. I'm a little uncomfortable about meeting her, but Dianne encourages me to sit on the bed and wants to hold my hand and be close.

I'm doing my best but feeling decidedly uneasy being back in a place like this. What am I doing? I've had four years of hell, why would I be here again? I'm catastrophising about the possibility of Dianne needing chemotherapy and I'm consigned to be a carer for my entire fifties. That would be insane. This isn't Nan. I've done a lot to help her to this stage, but how do I pull back? Somewhere I must think of myself and my own wellbeing. That's what everyone is telling me anyway, but what would people think if I suddenly stood up and walked away now without returning?

As I sit facing her laying half upright on the bed, I notice the suction unit on the wall. I'm transported back to renting our own unit to deal with Nan's secretion problems after the cerebellum bleed. The last twelve months were the hardest. But there were the first twelve months too. In truth, it was all hard. These periods were the most dangerous and frightening, bookending two comparatively stable years in the middle.

This hospital setting takes me back to that night at Albury Base. I'm back in the room with Nan on my arrival. A balding, fair-headed guy in his forties walks in and announces he is a doctor. The guy I spoke to on the road. I'm introduced as the husband. He tells me they are still waiting for an intensive care bed in one of the cities. Nan needs neurosurgery to deal with the bleed but there are no neurosurgeons here in Albury. If you want to live in the country, don't be there if anything serious and time-critical happens.

They are trying to find somewhere in Melbourne, Sydney or Canberra. The intensive care wards are all full because it's flu season. 'FLU!' I think to myself. We've got a life and death situation here that is way more critical than that. He says Canberra hospital is investigating the possibility of converting an operating theatre to an intensive care bed for her.

He again tells me they are giving her every chance. They've put her into a coma to let her body and brain rest. Drugs, I guess. But the situation is very bad. Her bleed is very large, and her chances are slim. He tells me this in such a matter-of-fact way with seemingly so little compassion it's as if we are discussing something of little consequence. Like whether my CD player can be repaired.

He leaves the room and goes about whatever he goes about. Wasting time on other patients. Can't he do something for Nan? Can't we? I feel so incredibly helpless. She just lies there. Perfectly still. I'm not sure she would still be able to breathe if the machine wasn't doing it for her. I'm the opposite. I can't sit or stand still. I can't stay in the room. I can't be out of the room. I can't do anything. I can't do anything right. I can't do anything wrong. I know time is of the essence. I look at her. How can she be like this? Are they sure this is what has happened? I know they are.

I join Jill, Frank and their daughter Lucy in a nearby waiting room. They tell me they had to break into our home through the glass door at the back. They could see lights on but couldn't get Nan to answer when they knocked at the front. Frank found a rock in the garden to smash the glass. As they went up the stairs looking for Nan, they found Hester our Labrador in the study. Frozen. Terrified. A harbinger of the tragedy that awaited them on the next floor. After ascending the final six steps to the upper level, they found Nan unconscious on the floor of the ensuite. A large vomit lay next to her. They called an ambulance and tried to rouse her, unsuccessfully, while they waited.

Lucy decides to leave. The rest of us wait. By this time it's 2am. Another hour ticks by. The doctor comes in briefly to tell us there is still no update on a bed. The waiting continues, as does my ritual of helpless and useless actions. Moving between Nan and the waiting room. Sitting, then standing. Touching her, talking to her, asking her to wake up. Anxiously checking the clock.

At around 4am the doctor returns to tell us they have a bed. It's not in Canberra where I expect. It's at a hospital in Kogarah, Sydney called St George Public. I've never heard of the hospital nor the suburb. I was hoping for Melbourne or Canberra where I have sisters. I have some friends in Sydney but my closeness with Nan means I haven't maintained the connections that well.

I start worrying about practicalities. Sydney seems so far away. Ridiculous with hindsight given the amount of international travel I've done. It's the stress and fear talking. When you're out of your mind with anxiety, even the tiniest things tip you over. They could have said the hospital was somewhere else in Albury and that would have seemed like another universe away.

The doctor tells us they are sending an air ambulance down to collect her. Just as well Nan is unconscious. She hated flying and wouldn't get on a small plane like that. She has no choice. I am wondering how I will get there. We've been up all night. I can't drive another 600 kms. He says I will be able to fly up with her. I hate small planes. I don't want to do that. A moment of selfishness on my part.

I opt to go home and pack some more things. I want to see the dog and cat. I want to check the house. It's probably going to be a while before I get back. Qantas has a morning flight from Albury to Sydney leaving at 6.30am. I ring and make a booking, mentioning to the person at the other end that I have an urgent medical situation with a family member. That snaps her to attention despite the early hour. She makes my booking and then sincerely and compassionately tells me she hopes things go well.

I leave for home and tell Frank and Jill I will grab a cab back to the airport. They will stay with Nan until she is collected and then meet me there before the flight. I go to Nan and whisper to her that I love her and ask her not to leave me. I will see her in Sydney. We will get through this. I kiss her. I'm still expecting her to wake but there is no reaction.

Our home then was a large split-level dwelling in West Albury. Given it's winter, it's still dark when I pull up. There are lights on and the curtains in the lounge room and study are not drawn as they would be on a normal day at this time. I can see Hester in the study. I enter the house. Strangely, she doesn't come to me, so I go into the study to her. She is sitting but with head bowed. I touch her and encourage her to come out the back with me so she can go to the toilet. Uncharacteristically, she doesn't move. I try her again. Still nothing. Just like Nan in the hospital except she is conscious.

Hester is frozen stiff. Terrified. Her body is tight. I pat her and try and calm her. No change. I nudge her more strongly. Her feet and legs are welded to the spot. I push her harder. I try and drag her. She's not going anywhere. She is replicating Nan's condition. 'FUCKING COME ON!' I scream.

I have hardly ever yelled at Hester in her entire life. She was just the most perfect and sensitive dog. Even as a pup she was rarely destructive. So well-behaved. So incredibly in tune and in touch with us. The third member of our exclusive club. Our unbreakable bond. Years earlier, we had decided to only take holidays where she could come with us. We knew she hated being in the kennels, and we missed her. That meant regular trips to dog-friendly accommodation in Apollo Bay.

I'm exasperated. I don't know what to do. I consider picking her up and carrying her downstairs, but realise she is so stressed by the evening's events and whatever has happened to Nan that I won't trouble her any further. She is old and has had several medical issues too. I give her a couple of gentle pats, reassure her, and leave her in the study. I make my way up to the bedroom with my suitcase and start to grab some additional clothes and whatever else I feel I need. I have a quick shower and clean my teeth hoping that will help me feel a little better. The gains are only marginal.

Next step is to check on the cat. Beryl is a tabby kitten we had taken in only a few months before. She is staying indoors only, and

I wonder whether she has escaped outside with everything that has happened. I find her still enclosed in the laundry. I put some more food out for her and close her back in, thinking Jill and Frank will work out what to do with her after I am gone. There isn't time and there is no other solution right now.

It's time to make my way to the airport. I call a cab and notice the back door where they broke in. The glass is shattered and lying on the floor in front. One whole panel of glass is missing. Again, nothing I can do about it. The theme of the day. Returning to the study to check Hester, she is now lying on her front, but still frozen stiff. The cab arrives as I give her one last pat and then it's time to say goodbye for now. I hug her and tell her I love her. Her mummy is sick, and we need to try and get her better. Frank and Jill will come and get her later. I'm reassuring the dog just like reassuring Nan earlier on. It will be the last time I see our beautiful Hessie.

I can remember nothing of the cab trip to the airport. I am just there. In a daze. Making my way to check in. I do that and stand in the area before security screening. I notice a woman I worked with standing nearby. I don't want to talk to an acquaintance. I can't do that. I avert my eyes and move away.

It's time to start notifying my siblings of what has happened. I ring my elder sister Christine. I know she loves Nan too. They all do. The phone rings out. Frustrating. I try again but the same result. I decide to ring Michelle as the plane will be boarding soon. Bernard, her husband, answers.

'Bernard, it's David.'

'Hi, David,' he replies. I can hear the surprise in his voice as to why I would be ringing so early.

'Is Michelle there?'

'No, she's out walking the dog.' I can't reach any of my family it seems. Why does everything have to be so fucking hard?

'I've got bad news. Something terrible has happened. It's Nan …'

At that point, I burst into tears. I'm unable to get any more words out clearly. I try and start the sentence again, but the same thing happens. I'm shaking. I walk outside of the airport to be in a less public place. The cold August morning air provides a soothing calm.

'I'm sorry Bernard. Nan has had a big stroke. A brain haemorrhage. They are uncertain whether she will survive.'

I lose it again and resume the fight between trying to talk and starting to cry. The crying is winning. The talking momentarily seizes control to finish our conversation.

'They are flying her to Sydney for surgery. I'm at Albury Airport. I'm about to catch a flight to Sydney as well. I don't know what's going to happen.'

'I am so sorry David,' Bernard responds.

'Bern, can you please get the message out to the family? I tried to call Christine but couldn't get on to her either. I need to go for my flight. I'm sorry, I'm too upset to talk any further.'

'I'll do that David. You take care. I hope it goes well. We will be praying for her.' Bernard and Michelle remain the most religious couple of our Catholic-raised family.

I thank Bernard, hang up and get back to the matter of sobbing uncontrollably about my darling. Have I talked to her for the last time? Is she still alive? Walking back into the airport terminal, Frank and Jill have arrived to see me off. As I stand with them, I notice the woman acquaintance from work standing very nearby. There is no way she couldn't have noticed me but she's not looking. She knows something is horribly wrong and she's the one now averting her gaze. She would never have seen me or imagined seeing me in this kind of state.

Frank and Jill tell me that the air ambulance arrived and collected Nan and she is on her way to Sydney. It's time to board and I say my goodbyes. It's the kind of grave farewell soldiers probably make to each other before entering a battle. A deep sense of foreboding. The knowledge someone wouldn't survive. The hope that all would. In this case though, our anxiety is for Nan.

I board the Qantas plane and take my seat towards the rear. I throw the book and music I optimistically carried on with me into the seat pocket and buckle up. I'm hopeful no one will sit next to me. I want my space from the rest of the world. I'm not small and whenever I get on these regional planes with their tiny seat allotments, I seem to draw the short straw and have some large man or woman placed next to me. We spend the flight with our elbows arguing over the shared arm rest, struggling for comfort.

A woman approaches and is about to sit next to me before she realises she has the wrong row. A few more minutes pass. Everyone is on board. The plane is closed and takes off. I'm fatigued from not having slept a wink overnight. But once airborne, the flood of tears starts like my own haemorrhage. Bursting out of me uncontrollably. Unstoppably. One wave after another. Each coming with more force. I check to see if anyone nearby notices. No one is even looking, so I just let it happen.

No sooner do I regain control, than another wave bursts through. My whole body is consumed and overtaken by the power of this grief. It's got to come out. I wonder how I will be able to cope with what's coming up. I wonder if I will ever stop crying again. The whole flight is spent this way. Crying and crying. How can there be so much fluid to cry out? I wonder if there is a limit to how many tears your body holds. There doesn't seem to be.

As we approach Sydney and descend, there is the usual delay waiting for clearance to land. The world never gives you a break. It just goes on its own way. There is no air traffic control deity giving us a priority land. I hope at least they gave Nan one when her plane came in.

When we eventually touch down and disembark, I grab my mobile and turn it back on, scanning for messages. There is a voice mail from a number I don't recognise. It's a doctor at St George Hospital. His message tells me they have Nan, and he needs me to call him on his number urgently. I ring him but it goes to voicemail. I leave the message that I have now landed and am on my way.

As I walk through the terminal to get my bag, I decide to ring Grant at the TAFE where I had been working only twenty-four hours ago. It feels like twenty-four years ago. He answers and I cut straight to the chase.

'Grant, it's David. I'm in Sydney. My wife has had a massive brain haemorrhage. She needs surgery and I'm with her. It's a life and death situation. I won't be coming back to the contract. I'm sorry. There's nothing I can do.' He's disappointed and expresses his concern but accepts there is nothing he can do either. He wishes me luck and we say goodbye.

I grab a cab to St George public and as we round Sydney airport runway heading south, my phone rings. It's Nan's mother, Joan.

'Hi Joan, I'm in a taxi on the way to the hospital. I've just landed,' I answer. I'm already feeling guilty for being away working and not with Nan when this happened.

'Oh, aren't you there yet?' she responds.

'No.' Another huge wave of tears knocks me over like an unexpected wave of surf. I can't get my words out. The taxi driver looks at me with great concern and compassion. He strokes my arm wondering whatever has happened.

I can't control it. I utter something to Joan about letting her know when I know something and tell her I must go. She says something about me needing to be strong for Nanette. I tell her of course I will. I will do anything. I hang up. The driver is a very nice man. I think he is Islamic. He continues to offer whatever comfort he can while still driving. Probably not often that a fifty-something man is crying uncontrollably next to him in his cab. He drops me at the hospital, and I make my way in, not knowing anything. Not knowing what comes next or what to do. Marching into battle.

ST GEORGE

I'm looking across my lounge room at the piano. It sits in the room that would have been a dining room for previous owners of this apartment. Not for me. This piano is a lifer. A bit extravagant perhaps to have a six-foot grand in an apartment, but there was no way I was parting with it.

I think of my favourite jazz pianists of the fifties: Bill Evans, Bud Powell, Lennie Tristano. All living in apartments in New York City. Bill had a seven-foot grand. Bud and Lennie no doubt something similar. I imagine living near those titans and hearing them practise daily. Geniuses that paved the way for how modern jazz piano is played. There were earlier players, but these guys evolved it and their ways became the way. I read somewhere that when Bill was younger, he would stand outside Bud's apartment listening to him work out. That's what it's like. Hours in the gym every day. Building muscle memory. Building ideas. Solving technical problems.

I head over to the piano and sit down. I run Ornette Coleman's *Turnaround*, doubling the melody in both hands two octaves apart so I've got a nice bass sound to thicken it up. It's a blues in C and I run some improv while walking the bass in the left hand. Walking bass is a new development for me. It's hard to do. I then alternate bass roots and chords in the left underneath the improv and return to the statement of the head. It's a nice sounding piano.

My piano is surrounded in that room by Nan's artworks. I think of it as a gallery. Like the rooms in the Musee d'Orsay where we sat many years ago surrounded by Van Gogh or Monet. On the long wall there are four painted works on pieces of board assembled to look like aerial views of paddocks. Two in green shade, two in reddish-brown. On another there is a two-metre-long collage of dyed fabrics. The colours are those of the outback. She has meticulously stitched patterns all over it.

I have Nan's art throughout the rest of my home in addition to the pieces we acquired by more well-known artists. 'Your home is like a shrine to Nanette,' Dianne once said disapprovingly when we were talking through my reluctance to commit. It is that. I've deliberately done that and it's staying that way. It gives me comfort. It's what she's left behind. Art survives us. Something of her is still with me. I can't and won't give her up. Not for anyone.

I played guitar from my early teens. During my twenties after my own illness, I concentrated on classical guitar for five years. Then I said to Nan that I wished I knew how to play piano. It's a great instrument and the music for it so profound. On the morning of my twenty-seventh birthday, I returned home to find an upright piano wrapped in a big yellow bow. Typical of Nan. A brilliant gift that kept on giving and she managed to orchestrate giving a piano as a surprise. Not such an easy thing to do. I'd say it was the greatest gift I ever received, but actually, that was Nan. And then Nan number two, the miracle of St George.

That day I pulled my roller suitcase into the entrance of St George Hospital, I wasn't to realise that I would hardly press a piano key again for another fifteen months; easily the longest break I've had from piano since I took it up.

* * *

The entrance hall to St George public is a busy place. Multiple corridors meet at the point where the information booth is located. There is a gift shop located to the right filled with bright coloured flowers and balloons. Two middle-aged women sit behind a counter answering phones and disinterestedly directing people to various parts of the hospital.

I walk up and advise I'm looking for my wife, Nanette Hoysted. Without making eye contact, the woman searches for Nan on her computer and tells me she will be in Intensive Care. I drag my suitcase over to the lift and head up. When I exit, I see some large double doors with a sign indicating 'intensive care'. I attempt to push them open, but they are locked. Someone standing nearby tells me I need to push the intercom and ask to be admitted.

I do that and when a voice answers I tell them who I am and I'm looking for my wife who I believe is here. After a few minutes, the doors open and Brenda, a forty-something woman with short brown hair comes out. She smiles and has a kind face.

She tells me she is a social worker and takes me into the ICU. She asks me to disinfect my hands and we move into a small meeting room to talk. It's not a room to be comfortable in. The chairs are basic, upright and unwelcoming. However, I'm happy to sit again after the night I've had.

She tells me Nan is in surgery and might be a couple of hours as she has only just gone in. Brenda doesn't have any details on Nan's condition but instead asks me to tell her what's happened overnight. I relate the story and that I've just come from the airport having flown in from Albury. Fatigue and reality are starting to bear down on me. I'm morphing between fear and sadness. I'm completed drained.

Brenda asks me if I have somewhere to stay, and I don't. I have a suitcase with minimal belongings and I'm in a city that I don't know that well; I feel like a homeless person. I don't know where I'm going to sleep tonight. I don't know where Nan is and I don't know how she is. Right now is when I feel most alone.

'Are there some hotels with accommodation nearby?' I ask.

'I can get you a list of hotel options in this area. There is also a place across the road that is usually available for visiting cancer patients and their families. Let me talk to them and see if they are able to help out.'

I thank her and she asks whether I've eaten anything. I haven't. I didn't eat on the plane, I was too busy crying. She encourages me to get something to eat and offers to hold my suitcase while I do that.

I find a café nearby that's mostly empty because it's only 9am. I'm happy for it not to be noisy. The café is run by a middle-aged, Middle Eastern couple. I take a seat and am presented with the menu, and even at this hour, and despite my inability to process anything more, they advise of some specials and amendments to the menu. I ask for bacon and eggs and a glass of milk.

As I sit there staring into the light outside, I feel another wave of despair overtake me. Another flood of tears streaming down my face. I pull out my handkerchief. It's still wet from the flight, so I start grabbing serviettes. I have never cried so much in my life as I have in the last couple of hours. Nothing like this when my dad died eight years earlier. This is a new level of sadness beyond anything I've ever experienced. The greatest person of my life, the woman I love and adore, is on the verge of life and death.

The crying continues interminably. I expect that by letting it out I will feel better. I don't. I just feel worse. It's not solving anything. It's gaining momentum, taking greater hold. I'm rolling down an infinite slope of grief.

With my elbows on the table, I guess my shoulders are shaking and the owner has noticed and comes over to try and console me. Given his café is outside one of Sydney's key trauma hospitals, he's probably seen it before.

He asks me what has happened, and I tell him. Tell him that Nan is undergoing surgery right now. I don't know whether she will live or … I can't say that word. Even now, it's hard to. To his credit, he stands there comfortably and listens. He's not frightened away by the moment or the sadness of a stranger. He says everything is in the hands of God. He seems to be Christian. I should pray. I tell him I will. I don't anymore, but this was no time to piss God off. The owner serves my food and I begin eating.

Food, or at least the process of eating, helps immediately. Mainly the distraction of doing something that requires coordination and some concentration, not yet the sustenance. I finish the meal and then decide to ring Jill and tell her I am here and what I know: nothing. I'm at least in the right place.

I've accounted for most of an hour since I left intensive care. I can't stand it any longer so I head back. I seek out Brenda the social worker and she introduces me to one of the nurses. Nan still isn't out of surgery, and they encourage me to go and wait in the room we had met in. They think she won't be much longer.

I return to the room. I'm struck by how utterly characterless it is. A dimly-lit beige shade of beige. Having been awake for more than twenty-four hours and with some food on board, I start to doze off. I sleep and wake with a start, about ten minutes each at a time for a while and then the door to the room opens and in walks a tall, young, Chinese man in blue scrubs.

He introduces himself as Johnny. He's one of the neurosurgery registrars and he has just come from operating on Nan. He explains they tried to contact me but when they couldn't reach me, they made the decision to operate. They had to to save her life. Johnny tells me they normally prefer to have consent from the family in cases like this. It might be the family doesn't want the surgery and is happy to let the patient go. I explain I was in transit myself, but of course I wanted anything done that could be done.

I ask how she is. Johnny tells me the haemorrhage she suffered was huge. Seven centimetres by five centimetres by four centimetres. A gigantic hole to blow in anyone's brain. Her chances are slim. But at least she is what he considers to be young. She has just turned fifty-four. She would love to hear herself described as young. I imagine her batting her eyelids and turning her head to the side in a feigned response to flattery.

He wants to know more about Nan. Does she work? What kind of work? What kind of interests does she have? I explain that Nan does some casual art teaching and that she is an artist. A very good one. I tell him she's been looking after her mother since she was widowed. I don't feel I'm giving her enough credit by saying that, so I add she is double-degreed. Media studies and then fine arts.

'She is highly intelligent,' I hasten to mention. 'She is extraordinarily well-read. She has a photographic memory. Her written skills are second to none in anyone I have ever known. She has a massive vocabulary. I have rarely encountered a word in over thirty years that she didn't know the definition of. They skipped her a grade at school when she was a kid, and she had only just turned seventeen when she finished her HSC. She had one of the better passes in her class despite not doing maths and much science and being younger!'

'Not only is she highly talented,' I add, 'she is an extraordinarily good and kind person. She is self-sacrificing and modest.' I am formulating my 'Save Nanette' campaign. I would get plenty of opportunities to run this in future, but this is where it commenced.

The registrar has heard what I said. He responds that this is good for her chances. They know that the more intelligent you are, the better your chances are of surviving something as extreme as this. I reiterate that she is very intelligent. He is giving me some hope and that is restoring some energy. Temporarily at least.

'Has she been well?' he asks.

'Yes, as far as I know.' There is a creeping reservation in my mind as I answer this. Some of the things she had said.

'Has she had any issues with blood pressure? Is she on any blood pressure medication?'

'She wasn't on any blood pressure medication. I couldn't get her to go to the doctor. She wouldn't even go for a regular check-up. She hadn't been to the GP much over the last ten years. There was one visit a year or so ago which was to do with menopause and some menstrual changes she was experiencing. But she wasn't on any blood pressure or other medication.'

At this point I recall our dinner conversation two weeks earlier. Nan indicated a severe headache that felt like she was going to have a stroke and me responding with 'For Christ's sake will you go to the doctor and at least have your blood pressure checked?' I tell him about this.

'Was she active. Did she exercise?'

'She led an active lifestyle, but she wasn't exercising. She had stopped walking once our dog became old and wasn't capable of long walks. Only a couple of days before, I had said to her she needed to get some exercise.'

She responded in her usual way that I was suggesting she was fat. She had put on weight. I said it was a matter of health. She had listened and went on a couple of walks after that. I can picture Nan walking up the hill toward our place as I was returning home in the car the very day before her stroke. But by then, it was too little too late.

'Has she had any strokes before or is there any family history of strokes?' Johnny asks.

'She hasn't. I know that her paternal grandmother had strokes, but this was before I knew Nan. Her father died at 70 of a heart attack.' I start to wonder about that day, two years before, when she was sick …

He then fires off a series of additional questions that they need to understand.

'Is Nanette left or right-handed?'

'She's right-handed.'

'Good, that means the stroke is on her non-dominant side.

A stroke like this on the left side of her brain would certainly have killed her.'

'Does she drink and if so, how much?'

'Yes, she drinks. Probably 2–3 glasses a night or thereabouts.'

'Does she smoke?'

'No.'

'Does she do any street drugs?' This question is so ridiculous for Nan that it makes me laugh for the first time since yesterday. I shake my head at the idea.

'No,' I respond. 'That's definitely not her or my thing at all.' He smiles in response. He can see I'm amused at even the suggestion.

Johnny tells me that she will be brought to a bed here in intensive care soon and I will be able to see her. He gets up to leave, shakes my hand and I thank him.

I'm left alone, again. It isn't long though before I'm notified that Nan has returned from the surgical theatre and I can go and see her. I'm extremely anxious about what to expect even after seeing her earlier that same morning in Albury. I'm brought fully through the intensive care unit this time.

There is a sunken bunker in the middle of the room. It's full of computer screens and monitors. Four or five doctors are stationed there. Men and women. Some sitting, some standing together. From that point they have a visual on all the patients, as well as ready access to their vital signs. The patients' beds are placed around them against the walls. There is a nurse stationed at the end of each bed. A one-to-one ratio of nurse to patient. On the other side of the corridor leading into the unit there are three or four separate rooms. I later find out the patients in there are isolated either because they have contagious diseases, or they are at the end, and they and their families are given whatever privacy can be offered in a place like this. The unit is well-lit.

I'm directed towards Nan's bed and my body and legs feel incredibly heavy as I walk the final ten metres or so over to her. My motion feels slow. I'm walking through water, certainly not on it. The sight of her is confronting. The bed head is propped up. She lays there not quite on her back. Over to one side just a little. There is a ventilator tube in her mouth. A feeding tube in her nose. There are other lines connected to her arm and a line from her catheter to a bag collecting urine at the side. Equipment and monitor screens surround her. The ventilator unit is over to her left. Her nurse is stationed at the foot of her bed with a computer and keyboard for entry.

As I approach, I'm introduced to Nan's nurse Kim, and she greets me warmly. She invites me to sit down but I can only focus on touching Nan. I need the physical reassurance that she is there and I'm not dreaming this. I lean down to kiss her. I can't kiss her lips and it's tricky to even get to her cheek because of the ventilator tubes. I notice her head has been shaved above her forehead to the right. That's where they have cut her, so I keep clear of that. There is a drain coming away from there. I find a spot on her face to kiss. I can smell her. I take in her unmistakeable scent. Not perfume. Her smell: 'Eau de Nanette'. I draw it in; I'm nourished by it. It tells me she is alive. I touch her shoulders, her arms, and her legs. I'm a doubting Thomas who needs to feel her, not just see her. I stop short of the need to feel her wounds out of respect for her wellbeing and mine. I tell her that I am here and that I love her. I will never leave her and ask her again not to leave me. Tears well in my eyes but it doesn't go beyond that.

Kim puts a chair behind me and encourages me to sit. I do that, but the framework underneath the bed means it's difficult to achieve the right angle where I can comfortably access Nan. I have to weave my hand through the bars on the side barrier in order to find her hand and grasp it. Can't find the right place for my legs to go. My spine is twisted.

Kim reaches around me and lowers the side bar to allow me better access. It's OK to do that when we are both there, but they have to be up when not. I'm too frightened to touch anything in fear of breaking something, or suddenly causing the bed to collapse and Nan to be catapulted onto the floor.

Kim is never idle. She moves from one task to another. There seems to be a lot to do, even with a one-to-one ratio. Recording readings from the monitors on her computer, checking Nan's urine output, responding to little alarms from her feed or fluids or the ventilator. I'm not yet used to the routine, so her every movement is a cause for anxiety.

The lowered sidebar allows me to move closer to Nan. I can rest my head on the bed close to her. I pull my arms around the top of my head trying to close off the light and the world we are now in. Nan is still in an induced coma to allow her body and brain to rest. But she is here, she is alive, and we are together.

Not all the life we spend with our loved one is active. We sleep, we rest. Sometimes we just be together. At this time, this is as much as I can hope for and it's enough. I can feel and hear her breathing. The ventilator drives it very evenly. More evenly than the natural breath.

After about an hour, there is an announcement on the public address system that I don't hear properly. Kim translates for me that it's now a lunchtime rest period for the patients of intensive care and that I need to leave. Nan has been unconscious since I've been here and I'm not disturbing her, but I accept whatever they ask. They know better.

It will be a two-hour break over lunch time. I don't need to eat again, but I look for the social worker to find out if I have some accommodation. She's managed to secure two nights at Bezzina House. Brenda grabs my suitcase and gives me a slip of paper with their phone number and the booking details. She tells me to ask for Natalie.

I head out the front of the hospital and cross the road to Bezzina House. I enter the office and Natalie is fortunately there to greet me. I give her my name and she confirms they can have me for two nights, but they are booked solid after that. I pay upfront for the two nights and she gives me a key and directs me to my room. Before I head off, Natalie tentatively asks me what has happened to bring me here. I explain my wife has had a very big stroke and is in intensive care.

This time I say I don't know if she will survive. I don't have to use the 'D' word.

The room is a small suite with a separate bedroom, lounge, bathroom, and kitchen. It's ideal being so close to the hospital. The complex also provides laundry facilities and a library/common area to sit if you have the inclination. I won't, but I will use the laundry once I understand how to do that.

I dump my bags and throw myself on one of the two beds for a rest. I've got an hour and a half left before I can go back to Nan. I decide to ring Joan again and let her know that Nan is back from surgery. I'm still feeling guilty about not being home with Nan when this happened. Joan doesn't mention anything about that. She just wants to know how Nan is. I tell her what the registrar told me: the bleed is huge, her chances are slim but she's young and highly intelligent and that might help. She asks me to call her. I detect her tone is already very pessimistic. Like Nanette, she runs on intuition more than facts. I'm hoping her intuition isn't correct.

I decide to ring Frank and Jill and give them the same message. Frank answers. He asks whether there are people I want him to contact. I tell him I've put the message out to my family and then remember a few close friends that should be told. Some of Nan's, some of mine. The idea of sharing mobile numbers is too hard right now so I tell him we will do it tomorrow. All I want to do is lay back on the bed and wait for the time to pass until I can go back to Nan.

INTENSIVE CARE

I am back outside intensive care at 3pm when it's scheduled to reopen. There is a waiting room just nearby: a small room with glass walls so you can see in and out. Most people sit in there in small clusters.

I first notice a group of Islamic women who are wearing hijabs. To my left is a red-haired woman in her sixties. She has a friend or relative of similar age and appearance sitting with her. Opposite me is an Asian family. An elderly woman, and a man and a woman both in their thirties. I don't know whether the younger man and woman are husband and wife or brother and sister. They speak quietly among themselves. I can't hear them well enough to pick the language. A stocky, middle-aged man with thick, grey short-cropped hair sits slumped on the floor to my right. He looks like he has had a hard night and is very sleepy. Everyone is containing their interactions to their own immediate circle. Except the grey-haired man and me. We are alone.

Eventually, the ward is reopened and we all file in to be with our loved ones.

I find Nan turned to her left side. I grab my chair and place it there to be looking at her. It's even more tricky to get comfortable around the medical equipment on that side.

Nan is still motionless. Breathing with the ventilator. She looks peaceful. Quite serene. She doesn't appear to be dreaming. No eyes flickering or movement of her body at all. What is it like to be in a coma? It is so strange to behold. I've never seen it other than on TV before. She looks like she could stir and wake at any moment.

Is she experiencing anything? Can she hear me when I talk to her? Does she know who I am? I reach out to hold her hand. Her skin feels cool from the air conditioning. It's soothing for me to touch her, and I hope it is for her too somehow. I have to believe it is.

Kim is still nursing Nan. She is doing a twelve-hour shift. She moves to Nan's side and explains to me that she needs to perform a small procedure that is not pleasant to witness. I offer to leave but it will only take a minute or so.

They need to make Nan cough. Pneumonia is an ever-ready enemy of the immobile. Kim withdraws a long tool of flexible wire from sterilised packaging and inserts it down and beyond the ventilator tube into Nan's oesophagus. It tickles and disturbs Nan's throat. Her body starts to convulse as best it can. She grimaces, her face reddens and there is the muffled sound of coughing from deep beneath the ventilator tube. She looks uncomfortable. Kim probes again and another coughing spasm occurs. The convulsion of Nan's body is slow and her movement snake-like from toe to head. Kim was right: it is deeply unpleasant to witness.

I'm conscious of the condition of her recently operated-upon brain. Is this too much for her? In the end it's cruelty for kindness.

'I'm sorry Nan,' Kim apologises. 'I need to suction you as well.'

She pulls the suction unit from the wall, turns it on and starts to clear Nan's mouth from anything she has brought up. There doesn't appear to be anything much. The procedure is over, and Nan seems to settle more quickly than I do. The redness gradually disappears from her face. They reposition her and check her diaper pad every two or three hours.

Around 6pm my phone rings and it's Patrick, a lifelong friend. He lives in Sydney and he's known Nan as long as I have. He's very fond of her and she of him. I can hear the genuine compassion from Patrick over the phone. He's saddened to hear what's happened and he knows how close Nan and I are. He offers to come in. I initially resist but then accept it. I tell him visiting hours end at 8pm and we agree he will come just before then and we can grab something to eat. When I hang up, I'm happy to know Patrick is coming. He's a great person and I know I'll feel less alone, even if it's just momentarily.

A little before eight, Patrick texts me that he's arrived in the waiting room. As we greet, I'm sure the look on my face tells him everything. I'm exhausted and stressed. We are both shaking our heads in disbelief. I give him a brief summary of what to expect and then take him back in to visit Nan.

When we get to the bed, I lean down and tell Nan that Patrick is here to visit. Pat reaches in and kisses her on the forehead. He holds her hand and speaks gently and kindly to her. I can see the impact it has upon him. He looks at me and laughs and shakes his head with nervousness and exasperation. It's so strange witnessing his interaction with Nan. It's like listening to someone speaking on the phone but only hearing one side of the conversation. Is she hearing and answering in her own mind I wonder, or is she completely oblivious?

When it reaches 8pm and visiting hours end, Patrick and I say goodnight to Nan with a kiss, hug and hand clasp each. We head out the back of the hospital into Kogarah. We are walking around aimlessly trying to find somewhere to eat. I'm recounting the last thirty-six hours to him and can't get very interested in food. We decide on a fried chicken place because it's quick and easy. Patrick orders for us and I sit down and wait.

I can't help looking at a young Islamic guy sitting nearby. I'm more than a little uncomfortable about their religion since the events of 9/11. Andrea, a work colleague of mine, was killed in the Bali bombing of 2002. I'd been about to offer her a job in my team when I learned she was missing. The Islamic man is in his early twenties, and he's dressed in a luminescent white robe with a matching hat. I'm fascinated by his appearance and how a young guy like that publicly displays his religion. I and most of my cohort raised in the Catholic system have long since shunned our religious roots. He sees me looking at him.

'G'day mate,' he says in an Aussie accent.

'Hi. How are you?' I respond. That's the end of the conversation, but some barrier or resistance in my mind is disturbed a little by that briefest of encounters.

After Patrick and I eat, I head back to my unit at Bezzina House. I'm exhausted and climb into bed. It's my first night in a bed since this happened. In the dark and attempted silence that a busy city address offers, I think back over what's happened. Still in disbelief, I expect to wake every hour, wondering whether the hospital will ring to advise of Nan's passing. Instead, I fall into one of the deepest sleeps of my adult life. My own coma.

* * *

I arrive a little earlier than the opening time next morning and head to the waiting room. The grey-haired man from yesterday is sound asleep on the floor and hasn't changed clothes. I guess he's pulled another all-nighter. He sleeps through other arrivals when the ward finally opens.

I'm relieved to find Nan the same as yesterday. She hasn't left me overnight. I ask today's nurse whether there has been any change.

'No, she's had a calm and comfortable night David,' responds Siobhan. I assume my seat at her bedside as Siobhan goes about her tasks in the same fashion as Kim yesterday. It's not long before she comes in close to Nan, holds both her hands and attempts to elicit a response.

'Nan,' she calls out quite strongly. 'Will you squeeze my hand please Nan.' She waits a few seconds and then tries again. 'Nan, squeeze my hand. Squeeze my hand please Nan.' There is no response, so she tries something else.

'Nan, can you poke out your tongue please? Poke out your tongue Nan.' She again waits a few seconds before making the request again. Nan doesn't respond. Siobhan then pulls back the sheet so she can grasp Nan's feet and asks her to wiggle her toes. She asks again and no response.

Siobhan advises me to keep trying this with Nan while I'm sitting there. Nan might recognise my voice and respond better than to a stranger. I try the routine Siobhan has just done but there is nothing. No movement, no squeeze, no tongue poke for me either.

I'm advised that there will be a family meeting today. I'm not sure what to expect, but at the appointed time I make my way to the characterless meeting room at the entrance. There are four or five men waiting for me inside as I take my seat. We are seated at close quarters.

The man taking the lead is very well-spoken. Andrew is head of intensive care. He is also a trained neurologist. He introduces Sayeed who is sitting to his left and behind. He's the consultant neurosurgeon who performed Nan's surgery. There is no sign of Johnny the registrar that I met the day before. There are two other doctors who are introduced to me, but they are bit-part players in the scheme of things.

The room is dim. Their complexions are grim. Grim is the theme of the day. I'm seated with the Brothers Grimm, but this is no fairy-tale. It's more like a war council or meeting of mob leaders. A homicide interview with a perpetrator. Marriage mediation. But none of those can possibly be of the weight of this room. Both sides are tense. Lives are, or more specifically, Nan's life, is at stake.

Andrew starts to talk. He tells me that with the size of Nan's bleed and the absence of any response from her to date, her chances of survival are low, let alone prospects for her future life. It's a duel and he's inflicted the first wound. I quickly lose focus. I'm bleeding and bobbing around on the surface of consciousness. I'm in a silent movie without subtitles. Rather than speeding up, this movie seems to be in slow motion. I get it though: this is to prepare me for the worst.

As he further describes Nan's condition and chances, I'm wounded again. And again. I have no option but to fight back or I will go down. I have no idea what I said, but I notice Sayeed (who had remained silent throughout) recoils. I'm not ready to give up or give her up is the point and they understand that. They retreat, as do I, both knowing there will be more of this unless she responds in some way or wakes soon.

The meeting ends within ten or fifteen minutes, and I go to the only place of refuge, back to Nan's bedside. As I walk back through the carnage of intensive care, having survived that battle, I'm still in slow motion. I don't seem to be able to hear what's going on around me, but am very aware of my own heartbeat. Am I actually physically wounded? It feels like they took some of me. I don't feel whole.

I sit down next to Nan again and hold her hand. Drawing from her and hoping I'm not taking from her. She's given so much in her life to me. I tell her we need to keep going. We need to fight hard. I will be with her and will not leave.

* * *

My phone rings and it's Jill. She's here at St George. I didn't know she was coming, but I'm pleased to hear that and I walk down to the reception to greet her. Like me, she has a roller suitcase with her. We hug and then head back up to intensive care. I inform her of the meeting I've had and that the medical team are pessimistic about Nan's chances.

When we get to Nan, I introduce Jill to Siobhan then Jill leans down to kiss Nan and tell her she is here. She tells Nan that Joan is OK. I know why she does that: Nan has been her mum's carer for so long. It's reassurance for Nan but I'm not bothered about anyone else. Only Nan.

We grab a second chair and take our places either side of Nan, talking across her. We talk about the previous day, where I'm staying and so on. We talk with Siobhan about being an intensive care nurse. They are specifically chosen and need to do additional training for the role. I'm sure a key aspect they are chosen for is their ability to relate to families in dire situations like this. She is natural and easy to talk to. Just like Kim was yesterday.

Siobhan has children and this is her last day this week. I'm disappointed to hear that. She's doing a nice job and I'm comfortable with her. I want some stability as Christ knows there isn't too much of that now. She reassures us that everyone who will nurse Nan here will be great.

Siobhan suggests we get some photos of Nan, her family and pets, and stick them up around the bedside. That's to give staff looking after her the full picture. She's more than her current condition would indicate. She matters to people. We are then encouraged to take some photographs of Nan as she now is. That's to look back on in the future for perspective. I'm not keen on that and don't photograph her. Would it be a photo to one day show she had no chance? Or a photo to one day show how far she had come?

Jill and I sit with Nan for hours as Siobhan goes through her routines. We leave when it's time to turn her and change her pad. 'Freshen her up,' as they like to term it. We return to experience some more of the cough stimulation. It's confronting for Jill, and she looks over to me with concern. It's confronting for me too, but I'm already toeing the line and explain it's to stop fluid settling on her lungs.

It's nearing 8pm and time for us to leave, but there is a problem. A young doctor I haven't met before arrives to tell us they have detected a pressure build-up in Nan's brain. It's dangerous and needs to be addressed urgently. They think that blood and fluid since her bleed and surgery are not dissipating properly, and they need to operate to put an extra drain in. He presents me with a consent form to sign on her behalf. Before I sign that, he tells me of the risks. Infection, strokes and even death are possible. There is no alternative, so I sign it with a shaky hand and before he heads off, I ask him how long it will take and when they will start.

'We will collect her very shortly and it should be done within a couple of hours.'

Jill and I look at each other with a glum resignation. I reach over to touch Nan and tell her they need to do a small procedure to make things better. Siobhan has already begun disconnecting any equipment and it's not long at all before they arrive for her.

We are left with the spot where her bed once was. Now a gaping hole. It's the visual equivalent of what I'm starting to feel inside. A void. Half of me gone. But she hasn't really left. *They are doing what they can* I tell myself. Jill and I sit awkwardly there without Nan and the bed between us. We decide to go and get some dinner while we wait. There is an Italian-style café nearby so we decide on pizzas. It's hard to make much conversation and instead we concentrate on eating when they arrive. Once done, I'm keen to return in case they are out early. It isn't the evening for a long dinner and chat.

Arriving back at the rear entrance to the hospital, we find it locked due to the later hour and have to walk around the front to gain admission. Despite visiting hours having concluded, there are still plenty of people milling about in the main entrance foyer. As we enter the lift, we are joined by a group of Islamic men including one who I guess is an Imam. He is tall and wears a one-piece neck-to-toe robe of some splendour. On his head is a large white circular cloth wrap. It's larger at the top than at its base. The other men in the lift are clearly deferring to him. Somebody has some clout here if a guy like this is visiting. I want to ask him to do something to help Nan. To prompt whoever it is they ask. I'm not wedded to anything or anyone in terms of religiosity these days. Any port in a storm. I manage to resist.

We need to wait about another hour before they bring Nan back to intensive care. She is now sporting a new tube from above the left side of her forehead. I'm told it is a drain and there is a bag on the end of it where they collect the fluid that comes out. There is some kind of gauge on the end with which they can keep an eye on pressure. We are advised the surgery went well. Normally such news would be greeted with relief, but in the circumstances, there still isn't much to be relieved about. The let off from stress is partial.

We wait and talk to Nan for a little while before deciding it's late, we are tired, and there isn't anything more we can do tonight.

Back in the unit, I retire to the bedroom and Jill gets ready to sleep on a foldout bed in the lounge and kitchen area. I call out goodnight and quickly drop off to sleep.

It's not long before the phone rings loudly. I'm out of the bed and in the next room with a single movement. My heart is beating wildly. I'm terrified. This must be the call I've been dreading for the last seventy-two hours. I guess she just couldn't survive the surgery. Jill has answered the phone. It was hers ringing.

'David, it's Bruce,' she quickly tells me once she hears the other end. Bruce is Nan's brother. He and his wife Joanne had just arrived in Sri Lanka for a holiday before all this happened. This is the first we've heard from him. Frank got a message to him somehow and he wants to know what's going on. I return to my room and sit on the edge of my bed with my head in my hands, trying to settle again. My heart is still racing and I'm taking deep breaths. I hear Jill talking Bruce through what has happened with pauses for him at the other end. They seem to cover the update on Nan and then there is a pause by Jill, and I hear her respond, 'he's devastated.' She's obviously telling Bruce how I am. She hangs up and confirms what I already know. That it's Bruce calling from Sri Lanka.

'Is he coming home early?' I ask.

'Probably. He hasn't fully decided what to do. They are looking into how to do that.' I don't mind admitting to Jill that the phone ringing at this hour frightened the shit out me. Her too.

* * *

Another long and deep sleep by my standards, but I'm waking each morning like I need another night. I'm exhausted by the trauma and the grief. Each morning upon waking, my first sensation is the pain and sadness for what's happened. I feel it start in my gut, but in reality, it engulfs all of me like fire or a flash flood. In the privacy of my own room I can cry to myself. Or when alone at Nan's bed. I cry regularly throughout the day. Always when alone. I don't know why, but I now seem to be able to hold off bursting into tears in front of others.

We need to move from Bezzina House and find somewhere else to stay. As I check out, I ask Natalie to book me a room there for any days possible over the next few weeks. It's so much easier to be across the road from the hospital. She won't have anything until next week, so we need to pack up and leave.

Nan has again had a peaceful night despite the events of the previous evening. With the exception of the additional drain in her head, she looks calm and unchanged. Jill and I wish her good morning and sit and talk across Nan for a while before I decide I should call Nan's mum Joan again and let her know what's gone on. I leave the IC unit to do this. When she answers I say, 'Joan, it's David here.'

'Yes,' she answers very tersely. I know it will be stressful for her waiting for our calls. I tell her about the additional surgery overnight and why it was done, but that Nan is the same and comfortable this morning.

'David, does she know you?'

'She's in a coma, Joan.'

'Still?'

'She's been in a coma the whole time. As far as I know she is on drugs to keep her that way.'

'You mean she hasn't been awake at all?'

'NO.'

This is frustrating. How could she have the message so wrong? She's eighty-four but normally on the ball. I guess it's the stress of what's happening, and the absence of Nan and Jill there for regular contact.

'Well, this is no good, David.'

'Joan, she's had a huge brain haemorrhage. She's not going to just wake up and jump out of bed.'

'No, No, No,' she insists. 'I know what I'm talking about. You think I don't, but I do. I've seen these situations. This is bad. I'm her mother. I know she wouldn't want this. You need to make a decision David.'

'It's only been a few days, Joan. She needs to be given a chance.' I am trying to remain civil and respectful. I've always had a good relationship with her but I'm quickly losing my patience.

'She won't be the same person. I've seen this before. You listen to me.'

I can't be bothered arguing or rationalising or trying to talk her around. Everyone here is doing their best and hoping Nan can come through, yet her blind, 84-year-old mother is abandoning ship already from 600 kilometres away. That's all we need. I told her the previous day about the pessimism of the doctors when I met them. I felt up until then that truthful communication was the best thing to do within the family.

'You listen to the doctors and do as they say,' she demands, 'and call me again later.' I'm not sure who hung up first. I don't think either of us even bothered to say goodbye. I'm pissed off by the call and decide on a few minutes of fresh air before returning to the IC unit.

'Well, that was fun. Not.' I tell Jill on my arrival.

'Why?' I give her the details. Jill tells me she will call her for another update later in the day. The nurses continue the regular neurological tests to see if they can elicit a response from Nan. The outcome is the same. No response at all. The timing of that testing is not great given the phone call I've just had. We've been advised of another family meeting for tomorrow. Those three things are building the pressure. I start to despair over Nan's chances. Is Joan just saying what everyone else is thinking? Is that what Jill thinks too?

It's one thing to build your own mental impression from 600 kilometres away of how Nan is going. It's another to sit here with her and look at her all day. Watching her breathing with the respirator. Feeling her skin and feeling her hair. Hoping her eyes will flicker. Hoping she will move her hand towards her face. I look at her and still love her. She's still alive and she's still my Nan. My response is to lean forward and kiss Nan on the forehead. Tell her I love her yet again, ask her gently to wake up for me, take her hand and sit there holding it. The rest of that day passes with what has quickly become the routine. We grab a bite to eat a little earlier for a break in the evening and then come back to Nan before visiting hours are over.

* * *

We need to move to a new hotel. I have booked us into a Formula One hotel near Sydney airport. We bid Nan goodnight and catch a taxi there. It was a last-minute decision and it's awful and depressing. Tiny little rooms and basic functionality. Cheap. It will do for one night only. It's there for outgoing or incoming travellers and is surrounded by roads and carparks. The only nearby eating option is Hungry Jack's at the other end of the car park. I grab some burgers for Jill and me and afterwards we return to the hotel to our rooms.

I'm waiting until it's bedtime and my phone rings. It's my former boss and colleague Jonathan calling from England. He and his wife Michaela spent four years based in Albury–Wodonga and we had several social occasions as couples. They are very fond of Nan and very concerned for her. The events of the day have left me despondent about Nan's chances. I tell him I don't think she's going to make it, but we will hang in and hope. They are hoping and praying for a good outcome for Nan. I tell him I will let him know how we get on and hang up. Before going to sleep that night, I have a very long cry.

I get into bed. The hotel is noisy given its proximity to Sydney airport. Planes are arriving and taking off frequently even at that time of night. My sleep is fitful.

A CALL AND A RESPONSE

Thirty years to the day before Nan had the stroke, 25 August 1984, I had surgery to remove my cancerous left testicle. It was a Saturday. Three days before that, I told Nan it felt swollen and hard. She checked it herself and thought I should see a doctor. Next day, I saw her GP. The day after that I saw a urologist, Robert McGregor. McGregor immediately confirmed it was testicular cancer and that my ball needed to be removed.

'I've got cancer?' I questioned him in panic.

'Yes, but it's very treatable. Your chances are good. Don't be thinking about Peter Crimmins (a prominent footballer who died eight years earlier from testicular cancer). A lot has changed. You have a 90 per cent chance of survival.' *Or a 10 per cent chance of dying* I thought to myself.

I went from his consulting room directly to the handbag and travel goods business that Nan and her mum owned. I knew I would find her there. Joan sent me out back where Nan was unpacking a delivery. She took one look at me and knew something was wrong.

'I've got testicular cancer,' I said.

She started crying and so did I. We were young. It was a month before my twenty-third birthday and a month after her twenty-fourth. When Joan found us, she was also concerned and supportive, but more in control of her emotions than us. Nan left with me to tell my parents and stayed the rest of the day. She was there by my side the next day for the surgery and the day after that when her parents visited me in hospital.

We drove to Wagga for scans, and I was sent to Sydney to see a prominent oncologist. I was given the option of a 'watch and see' period or the alternative of major abdominal surgery to remove a lot of glands which is where this cancer would spread to next. The surgery provided better chances of survival than the watch period, but it would impede my ability to have children naturally. Nanette urged me to have the surgery.

'What do children matter? That's too far away to even think about. You've got to survive. That's what is most important to me.'

We had been together about eighteen months by this time. I understood that family and loved ones were what mattered most to Nan. I remember her doting on her young nephew and niece and knew she would have been a great mother. She was already clear in her mind we would be married so this was a massive self-sacrifice on her part.

My surgery went for seven hours and there was a long recovery period. Nan stayed in the same hotel as my parents, and they were together more than they had been in the past. This may have scarred others, but she took it in her stride. She was always such great support to me, and this experience bonded us even further.

I remember my dad at the foot of my hospital bed. Misty-eyed, unprompted and somewhat incredulously announcing, 'Gee she's a good girl David.' He didn't verbalise it, but he meant 'hang onto this one'. We married 28 February 1987. The day after our wedding day, Dad spent so long singing Nan's praises to his brother Martin, that Martin told him he was in love with his daughter-in-law.

* * *

The family meeting is scheduled for 5pm. By mid-afternoon that day, Nan hasn't responded to any of the regular prompting from the nurses or me. I'm losing hope that she will wake up or recover. Why do I have to make a decision? Why can't we just give her whatever time she needs? It's only been a few days. My phone rings and it's Joan again.

'Have you had the meeting?' she asks.

'No, I told you it's not until 5pm.'

'You need to let her go David. I know it's not easy. It's what Nanette would want. I know it. She's my daughter. I know she would not want this, I am sure of it.'

'I don't know how you can be so sure of that Joan. She once told me that if ever she was in a life-threatening situation, she'd want to be given a chance.'

'David, she won't be the same person. She might be suffering.'

'She's unconscious Joan. She doesn't look to be in any discomfort at all.'

I'm torn between being furious with Joan and starting to wonder if she is right. It's a terrible decision to make. Nan is here and she is alive. If I agree to it, they will stop the machine and Nan will die. How can I decide to end her life? We don't know with certainty she won't wake up. We don't know that she will either. We don't know what kind of recovery, if any, she might make. Letting her go is like a pre-emptive abortion in case the outcome doesn't suit my lifestyle.

While talking to Joan, I'm pacing up and down the corridor outside the intensive care waiting room. There are half a dozen Muslim women sitting in there talking and waiting and I want some privacy. Tears are streaming down my face while I'm talking, and Joan is pushing this line of argument. I try not to let her hear the emotion in my voice. I decide I have had enough.

'Well Joan, I will wait and hear what the doctors have to say. They will know better than any of us.'

I know she isn't going to listen to what I think but she might respect the opinion of doctors. It's just a strategy to get her off the phone and out of my hair.

I hang up and pace the corridors for a while longer, anxious about the forthcoming discussion and what to do. I'll treat it like the many discussions and decision-making situations I had in my job. Hear the facts, ask a lot of questions and go from there.

Returning to the waiting room to take a seat, I notice the six Muslim women deep in discussion. They are speaking Arabic, so I don't understand them, but I know they are talking about me. They keep turning from each other to look at me as they speak. I don't really care. Say what you like. I just want to sit down until I'm allowed back in. Suddenly, one of them breaks into English.

'Is that your wife in there?'

'Yes, it is,' I respond.

'We are wondering what has happened to her?'

I look up at them. The hijabs make them all look alike and hard to distinguish. Despite that, I notice that some of them are prettier than the others. They are all in their twenties and thirties except for one who is closer to my age.

'She had a big stroke a few days ago. A brain haemorrhage.' There is much nodding and sounds of sympathy and understanding.

'Is she going to be OK?' another woman asks.

'I don't know. It's not looking good. She is in a coma. She hasn't responded in any way.'

'Have you been married long? Do you have children or other family here?'

'We've been married twenty-seven years. We don't have children. We just have each other. My wife's sister Jill is here with me.'

'What is your name and what is your wife's name?' asks the older woman.

'My wife's name is Nanette and I am David.'

'I'm Rania,' she says. 'God bless you, David. God bless Nanette. Keep fighting for her. She's lucky to have you.'

'Thank you, Rania.'

'God bless you David, you fight for her,' Rania repeats again.

There is violent agreement from the rest of them in the room. I suddenly feel a new strength. A right to fight rather than feeling like I have to let her go. Not everyone thinks this is all in vain. I am touched and emboldened by their intervention and kindness. I thank them all and wish them well.

When I'm in the corridor again, one of the younger women has followed me out. She wants to talk some more. She says she wishes she had a husband like me. Her marriage has just broken up and she sees what Nanette means to me. She wishes she had that kind of relationship. That kind of love. I thank her for the compliment but am a little taken aback as we stand there alone outside intensive care. It's strange to be having a discussion like this. I wish her the best and tell her I hope she finds happiness. I never saw her again.

* * *

At 5pm, Jill and I walk the fifteen metres or so from Nan's bed to the meeting room. On entry we find Andrew along with a tall, slim Indian man with a moustache. His name is Raju and he is a registrar in the intensive care unit. Again, a couple of junior doctors are present as well. Not the same ones as the previous meeting. I guess these are the guys on shift this day. I introduce Jill, and Andrew invites us to sit down. He's nice, polite, and erudite. Not at all arrogant.

These are difficult discussions to have. Andrew begins by giving more background on the extent of Nan's brain haemorrhage. It's huge. It's on the right side of her brain. She remains unconscious and unresponsive, and the belief is that her chances of any recovery are very slim. It's not even certain whether she will regain consciousness. He asks us to talk about Nan and her life. Her interests, work, etc. We didn't get that far in the previous meeting, but it's a good way to get us talking.

I begin by talking about her art. 'Nan is an artist. She does some casual art teaching at the TAFE college in Albury. She previously operated a couple of retail businesses, but when they closed a long time ago, she studied an art degree. She is also a carer for her mother who is blind and widowed.'

'She's very intelligent and extremely well-read. Her first degree was in media studies with a heavy English literature component,' I add.

'What kind of an artist is she?' Andrew asks.

'She mainly does printmaking. Scratching out plates and using inks to print the pieces. She's done work with textiles as well. She's had some exhibitions of her art in our local area and in Melbourne too. She normally works those up annually.'

Andrew takes quite a long pause before responding. 'Do you understand that she won't be able to do any of that now? Her life as it was even a week ago is over. This insult to her brain is life-changing.'

'She will not walk again. She will not be able to teach again. She will not be able to drive again. She will be in a wheelchair. Very likely she is destined for a life in institutional care. That's only the beginning of the impacts to Nan.'

It's our turn to pause as that sinks in. It's a hammer blow. My brain tries to push it away as not true, but I know he's not making it up. The very worst thing I could have heard was that she was gone. He hasn't said that. But the detailed verdict is very disturbing. Very confronting. We are on the back foot and remain silent and listening. Andrew then asks us for our reactions, or more pertinently, what Nanette's reaction would be.

'Did Nan ever declare a position on treatment if she was in a situation like this?'

I'm considering my words and then answer. 'Well, we never discussed anything as specific as this. I mean, how could you ever predict what's happening here? It's come out of the blue. There is one thing I remember her saying which is relevant I think.'

Andrew is listening intently.

'We were watching TV a few years back and there was a show about people in life-threatening situations. We discussed it a little and I asked her what she thought. She said that if ever she was in a situation like that, she would want me to make the decision because she knew I would want her to live and I would give her every chance. The main point from that Andrew, is that Nan would want a chance.'

Andrew nods and then responds. 'So, what do you think? Having heard what I told you, what is your reaction?'

'I don't really know. It's only been a few days. I mean, isn't she on drugs to keep her in a coma? To allow her body and brain to rest?'

'They've been stopped. That's not why she hasn't woken.'

That's one of the few remaining hopes snatched away. While we pause to take that in, Andrew jumps in with another point.

'Let me just put this option out there for you to think about. I repeat, she's had a massive life-changing stroke. Her quality of life will be drastically reduced. If you are at the point where you think we should not go further, we can end this for Nan and for you. This does not have to go on forever without end. There is a way out.'

'What, you mean you turn off the ventilator and she stops breathing?' I ask. 'I mean, isn't that terrible for Nan? Would she be gasping for air? I don't want her to suffer.'

'No, there are a number of steps we can take that enable this to be very peacefully and painlessly concluded.'

I'm wondering how they can be sure of that. No one has ever been through that and is here to tell of the experience. I'm even wondering whether it is legal to do it.

'We can do this. If families know that the patient would not want treatment to continue, we can give the option.'

'Andrew, if stopping the ventilator means Nan would pass away, are you telling us that she is already brain dead? I've heard that term. Is it just the ventilator doing the breathing for her?'

'So, brain death is a situation that can occur, but Nan is not brain dead. She is definitely not brain dead.'

'So, in that case, stopping the ventilator alone is not necessarily going to end Nan's life? That means we would be making an active decision and taking steps to do that? I feel very uncomfortable about deciding to end her life.'

'David, the problem is people in these situations can linger on for months or years and that's not in anyone's interest.'

'How long do people normally take to wake up after something like this? What is normal? I have had no experience in this kind of thing. Does the amount of time unconscious mean anything to recovery? Is it a problem to remain in a coma for a long time?'

'Well it varies to tell the truth. People can wake up quite quickly, within the first few days even, or else take weeks. The length of time unconscious does seem to indicate the likely recovery. So, we know that the longer it takes to wake, the poorer the overall recovery or outcome is. If the patient wakes within the first few days, the better the outcome.' Andrew then looks to Jill for her view.

'I'm very worried about something like locked-in syndrome. I think that would be horrible. I would hate to think that Nan could be in a situation like that. Unable to move or speak or indicate what she was thinking or feeling. That would be terrible.'

I'm alarmed by the possibility that Jill has raised. I don't want that either. There is another reflective pause in the room. We are all looking at each other.

'Andrew,' I say. 'I need some specifics. If Nan does wake up, would she be able to see, hear, speak, understand and communicate, write and at least have some movement?'

'If she wakes, then yes, she should be able to speak, to hear, to understand and communicate. She would be paralysed down her left side, but given she is right-handed, she should be able to write and use that right hand. In terms of vision, there would be some visual impacts, but she wouldn't really be bothered by that.'

'What kind of visual impacts? I don't understand,' I asked.

'So, she would lose vision on the left-hand sides of both eyes. She would be able to see out the right side. But, to give you an example, I can't see out the back of my head, but that doesn't trouble me. My brain doesn't expect to be able to do that. It's not part of our normal visual field.'

'Andrew, what would be the impacts to her personality? Are you able to predict that? Would she be the same as she is now? I have heard about people having strokes and then behaving very differently to how they were.'

'That's something we don't know,' he responds.

But the verdict on communication is enough for me. That's hope. There's a possibility that Nan could have something of a life beyond here. We all pause and reflect again and then I make my call.

'Andrew, I know that the most important thing in Nanette's life is her family. It's not career, it's not about being active. There is her art, but even that is of secondary importance. Her life is about us and being with us and feeling loved and giving love.'

'Considering everything we've heard here and thinking about what Nan said about wanting a chance, I want more time. I want another week. I want her to have the chance to wake up and be with us, even if that isn't for very long. I couldn't live with the thought of ending this too quickly and not giving her every chance to come back. To me, it's only been a few days. I hear what you said about the size of what's happened and her chances, but I want another week at least. What do you think?'

I see Andrew nodding and he's taking his time. He knows I mean it. He's looking from me to Jill who is silent. He agrees to it.

'OK,' he says. 'I have to say, other medical staff here would take a much harder position on this, but I think another week is fine given the discussion and the circumstances.'

That's a little unnerving to hear. It concerns me that the judgement could be subjective, that different people would have different opinions. These people would proudly declare themselves as scientific and rational. Yet these are very grey areas, and where there are varying opinions, and any degree of uncertainty, how could anyone claim to be more correct than anyone else? The reality is no one actually knows for sure. It's a game of probabilities and likelihoods.

After a pause, he shakes his head, breaks into a friendly smile, and says 'I'm sorry, I have to ask. What do you people do? What kind of work? These discussions are often terrible. I mean, we get screamed at in these circumstances, but this is one of the most rational and considered conversations of this nature I've ever had.'

Jill explains she has been a teacher all her life. I tell Andrew about my corporate career and executive jobs. I don't quite know what he expected, but I'm glad he found us sensible and rational. I feel very empowered by having argued for and won more time for Nan. What could be more important than the life of the person you love most?

Andrew then tells us he will be away for three weeks from today and that the lead of intensive care will be taken up by a woman called Rita. He emphasises she is a very compassionate, kind and capable doctor.

When we leave the room, Andrew takes me to a screen where he shows me the CT scans of Nan's brain. They are black and white, like photographic negatives. It's my first view of images like this and it's hard to discern left from right. Andrew points to Nan's eyes for orientation, but even then, it's hard to know if the shot is from the top or the bottom and thus the left/right confusion.

As he moves through various angles and images he points to a large, misshapen white area in Nan's right hemisphere. That's the site of the original bleed. It looks to be huge and to have consumed thirty per cent or so of the space there. He stresses that this is now damaged brain and it will not recover or repair. Andrew points to the division between the left and right hemispheres. They call it the midline. The bleed has caused her right side to swell and push over towards the left, placing pressure on that side as well. I can clearly see that on the scan. He calls this midline shift. He then takes me to other images that show more damage to the back of her brain in the left hemisphere. These are infarct strokes that Nan suffered as a result of her brain swelling against her skull.

Any temporary high I carried from the meeting has now been firmly swept away. The scans are very disturbing to behold. I thank Andrew for his time and go outside for a break. I'm feeling a little bit sick from the discussion and the images, and need some space and fresh air.

When I return to the unit, Jill has told her mother that the medical team agreed to another week. I knew she would find a diplomatic way to get the point across. I'm beyond diplomacy. I don't have the energy to be constructing palatable explanations for anyone. Jill also said she had a few moments with Andrew before I got back.

'David, I told Andrew you would do anything for Nanette.'

'That won't hurt. Thanks for doing that,' I respond. 'I really would.'

Jill decided she would go back to Albury. I'm very grateful she was here with me these few days. I find a hotel in the suburb of Arncliffe, a couple of suburbs from Kogarah, and after spending a few more hours with Nan, I grab a bite to eat and then catch a taxi there. A good-natured man is waiting at reception when I go in. Moving hotels every couple of days isn't much fun but I'm relieved to hear from Natalie at Bezzina House that she can take me back in for five nights the following week.

* * *

The next morning, I rise and have breakfast. The sun is shining outside. Sydney is much warmer than home. I decide to try the train from the nearby Arncliffe station. It's three stops to Kogarah station and I walk from there to the hospital. It's almost officially the start of spring. I'm enthusiastic, buoyed by the week's reprieve. I can focus on being with Nan and talking to her. Trying to coax her back to this side. Hoping that somehow she can hear me and know that there is love and care waiting for her here.

I wonder if she is in that famous tunnel and experiencing that deep inner peace. Is she drawn towards a light? Surrounded by deceased loved ones? Her father? Her grandparents? The children she never gave birth to? Are they beckoning to her that it is her time? Are the pets of her life there? Her dogs and cats? Is she nuzzling against her big bay horse Sam? Feeling the shaggy winter coat of his powerful neck against her face and body. Putting out his lucerne hay and horse muesli. Hearing the sounds of his nickering with joy. Seeing the steam rise from his semi-damp back when she pulls his coat off to bask in the sunshine. Saddling him up for a ride through the hills of nirvana. With boundless, beautiful trails to traverse in safety and constant happy surprises at every turn. That would be a compelling pull for Nan, but I hope there is still enough on this side to coerce her to stay.

I meet Rita who is taking Andrew's place in charge of intensive care. My initial anxiety over a new IC lead evaporates quickly. Rita is lovely: warm, engaging, tactile and hopeful of a positive outcome for Nan.

Nan's condition is unchanged. She remains immobile and unconscious. The nurses continue the usual monitoring, attention and prompting. At one point, Raju the registrar comes over to Nan's bed. He decides to do his own prompting of Nan, asking her to squeeze his hand and poke out her tongue. He starts off gently but then urges her strongly, trying to be heard through the fog of delirium. I start to think of Nan's university friend Sanjay, who I never met but she was fond of. Hopefully something in Raju's accent will hit a chord of familiarity. Raju tries a few times without response and then decides to sit and relax with us both for a few minutes out of his busy day. We talk about what has happened. He is gentle, caring, and compassionate. I am very drawn to him. I told him Andrew took me through the scans and I saw the additional infarcts.

'Yes,' he replies, 'that's what we think is the tragedy in this. That she lost so much time from when the bleed happened until she was here and operated on.'

'It doesn't pay to live in the country,' I reply.

'Well, it can happen on the steps of the hospital and we are unable to help, but in this case, lost time was critical. She sustained further damage because of that.'

Raju moves off and I'm left to contemplate as I sit with Nan. The day passes without change in Nan's condition or any response. As does the next.

It's now Saturday evening, and I'm standing at Nan's bedside almost ready to leave for the day. The nursing head for the unit approaches. We've nodded to each other a few times before, but this time she decides to stop and ask how things are.

'We aren't getting any responses,' I reply despairingly. She comes over to me and strokes my arm as we look down at Nan. Her comforting touch is almost too much. My resistance is fractured, and I have to hold back tears. She then says something I've never forgotten. 'There's a saying I like in these situations: Good things happen slowly. Time without new problems is a good thing. We will know it and it will happen quickly when something is wrong.'

It's another message to give me hope, delivered by another anonymous angel. The nursing manager is called off to another situation. She was with us long enough to say just the right thing. To leave a lasting quote, a potential mantra.

But then Sunday comes and that's one day before Monday. This Monday will be one week since Nan had the stroke. By Sunday afternoon, there has still been no response at all from Nan to the many attempts by nurses, doctors, and me asking her to simply squeeze our hands. My mood has deteriorated considerably with each day since that hopeful time after the family meeting. I'm amazed how quickly those few days went by.

In the afternoon intensive care rest period, I decide to take a break in my hotel room. My phone rings and it's my brother Bill. I hadn't talked to him since this started. We had communicated via text. I tell him it seems all hope is lost. It's almost been a week and there has been no response.

'Do you want me to come down?' he asks.

'Well, I'm not sure, that's up to you … actually, it looks like there's going to be a funeral. It would probably be better if you waited and came for that. I think all of this is going to end over the next few days, so the funeral will be later next week.'

When it's time to go back to the hospital, I decide on the train again. I had walked the distance a couple of times between the Arncliffe hotel and Kogarah but didn't feel like it this day. As I stand on the station at Arncliffe, I'm aware of a strange feeling in my body. I feel like half of me has been taken away. Just like Nan, it's my left-hand side. I can still walk and move, but I feel hollowed out. An absence. A loss. A physical reflection in my body of what's happened. A huge part of me gone. I've lost her. I'm sure of it.

I notice a diesel locomotive approaching the platform. It's not slowing down and clearly is not stopping here. It seems to be moving in slow motion but it's definitely going fast enough. It seems to take an age to get to me. I'm contemplating, and step towards the edge of the platform. She's gone, I'm thinking. I want to be with her. What's the point of continuing without Nan? Here's my chance.

Some remnants of Catholic guilt, the evils of suicide and the price of eternal damnation enter my mind. Then a dose of sheer reluctant cowardice holds me back a little. But the real hand of God moment comes from the thought that I can't go while Nan is still here. I will see it through. I must be there for her.

When I get back to the hospital bed, she is still there as I last left her. Breathing with the ventilator, looking peaceful. No change. It's hard to sit and look at her now. I'm feeling awfully guilty. I will be making the decision to stop care. The decision to turn the ventilator off and end Nan's life. What kind of husband am I? I try convincing myself that there is no hope, and I will be doing what is best for Nan. All that claptrap that is true in some cases but doesn't seem to be here. I lean forward to Nan and say, 'Nanny, if you can hear me, you really need to show us something now. Please, please, please wake up, respond, do something.' There is nothing. As the day draws to a close, I'm clear that on Tuesday I will agree to ending treatment and care. There is always some sense of relief in making a difficult decision, but that is only the most minute of rewards in this case.

When Monday comes, I go to the hospital for opening time and head straight to Nan's bedside. Unusually, there is no nurse in attendance. When she does arrive, a girl I haven't seen before casually says that there has been some development overnight.

'Oh, has there been a problem?' I ask, seeing Nan lying there as she has been for a week.

'No, something positive, I think, but I'm not sure what it was. It was before I arrived.'

It gives me a little hope but not much. I sit down with Nan and wait until I see one of the doctors. As I look up, I see a smiling Rita striding towards me.

'Hello David, have you heard the news?' she asks.

'Well only that there's been something positive, but I don't know what.'

'It's better than that,' Rita excitedly responds. 'Nanette squeezed the hand of one of our doctors on command this morning. She repeated it. Do you understand how significant this is?'

'She responded?'

'Yes, David.'

'You mean, she heard, processed and took an action?'

'Exactly! David, this is huge. I'm so happy for you.' Rita warmly embraces me, leaving no doubt as to the significance of this.

TAKE A DEEP BREATH

What? Who's that?
Oh, my head hurts
I feel drunk. Am I floating in water?
Is someone close to me? I can't open my eyes
I must be dreaming

Someone has my hand
'Nan, squeeze my hand'
I squeezed it
'She squeezed,' the someone says
I hear other voices
'Nan, can you squeeze my hand again?' says the voice
I squeeze again
'She squeezed again'
More voices
'Nan, can you wiggle your toes.'
It's a man with an accent. I'm wiggling them.
'She did it. She responded.'

They seem excited but I can't stay with them

The Sting song 'It's Probably Me' creeps in. Like all songs, I like it initially because of the melody and harmony.

'How can you not know the words to songs?' Nan would ask.

'Because I don't listen to lyrics. I'm a musician. I'm listening to the melody, the rhythm and the harmony.' Nan knew the words, even to old jazz classics that I learned to play. How could she know them? She absorbed them subconsciously just from being in the house when her father played his records of Ella or Sarah or Billie. But it's the words for me this time in the Sting song. And it wasn't Sting performing it when it comes to my attention. He's there in the front row though, because it's a tribute to him. It's a YouTube video and the performer is jazz singer Gregory Porter. He does it better than Sting did and when you watch Sting taking it in, I'm sure he thinks that too. He's trying to maintain the stiff upper lip and British reserve but towards the end, his eyes are moist.

'A solitary voice to speak out and set me free'

It was Raju that first found Nan of course, languishing on the bottom of a sea of consciousness, her air supply almost depleted or about to be depleted for her. Hanging by her fingertips from a cliff, about to let go or be let go of. Somehow, they connected, and she grabbed on to show she was still there and still fighting. Hearing, understanding, responding, and still within reach. It was only Raju that could find her again the next time, a day or two later. Despite my best efforts, she didn't respond to me. She didn't squeeze my hand or wiggle her one good foot. There would be six full days of trying on my part before I would experience my own success. I was starting to think she had been and gone again and I had missed my chance. It was better that she first responded to one of the doctors. It was a more credible statement when accorded to Raju than to her desperate husband who could be perceived as imagining it, or even making it up.

After Nan responds, the hospital responds back. She is rewarded with a tracheostomy. On the surface not a pleasant gift, but a show of faith from the hospital that they believe she now has some sort of chance.

'Do you really have to do this?' I cringe and ask a junior doctor when he presents me with the waiver form for the trache operation.

'It's best that we do. The mouth is the major source of infection for the human body. The longer we keep breathing tubes in there, the greater risk of Nan picking up some infection. She doesn't need that.'

'Is it going to be permanent? Will this mean she will need one of those electronic voice units to be able to speak?' I ask with some horror, but thinking with some delight that if she recovers, I could take the piss out of her when she used it. I imagine her telling me where to go via electronic voice in return.

'It shouldn't be permanent but it's the right thing to do for now. She should be more comfortable afterwards than with the tubes in her mouth and down her throat.'

I worry about any kind of intervention at any time given her fragile state. I want to leave well enough alone. Especially so soon after Nan has shown a response. It feels like we are throwing caution to the wind. But it's all a matter of trade-offs and I sign the form and waive the waiver away. Medical knowhow is not only about knowing what to do, but when. Best practice. It's not always the case because sometimes we have the misfortune of being on the bleeding edge. But a lot of what is done has been done before many times over.

'You wake the morning, in a stranger's coat'

It's a Sunday afternoon when they take Nan away for the tracheostomy, and I'm sitting in the intensive care waiting room. I hear a helicopter hovering low overhead. There is a window nearby which affords me a good view as the large, loud, and powerful craft descends to the landing pad. I'm joined by another bird fancier dressed in scrubs. We get talking and he tells me he is an anaesthetist who was previously a member of the air ambulance crews. He'd had some amazing flights across Sydney harbour. He is still in awe of the whole concept despite having been in it himself. I tell him I'm waiting for Nan to come out of surgery. He was in there and it's done and has gone well.

'They will bring her out shortly,' he says.

After watching the chopper land and the motors eventually cut, we see the teams descend. The patient is unloaded, and their stretcher rolled into the unit somewhere. The anaesthetist then decides he needs to get on and we bid farewell.

When Nan is returned to intensive care, the breathing tube is connected to a new hole in her throat. At least I can see and access her face better without the ventilator tubes in her mouth. I can even kiss her on the lips which I hope is more stimulating for her. I think she looks a little more peaceful and comfortable with just the feeding tube in her nose. She looks more like Nan.

I guess word got around that Nan gave a response, because some physiotherapists arrive the next day to check on her as well. She is still unconscious, so they can't do much more than ensure she is being turned regularly and have a listen to her chest with a stethoscope.

'You're here a lot,' one of them says to me. 'Would you like to try and help a little? Are you happy to participate in her care?'

'Yes, of course.'

'It would be good for you to regularly move her limbs around. Lift her legs, lift her arms. A big challenge for immobile people is the possibility of DVT. Blood clots. We don't want her to get anything like that. You and I are able to move around and stand and sit and that stops them developing, but Nan is lying here all day.'

She shows me what to do, lifting her arms and bending them at the elbows. Rotating them a little. Completing the various motions we can perform. Then her hands and her legs, bending them at their knees and lifting from the ankles as well. It's true what they say about the dead, uncooperative weight of another human. Nan is completely unconscious, and her arms and legs are surprisingly heavy to lift like this. It is a workout for me as well.

'How often should I do this?' I ask.

'Hourly if you like or as often as you are able. To be honest, the research suggests it isn't that helpful, because we really need to initiate our own movement rather than for it to happen passively. But it won't hurt, and it gives you something to do while you are here.'

I wonder if I am being given work for work's sake. Digging holes and filling them in again. Working for the dole. Anyway, I am fine with that. I hope it might be mentally stimulating for Nan to have her arms and legs moved, even if it isn't that helpful for clots. As I put my new skills into practice, I feel a little embarrassed and awkward doing it in a public place, but no one pays much attention. Everyone there has their own set of worries, or their own job to do, and people adjust to new routines fairly quickly.

'And your eyes search the room. One friendly face is all you need to see'

I am getting more familiar with the other patients and their families that are in intensive care. The Islamic family is watching vigil over Rania's husband. He has some kind of infection and his lungs keep filling up with fluid. The Asian family is mother, son and daughter. They are there for the father of the family who seems to be at the end. They are very sad but resigned to fate.

'He is deteriorating,' says the daughter to me when we have a brief exchange on the street and as we all did, check in on how each other's plights are progressing.

'Nan has responded to one of the doctors with a hand squeeze but nothing yet to me,' I say when it is my turn.

I start to suspect the stocky grey-haired man who is always asleep on the floor might be a homeless guy who has found a way to stay out of the weather. When he is awake, he avoids eye contact with any of us.

The sixty-something red haired woman is Colleen, wife of Garry, who is in the bed closest to Nan. Garry is a very large man well into his sixties. He seems to be semi-conscious, at best delirious, and is constantly trying to get out of bed. When the staff run to settle him down, he gets aggressive and lashes out. They lecture him with raised voices, telling him not to hit or grab them. Poor guy doesn't know what he is doing. He has to be restrained to stop him getting up and then falling down.

Like us, Garry and Colleen are from a country area and so are also away from home. Colleen is staying in Bezzina House, and she is a lovely person to talk to. When I speak with her, she is calm, but I know she is wondering how the hell this is going to work out. Despite tests, they aren't quite sure what has happened to Garry. It is clear there is no way he can go home like this anyway.

When I arrived that unforgettable Sunday morning, Nan's nurse, a small Filipino man, excitedly called me close to the bed.

'Here, I want to show you something,' he said. He pulled back her sheet.

'Get in close, hold her hand,' he instructed me. 'Tell her to squeeze your hand.'

'Nan, squeeze my hand,' I told her. Immediately and unmistakeably, she squeezed. Firm, not slight, no doubt. She squeezed. We repeated it and it happened again.

'Now grab her right foot,' he said.

'Nan, wiggle your toes.' She flicked her right foot back towards herself. Again, no doubt it happened. A clear, strong movement on command. At last, what a relief to receive a response for myself. A show of life, an indicator she was still there despite everything that had happened. Until then it was a matter of belief that she had responded. Faith and belief can only take you so far.

'Some would say I should let you go your way you'll only make me cry'

Responses of that type were infrequent and even dried up over the next week or two, and one male nurse of about my vintage thought it best to cast some doubt on what had really happened.

'Well it was one of the doctors that first experienced it mate,' I responded. 'In fact, he has experienced it a couple of times. I also felt it myself. It was strong and it was clear. There was no doubt in my mind, and it didn't come for almost a week after he first got it. I didn't make it up.'

'I'm not questioning whether you experienced something,' he replied. 'But there is some conjecture about whether a hand squeeze is really a great indication. It's viewed that poking out the tongue is a more deliberate action. An unmistakeable one. Squeezing a hand could be an involuntary reaction to being gripped or touched. Moving the foot can be similar. But a tongue poke, there is no doubt there.' *Yeah, well thanks for trying to extinguish any hope*, I thought to myself. I wondered whether he liked pulling the wings off insects in his spare time.

'Ask yourself, who'd watch for me? My only friend, who could it be?'

While Nan lies motionless and mostly unresponsive, there is no shortage of action in the intensive care ward. I notice it happening but am largely unaffected by it. There are Garry's regular attempts to get out of bed and break free and the usual back-up staff running to try and restrain him. A few beds over in the opposite direction, a man goes into cardiac arrest. Patients are constantly monitored, so the problem is quickly detected, and the response is breathtakingly fast. Half a dozen doctors and nurses rush to his side. They prepare the defibrillator. I can hear the urgency in their voices. 'OK, clear', a long haired forty-something doctor calls and they zap the man. His body recoils from the shock and they give him some time. No good so they try it again. Another zap. Someone is calling out to the patient. 'Come on, stay with us,' the long-haired doctor says.

The process repeats itself several times before they seem to have achieved the result they want. They stand back observing before gradually becoming confident that the patient's motor is running again. After a while, the team begins dispersing to do whatever they were up to before this all happened.

A couple of days later, the same man goes into arrest again. The same things repeat themselves, but it seems to take longer this time to crank him over. The first occasion didn't bother me to observe, the second even less so.

Sometime after that, I'm returning to intensive care after the lunch break. I buzz to be admitted. The nurse on the other end lets me in but asks me to come to the station on the way past. I feel a little uneasy about that change to the admission process. When I arrive there, she has anticipated my concern and tells me Nan is fine but there is a problem a few beds away with a disturbed patient acting out. 'It's reasonably close to Nan's bed but we thought you'd be ok, so we've let you in.'

'OK,' I say and take my place beside Nan.

This time it's a woman. She is screaming at the staff. Battering them repeatedly with a barrage of four-letter words. She's being held down by the team and she's warned that if she doesn't settle, she will be medicated. She is warned multiple times in fact. She's not bothered by any of that and continues with her abuse and screaming. After some time, the team have decided enough is enough and they elect to sedate her to bring a halt to things.

It seems compassion and empathy are finite resources. The ample trauma in my own life has numbed me and I don't feel much when I observe these other things going on with strangers. They are spot fires in my vicinity that others will extinguish. I've become immune to events that would have been upsetting to experience previously. Robert Duvall striding around that beach in *Apocalypse Now*, oblivious to the bullets and the grenades exploding around him. I have my own 1000-yard stare happening. Fearfully surveying the scene and the future, looking for an invisible predator. I'm not in physical danger, but Nan is.

* * *

There is a new-looking Nan awaiting when Jill returns. The breathing tube has been moved from her mouth to her throat. On this visit, Jill is accompanied by her son Alex. I guess with the knowledge Nan has given a response, there is some hope of experiencing it for themselves too. Nan adored Alex, and vice versa, since he was a baby. One of our early nights together was baby-sitting Alex while Frank and Jill had a rare night out. He was only about twelve months old then and we couldn't get him to sleep, resorting to taking him for a late-night drive.

As we walk into intensive care, Alex who is now thirty-two, is more uptight than I have ever seen him. He's only just holding it together. He loves Nan and he feels it. His first sight of Nan is very upsetting and he cries. He has to let it out. There is no stopping it.

That evening, the hotel merry-go-round continues, and I've made a booking for the three of us back at the hotel at Arncliffe. The same good-natured man greets me as we arrive to check in.

The three of us spend the next day with Nan, two at a time, adhering to the intensive care visiting rules. When end of day approaches and it's time for Alex to catch his flight home, he's upset again, wondering I'm sure if it's the last time he will see Nan.

My three sisters arrive a day or two later as well. They've driven up from Canberra. It's genuinely good to see them. Jill is still there too. One by one they come in to see Nan with me. We are not a demonstrative family by any means, but I know that all of my siblings are kind and good people. As they come in with me, I tell Nan who is with her.

'Christine is here Nan.'

'It's Michelle, Nan.'

'Angie is here Nan.'

Each of them speaks kindly to Nan assuming she hears them. They all tell her they want her to get well again and make small talk. But then the cruncher. Every one of them as they are about to leave says, 'I love you, Nan.' They are not in the room at the same time, only with me. We don't even say that to each other, but the circumstances call for it here.

We have lunch in the café out the back with Jill, they each make another quick visit to Nan when visiting hours resume, and then it is time to head back home. It is a day trip by road with Christine driving. I am sorry to see them go.

Patrick comes in every couple of days and checks in with me to see if there has been any change, and how I'm doing. He's a great friend. I'm receiving a lot of well wishes from other people as well and many want to say hello, but I just can't talk to anyone else. It's too sad and I don't have the energy.

Then, another great mate from my childhood wants to visit. I hadn't seen much of Peewee since he moved to Canberra. He is very religious, but Peewee is the real deal. He does charity work, cares for refugees and other social issues, and is a great friend.

It's nice to see him. He's also keen to visit Nan so we go in. He talks to her a little bit, and then silence. He has his hand on her shoulder and I think he is praying. I haven't really done that. All my urging has been to Nan, not to God. We were altar boys together, classmates at Catholic school, but my faith evaporated years ago.

We have lunch at a different café where I have a great steak sandwich and then we repeat a visit to Nan after lunch and Pete drives back to Canberra.

One visitor is adding to rather than easing the trauma, and she's attending by phone not in person. It's Joan. The regular daily calls have become a nightmare. There is scepticism about any good news like Nan squeezing my hand, or Nan coming through the latest procedure. She continues to push that Nanette wouldn't want this, and she steadfastly refuses to come to Sydney herself to be at Nan's side. She demands that I call her daily to provide updates.

'You don't understand why I won't come, do you?' she accuses me one Saturday evening.

'I don't really care what reason you might have. You should be thinking about what you can do for Nanette.' That's hit the mark and she's thrown off her line.

'If you like I can put you on speaker phone next to her so she can hear your voice.' To my surprise, she agrees to that and later that evening, I call her back from Nan's bedside.

'Joan, it's David. I'm here with Nan. I'm going to put you on speaker.'

'OK.' I can hear the reservation in her voice.

'Nan, Joan is on the phone to talk to you. You're on speaker now Joan.'

'Hello Nan, this is Mum.' The words come out slowly, painfully, like teeth being extracted from her. There is a long pause.

'I'm thinking about you all the time … I want you to get better … You've looked after me so much … I want you to come home so I can look after you …'

There is a long pause again. She's not sure what to say next and it is hard when having a one-way conversation.

'I love you Nan and I will go now. Get better Nan,' and she ends the call. With the pauses, the call probably only lasted a minute or two. She rings me afterwards and tells me how hard it was to do.

'Well,' I say, 'we don't know what she can hear, and everything is worth a try.'

I encourage her to do it again because she and Nanette have been so close, and Nan needs to hear from her.

'But if there's one guy, just one guy, who'd lay down his life for you and die,
… It's probably me'

It's approaching the end of September and four weeks since Nan had the stroke. We've only had a few hand squeezes. She's had two surgeries on her brain and the tracheostomy.

The only other cause for hope I had seen was a partial opening of Nan's left eye a couple of times. It may not have meant anything. There was no focus or movement of the pupil of that beautiful blue eye, but it was nice to see it again, to look into it.

My fifty-third birthday had been and passed; the first one in over thirty years without Nan wishing me 'happy birthday' and making a fuss of me.

Rita has rotated out of the leadership of intensive care, and Doris is now in charge. She is nice and compassionate too. Doris thinks it is time we try Nan off the ventilator. To see if she is ready to breathe for herself. It's a scary prospect, but I know that life on a ventilator isn't a life.

'We need to do it in a controlled manner,' explains Doris. 'It will be very taxing on Nan initially. She hasn't been doing this for herself for nearly a month. She would have some time each day off the ventilator. We would increase the amount each day over about a week and if that goes well, we can leave her off it. What do you think David? Are you ready to try it?'

'If she doesn't breathe, or there is a problem after a while, can you quickly get her back on?' I ask.

'Yes, she would be monitored the whole time she's off. We can turn the ventilator back on quickly if we need to.'

'Can you do it while I'm here?'

'Yes, of course.'

'It's a scary thought but I guess we have to try.'

We agree to start it the next day.

When the time comes, we are with Nan and the nurse makes the preparations. She, Doris and I all look at each other knowing it's time to flick the switch.

'OK?' one of them asks.

'OK,' I say.

The switch is flicked. The machine stops. Nan is parachuting from the tenuous safety of man-made technology into a wide blue yonder. Gusts of air turbulence lift and carry her.

Her chute opens. She is breathing on her own. One breath. Another. She keeps going. It's the most stressful hour-long first minute. They are monitoring how many breaths she takes. More than we would, but it's good. They are monitoring her oxygen saturation and heart rate as well.

I'm anxious but excited. Riding every one of Nan's breaths. Watching her chest rise and then fall. In limbo after each exhale waiting for the next inhale to start. It's a terrifying pause that I cannot quite take for granted, even after a few minutes.

Fifteen minutes in total, which is much better than was expected, but then it's time to put her back on the machine. She's working too hard. Her heart rate is up and she's taking more breaths per minute.

She's back on the ventilator and we look at each other with smiles and nods of relief.

The next morning, we try again, and Nan lasts for an hour before she goes back on the machine. She is surpassing expectations.

The day after that it's two hours and the day after that, she is doing so well that they decide she can stay off the machine. She is breathing unaided. This is a great step forward. It would be better if she was awake of course, but it's another indication she is still alive and still fighting. Good things happen slowly after all.

I excitedly ring Joan to give her the good news. She greets it with disbelief and uncertainty but then realises that it is good news. Then she has some news of her own.

'I've been talking to Nan's school friend Andrew who became a doctor. Do you remember him?'

'Yes, I've met him a couple of times.'

'He's a very senior professor of intensive care now.'

'OK.'

'He says that for Nanette to be unconscious for four weeks is bad. She should have woken up by now.'

'Well, I told you three weeks ago the doctors here said it is better if she wakes more quickly. So, I knew that. What do you expect me to do about it? She's breathing Joan. She wanted a chance.'

'Andrew said he's happy to talk to you. Ring him. You're not a doctor. You don't know.'

'What would he have to add that the people here in equivalent positions don't already know?'

'You ring him. You listen.'

'He's not here looking after Nanette. He doesn't know what's going on. He's completely removed from it.'

'Ring him, you're not a doctor.'

No, I'm only the husband. What does it matter what I think? The last thing we need is other opinions to take account of. I'm sure Andrew wouldn't really want to get too involved either.

'He's a neurologist. He knows a lot about these things.'

'Joan, he is not a neurologist. You are confusing him with the Andrew who works here.'

'He is a neurologist,' she angrily snaps back. 'You ring him. What is there to lose?'

Only my sanity, whatever energy I still have left and giving Joan some sense of control.

In the end, I rang Andrew. He was of course not a neurologist, but yes, he is an intensive care head and yes, he had 'treated a lot of patients with sick brains'.

He was very nice to talk to and very concerned for both Nan and me. He knew some of the team at St George and agreed that everything possible was being done. He offered to be there as a sounding board, and I did seek him out on many occasions. Over time he and his wife Ingrid became very nice friends. However, he is not in Sydney, and he knew we were in good hands.

'Good morning Nanny'
Davey, is that you?
'Nanny, squeeze my hand'
It's him and I squeezed
'Good girl darling, now wiggle your toes for me'
I'm wiggling
'Nanny, I'm so proud of you. I love you'
I'm here Dave, but I can't wake up

IT'S NOT A TUMOUR

I'm short of breath, can't get my air
They opened a window, there is air, and I can breathe again

It would be nice to enjoy the good news that Nan is no longer dependent on the ventilator. To be able to take another kind of breather on a safe plateau in our ascent upon the mountain of recovery. There had been so little that was positive within that first month.

But long human recovery and the economic reality of hospital resources and funding don't always work in cooperative tandem. There is a limit to hospital largesse and the regular need to play God on the kind of care that can be extended and to whom.

Now Nan is no longer in need of a ventilator, the decision is taken to move her out of intensive care. She remains in a coma, and I am advised that she will be moved to the next highest level of care, the critical care unit.

I meet with some junior doctors I had only seen in passing, and they reassure me that the level of care will still be good. We talk a little about the greatest risks to Nan other than her not waking up.

Pneumonia and blood clots are challenges due to her immobility, and there is also the risk of some other form of infection creeping in. It is clear that each of these would likely have fatal consequences.

She is moved one afternoon while I am at lunch. I enter her new unit and find Nan and her bed. The differences are immediately stark between this ward and intensive care. She is in a two-bed room. I can hear another patient in the other bed, but the privacy sheet is drawn around them so I can't see them. I hear now that he is a he, and that he is conscious, as he is having a conversation on the phone to a family member and reporting his condition.

There is no nurse stationed in the room. One comes in at regular frequencies, says hello to me, eyeballs Nan, administers her feeds and medications and checks on the other patient. There is no ventilator, and significantly less other equipment placed around Nan. My darling lies on the bed, peacefully. She is breathing freely and calmly through the trache tube.

I feel like I've just arrived at boarding school for the first time. Everything is foreign and I have no friends. I know none of the staff and they don't know Nan. Nobody here knows what we've been through other than a fifteen-minute handover between nurses. 'The husband is here a lot and he's traumatised,' I imagine one busy nurse telling another.

Our acrobatic act has just taken a step up in level of difficulty. The safety net has been dropped. I feel intensely anxious that there are now long periods without any medical staff in the room. Just me. Other than panic, what would I do if something went wrong? I notice a green button on the wall behind Nan's bedhead that says 'Nurse' and a red button of similar size that says 'Emergency'. I'm tempted to hit the red one to see what happens and how quickly it happens.

Over the afternoon, I hear the other patient make several phone calls of the same nature, retelling the story of what is happening and how he is doing. I find myself longing for the silence of unconscious and comatose roommates, and the rhythmic, almost musical beeps of the ventilators.

I dread the opening of the drawsheet and the inevitable introductions and discussions and 'what's wrong with her'. When it does happen, I try and be polite, but don't want to get too engaged. Don't want to build a connection.

I feel jealous that the other patient is sitting up and conversational and talking about leaving hospital soon. I also feel uncomfortable as he surveys Nan and myself.

'She's been in a coma for a month. She's given a few responses but hasn't woken up.'

'Wow. That's a long time. A lot for you to deal with.'

I don't need that pointed out and don't like us being the focus.

It's the next day before I see a doctor. I hear him approaching from down the hall. He has an accent and sounds Russian, and he's dressed in a suit and tie, much more formally than the doctors in intensive care. He also seems a little curt with the junior doctors.

He and three others walk into our room. He looks at me and straightens. Did he snap his heels together in attention? He introduces himself.

On that first meeting he is quite engaging and seemingly sympathetic. He examines Nan, offers some words of encouragement, and moves on to the next patient. I breathe a sigh of relief that he has gone. It was relatively painless.

When he arrives the next day, I'm more relaxed about seeing him. There has been no change to Nan's condition. He wants to talk some more. My relaxed state doesn't last long as he takes me through a grim wake up call. I hadn't really been asleep to the reality, but he needs to be sure of that.

'This is a catastrophic-sized stroke … A patient in this kind of state may not wake … If she does, her quality of life will be poor …

You have to ask yourself if it's worth it … Events like this cause massive divisions in families … People wind up fighting and hating each other over these situations.'

These are the essential messages he wants to get through. All the rest of what he said is blah blah blah. I absorb it but it hurts. I can't be bothered disagreeing with him or fighting.

He wants to review the most recent scan with me. There is something on it I need to see. He continues on to see other patients and says he will be back soon.

OK great, I can't wait, I think to myself and sit there feeling very glum.

When he returns, he takes me to a screen behind the nurses' station. He types in some commands and retrieves Nan's most recent scan. I see the familiar black and white images as he moves through various rotations and viewpoints until he finds what it is he wants to show me. He points to a place on the screen.

'See that circular image there?' he says and traces his finger around something white and circular that on this level of magnification looks to be about the size of a squash ball.

'Yes, I do,' I reply.

'The radiology report is suggesting that this may be a tumour.'

He is looking at me to make sure it has sunk in. We both know it has sunk in because my head is in my hands in an attempt to black out not only this image, but the entire world. A massive brain haemorrhage with the garnish of a brain tumour. How delightful. Is there anything else that God, aliens, providence or whoever else is out there would like to throw upon this poor little darling?

'Now they are not one hundred per cent certain. They have raised the possibility. We really need a neurosurgery view on this. Perhaps we need a biopsy of this thing to have it analysed.'

'A biopsy?' I ask. 'How would you obtain a biopsy of something like that in what looks to be the middle of her brain?'

He responds and uses the words 'small bore needle' at which I almost pass out at the thought of anyone sticking anything further into my Nanny's poor, already overwhelmed and overrun brain.

'David, this may be a good thing. This may be the solution. This may be a way out.'

Those remain three of the most objectionable sentences I have ever heard. I could never think in those terms. I decide not to fight him and look to make my excuses. I can't stand it any longer. I thank him for his time and move away.

Over the next few days, I do my best to avoid him but accidentally bump into him one morning. 'Still waiting on a neurosurgeon to come and talk to you. I've requested someone very senior for this. We will get the best if we can for an opinion and advice on what to do.'

'OK, thanks,' I say, barely stopping to take that in, my mind already breaking into a sprint to get away.

My eyes are closed but I sense light
There is a lot of noise and it's getting louder
I can feel my body moving but I'm not moving it

I'm still doing the daily lifting and moving of Nan's limbs to try and keep things circulating, especially her mind. It's been quite hard work and depending on my own level of tiredness, I may not do it as often as I would prefer. I'm also wondering if it's helping at all. Over a couple of days, however, I notice that her limbs feel much lighter, like she's helping me. Maybe I'm imagining it or getting stronger, although I'm sure that's not the case. But they are definitely feeling lighter. I report it to a nurse because there isn't a doctor around, and she listens patiently, but isn't able to offer any real rationale.

Almost another week passes before the meeting with the neurosurgeon is scheduled. The day before the meeting, I had a call from Joan.

'We need this biopsy done David. We need to know,' she demanded.

'Oh? We should jam a needle into poor Nanette's brain just so that we know, Joan? I'm not doing that. I'm not putting her through anything unnecessary. If it's a tumour and it's malignant, it will take her whether or not we have a biopsy done. I'm waiting to hear what the neurosurgeons have to say.'

I'm at the nominated office on the nominated Monday at 1pm to meet with a neurosurgeon. I have compiled a list of a dozen or so questions to ask about all this. I'm anxious about what I am going to hear. He's late but at about twenty minutes past the hour, a young guy of Indian descent arrives.

'Hi, I'm one of the registrars from the neurosurgery department,' he says.

I introduce myself and think *so much for getting one of the top guys.* This fellow looks to be hardly out of school. We begin talking about Nanette and what has happened, how long it has been, her minimal responses, she hasn't woken up, and so on. He's very sure of himself, in fact, quite cocky. I guess that's OK in a neurosurgeon. You hardly want them riddled with doubt. We quickly move to the primary topic.

'I don't believe that's a tumour on the scan,' he says.

'You don't?'

'No, we see a lot of strange images like this on scans after surgery like she's had. I think this is one of those.'

'Do you think it's necessary to biopsy it to be sure? I'm not very excited by that idea,' I respond.

'No. What would be the point? What would you do about it? You're not going to treat it with surgery or chemotherapy. Anyway, I don't believe this is a tumour so there is no need.'

All the questions I've written down are redundant just five minutes into the discussion, so I start to freewheel a bit.

'Do you think she will wake up?'

'That's impossible to tell. Clearly, it's been a while already. We are giving her a drug to try and wake her.'

'What kind of drug?' I ask.

'Well, it's not speed, but something that would work like that.'

'What is it called?'

'Amantadine.' It's just a word to me. 'It acts as a stimulant, and we are giving her as much as we feel is appropriate.'

I start to reflect on where this is heading and ask him how long this could go on for.

'Is there a limit to how long she can stay in the hospital?' I ask with a degree of concern.

'Well, she couldn't stay here forever.'

'What are the options then?' I ask, my level of alarm rising.

'Well, probably a nursing home or your own home if you have the resources, but home care is very expensive.'

Nan in a nursing home? She's only fifty-four. NO, surely not. 'How much would home care be?'

'She would need 24/7 care. That would be around $150k per year to have the right degree of help. There would also be some setup costs.'

'That's a large number,' I respond, realising that with the exit of the tumour, my ledger of things to worry about is immediately replenished with a new item. Our discussion concludes, I thank him and decide to call Joan.

'It's not a tumour. He thinks it's an unusual image on the scan after they've operated on her,' I tell her with a sense of vindication. I decide not to share the story on longer term care for the moment. She doesn't offer much response. It's a short call.

The nurses are changing me
They turn me side to side
Now they are washing me
I hear them say 'Nan'

Shortly after the meeting with the registrar, a middle-aged woman walks into our room and introduces herself as Julie. She's a clinical nursing consultant. I have no idea what that is and when I question, she says she is there to play a coordinative and advocative role on behalf of the patient inside the hospital. We talk about what's going on and then she asks whether I have any concerns.

'Well, other than Nanette's condition, I'm worried about being evicted from the hospital at some point. I have no idea how long the support will go on for and I don't know what will happen when it doesn't.' I tell her about the recent discussion with the registrar.

'Those guys don't always think about the impact to people of what they are saying. Don't be worried about that David. I am here to help you with that. No one will be kicking you two out.' I'm encouraged by that, but worried about how much sway a nurse will have against the hospital system. Anyway, I was more relieved than before she came.

Julie does an examination of Nan's trache site, says it looks to be in very clean condition and then talks about another possible ward move.

'David, it would be better if Nan was in the neurosurgery ward. You're a bit out of the way and forgotten about here. Also, there are some specialist allied health staff there. We have a physiotherapist who is outstanding in these situations. Her name is Claire. They do things like tilt-tabling which can be helpful to waking patients up.'

'What is tilt-tabling?'

'They strap the patient onto a table that is powered to elevate one end up to ninety degrees or even more if necessary. It is to simulate standing, but the patient is strapped in while this happens. The process of being upright can help a patient regain consciousness. Lying down all day means Nan is in a sleeping position.'

This seems to make a lot of sense and I let Julie know I hope we can move departments quickly.

'They are quite full up there at the moment but let me look into it.'

'Thanks Julie, I'm so glad you came. You've given me some hope. There hasn't been much lately.' She really had.

There's something in my nose
It's annoying, I'm pulling it out
That's better

It was shortly after being relocated to the neurosurgery ward that I was advised that Nan had pulled the feeding tube out of her nose.

'It's just as well she didn't pull out the trache tube,' said the nurse who told me what had happened.

I considered the possibly dire consequences if she had. She's not in intensive care now with a nurse at the end of her bed to immediately address it. How long might it have gone unnoticed?

'We've had to take the step of restraining her good working arm to ensure she doesn't pull the trache out. Is that OK with you David? We don't like restraining patients unless it's absolutely necessary.'

'It's completely fine and I understand it's the safe thing to do. Thanks.'

Nan pulling her feeding tube out was good news. The nursing unit manager who said 'Good things happen slowly' also said it would be great if Nan did something exactly like that: a clear and deliberate act. Better than any hand squeeze.

The hospital had for some time wanted to get the feeding tube out of her nose and replace it with a PEG (percutaneous endoscopic gastrostomy) tube to deliver liquid food directly into Nan's stomach, bypassing the nose, mouth and throat. Nan did half the job for them. They decided it was time to do the rest for Nan's comfort and to minimise infection.

Jill is with me when it's time for Nan's surgery. We are worried about it and know it will take a few hours, so we decide on a walk for distraction. I have not had any real exercise for the six weeks since this happened.

When we return to the room, Nan is there looking peaceful. The trache to her throat is still in place. I take a look at the PEG site and see an eight-inch tube with a ring at her skin and a clamp and an adapter with a cap at the end. Because they have cut into her and clamped it in and outside of her, it has a greater look of permanency about it than the feeding tube ever did. It's part of her now – a new orifice, another statement of permanent impairment.

* * *

On the following Sunday, I find two men in Nan's room at the foot of her bed looking at her chart. Nan remains unconscious, oblivious to their presence. I recognise the taller of the two is Johnny, the neurosurgery registrar who I met that first day. The other man is wearing a white Ralph Lauren Polo shirt. He's older. I eventually twig that it is Sayeed, the neurosurgeon who operated on Nan. He looks different without a suit, and I haven't seen him for some weeks. I greet him warmly and gratefully. I'm anxious to know what they have to say.

I go into positive spin mode and tell them about her limbs feeling lighter, Nan pulling out the feeding tube and the partial eye openings. But I know it's not really anything much, six weeks since her stroke.

Sayeed pauses for a while, reflecting. He is a quiet and conservative man, not cocky like that other young registrar was. He's looking at Nan again and I can see he is quite perplexed. They are at a loss for what to say and how to explain why she hasn't yet woken.

He cups his chin with his hand and nods slowly taking his time to answer and his answer is only about time. That's really all anyone can do now.

'We will just give her some more time and see how we get on.'

A NOD IS AS GOOD AS

Our beautiful and ageing Labrador Hester had been staying with Frank and Jill since the day we had gone to Sydney. Hester had several medical issues. Some years before, she needed minor surgery to remove a couple of lipomas from her front shoulder area. When the vet operated, he found that one lipoma was huge, and had wrapped itself around vital organs and arteries. He rang to say he didn't think she would have long.

Another time, Nan had found her in some distress, throwing one side of her head to the ground as she moved along in an agitated fashion.

'Dave, I think Hester's had a stroke,' Nan screamed.

We rushed her to the vet. They did scans and tests and concluded she had a vestibular problem which largely righted itself within twenty-four hours.

Then there was the discovery that there was something wrong with Hester's liver. She had to go on a special diet and couldn't eat meat, so every day for over a year, Nan cooked rice, sweet potato and other vegetables to deliver her protein in a way her liver could process.

Frank had very kindly assumed the role of Hester's cook and was making her meals as Nanette had done. He sent me some photos of Hester. I thought she looked older and sadder. Taken from her pack.

Frank rang one day to tell me he had taken Hester to the vet.

'David, I think it's time for Hester. I think she's reached the end.'

'Oh shit,' I said. 'Well if she has then she has. I'll talk to the vet.'

A young Irish woman named Christine had been Hester's vet for the last year or two. We liked to think of her as Hessie's personal physician. When I talked with Christine, she confirmed that something serious was wrong.

'I think she has had a neurological change, David.'

'A stroke?'

'I think so. She's just not there now. She's not the same dog.'

'Is it time to let her go, Christine?'

'I think so. David, this dog has had another two years of life because of the quality of care that you've both given her, but I feel she's reached the end.'

'OK, can you let me know when it's done, please?'

Christine did that. Losing Hester had been something I had dreaded for some time. We loved her. She was the most beautiful dog. Her connection with Nanette was uncanny. The night of Nan's stroke she was frozen. I couldn't move her. She knew something terrible had happened. Now, six weeks on, Hester also suffered her own stroke.

I wasn't as sad about it as I would have been in normal times. My emotions were prioritised. I loved Hester but the situation with Nan was far, far greater, and far more affecting.

I'm on a bed
I'm awake and my eyes are open
Where am I?
What has happened?
There is too much to take in

Just like that, Nan's eyes are open. Not one, but both. Not half open, fully open. Not just for a few seconds, they are staying open. She starts to blink with the frequency any of us do when we are awake.

She is on her right side on the bed. She's not moving her head to look around. Not trying to take everything in. Not waking in wonder and near fear like we do in a strange place or room. More like a footballer knocked unconscious during a match. Stunned. Uncertain. But she's not pained. She looks comfortable.

Her big beautiful blue eyes are moving very slowly to take in a small field of view immediately in front of her. Every now and then I notice the irises seem to drift to the left like she has lost focus or lost control of them.

I'm frightened to say anything. Frightened to interrupt her reverie. I don't want to frighten her. I don't know what she is experiencing. I don't know what Nan is like now. How has the brain damage left her? Eventually and carefully, I summon up some courage.

'Nanny.'

She doesn't look my way or respond. She just continues her little eye scan.

'Nanny, can you hear me?' I ask a little more loudly. There is still no response.

I decide to leave it and let her be. Eventually, she closes her eyes again. I ring the buzzer and wait for a nurse to arrive. She walks in and reaches across to turn off the nurse call button.

'Hi, what's up?' she asks.

'Nan had her eyes open for a few minutes. She didn't respond when I spoke to her. She did seem to be awake though.'

The nurse reaches down to Nan, calls her name, and tries to wake her. Nan doesn't stir.

'Well, it happened,' I say, wondering if they thought I imagined it, sitting here too long and slowly losing the plot.

'OK, call me if it happens again.'

It does happen quite regularly from there on. I'm able to get the nurses in to experience it as well and prove I haven't imagined it. But Nan isn't responding to us. Doctors are never around when you need them, and I just have to accept it is recorded on Nan's chart and discussed with the doctors when they arrive.

I wonder whether she can hear me, so I try to get into a position where she is looking directly at me. It doesn't make any difference when I speak. She doesn't seem focused on what I am doing or saying.

I grab some A4 pages, and write in large capital letters on them, each phrase on a separate page: 'CAN YOU HEAR ME?', 'POKE OUT YOUR TONGUE', 'NAN', 'I LOVE YOU', 'SPEAK TO ME', 'SMILE', 'RAISE YOUR RIGHT HAND', 'I WILL ALWAYS LOOK AFTER YOU'.

I show the pages to her one at a time, but none of them seems to register with her. I don't know if her brain is completely blown or if she is still coming out of the coma. Maybe she can't see properly either?

Nan seems to be awake, and for longer periods, but she is not responding to anything we say. When I put my hand in hers, she strokes my hand and fingers lightly with just her fingertips. Backwards and forwards. It's quite compulsive.

She looks to be revelling in the sensation of touch. Possibly a little fixated on the sight of it, so maybe she can see, or maybe her sight is distorted or different? Magnified or reduced, I just don't know. All I know is that I can't get her attention.

I have kept the family up to speed with these developments, preferring to speak to Jill now she is back in Albury rather than Joan. I'm getting more scepticism from Joan. I don't think she believes what I'm telling her is going on.

'You listen to the nurses and doctors David. You don't know anything. You're not a doctor,' she spits at me one afternoon.

'When did I ever say I was a doctor?' I reply angrily.

'Don't you be questioning them and asking them too much. The nurses will hate you,' she replies.

Great, I'm thinking to myself. No one here seems to hate me. I am doing what I can. The situation is deeply traumatic and frightening, and I have to withstand this daily barrage of scepticism and contempt.

I try telling myself how close she and Nanette are. I try reminding myself of the many years I have had a good relationship with her. I try and remember that she is older now. Eighty-four. What a shock this would be. But I don't need this.

A very nice middle-aged Chinese nurse called Ping starts looking after Nan for a few days. She is kind and tells me I am a good husband. I speak to another senior nurse about what Joan had said.

'Of course we don't hate you, David. It's fine to ask questions. It shows you care about what's going on. Some families just abandon patients in Nanette's situation. We have patients and families screaming at us. You never do that. But there is nothing wrong with wanting to know.'

Bruce is here now, and so is Jo
They've come to see me
Don't cry Bruce

Nan's brother Bruce and his wife Jo decided to cut their holiday in Sri Lanka short when they got the news. I was hopeful that new family members might help excite Nan forward. When they arrived, they were also able to experience Nan opening her eyes and the repetitive stroking motion of her fingers. They spoke to Nan quietly and lovingly. Bruce told her she was a very nice sister. I have no idea what, if anything, Nan was experiencing. She didn't respond or react to Bruce any differently than she had to me.

I asked that they call Joan while they were visiting and communicate what they had seen.

'She's become terrible to deal with,' I told them as we stood outside St George while they both had a cigarette break, and I took in a passive or two. 'She doesn't seem to believe what I say, but you can see her eyes are now open. You can tell her.'

They agreed they would and commiserated how tough this must have been. We were now six weeks in, and they were experiencing first-hand what the days in the hospital were like and how it felt to see someone you loved deeply in such a state.

We took a beach walk one afternoon at Brighton–Le–Sands. It was strange to see people on a beach: sunning themselves, playing with balls, frolicking in the water. Not a care in the world. It was a painful contrast to the life and death battle we were fighting less than two kilometres away.

When we returned to the hospital after the rest period, Bruce was suddenly overcome with emotion as we stood outside Nan's room while they changed her.

'I don't know how you do it,' he somehow got out among the tears.

'I love her. How could I not be here for her? I just adore her.'

There really was no choice. No desire to be able to choose. Nothing else mattered.

After a couple of nights, Bruce and Jo set off on the 600-kilometre trip back to Albury. They left me an old guitar thinking it might give me a healthy distraction. They meant well, but I didn't want it. I felt no inclination to play music or do anything else other than be with Nan. I tucked it out of the way in the corner of the room at Bezzina House where I now had accommodation for a month, thanks to Natalie.

> *The big nurse picks me up off the bed*
> *A man is there to help her*
> *They carry me through the air*
> *And put me in a big comfy chair to sit*

The nurses decide it would be nice to put Nan in a princess chair, a large, soft and padded chair that could be both reclined and wheeled around. It would give her some time out of bed and sitting upright. They called for porters who arrived with a hoist to get Nan from the bed into the chair. I left the room while they did that.

Nan now seems even more awake and focused, but she is still not responsive. Seeing her sitting up in a chair in her white hospital gown with a sheet neatly draped over her, she looks reasonably healthy. One might wrongly assume she was recovering from minor surgery.

Ping encouraged me to wheel her around the ward in the princess chair. I didn't feel confident enough to do it. I was anxious about misusing the controls and about taking Nan even one metre away from her hospital room.

I gave it a try though. For a large chair, it moved very easily. It was tricky to manoeuvre though within the confines of the ward corridors replete with people and equipment. We had a brief stroll around and then returned, me breathing a sigh of relief.

'Why don't you take her down in the lift and outside,' said Ping.

'No, I couldn't do that.'

* * *

Claire is the lead physiotherapist for the neurosurgery ward at St George. She is a blonde woman in her early thirties and has a very good reputation. When we meet to talk about Nan and what has happened to date, she is keen to try Nan on the tilt table. The intention is not only to see if it will make her more aware, but also to stretch her body, a benefit we all achieve naturally by standing and walking around. I am happy to try anything by this time that might bring Nan forward.

The table and the hoist are brought into Nan's room a couple of days after we talked. Claire explains that they must be very careful about Nan's blood pressure during the process and that she'll be monitoring it closely, making sure it isn't spiking too much, given undiagnosed hypertension is assumed the most likely cause of Nan's initial bleed.

When Claire and her assistants arrive, they manoeuvre the tilt table and the hoist into the room. Claire takes Nan's blood pressure and says it is at an acceptable level to start. They bring the hoist close to the bed, wrap the sling underneath Nan and connect it to the hoist. When she is secure, they use the controls to slowly lift Nan from the bed, bringing her torso and legs towards each other in a 'V' position. Once up high enough, they wheel the hoist to the tilt table, angle Nan properly over it and then lower her down into a flat position.

Nan's eyes are open, but there is no reaction from her while this is going on. As she is suspended mid-air, swinging a little with the movement of the hoist, I recall how she would enjoy lying in a hammock on a sunny afternoon. She looks quite content.

The team is careful to ensure Nan is safe on the table and then begins disconnecting her from the hoist and placing straps around her to secure her. Claire lets Nan settle for a few minutes and then decides to take her blood pressure again. It is still OK – the transfer process hasn't caused any real upset to her.

Claire starts the tilt table and as its motor whirrs into action, Nan's feet are lowered, and her head raised so that she becomes more upright. The table moves slowly but it is unnerving to watch. As she rises, so does my own blood pressure and anxiety. Nan wouldn't have been able to act to steady or protect herself should she fall.

After a short time, Claire stops the table to let Nan rest at this more upright position. After five minutes or so at that angle, she starts the table again to take Nan even more upright. When she checks Nan's blood pressure this time, the reading is too high. There is disappointment all round. It hasn't taken very much for us to push Nan too hard. Claire is clear we must stop, and Nan is lowered and returned to her bed to rest. We agree to try it again in a few days and see whether she can tolerate more.

Nan doesn't seem worse for wear after the experience, and as I sit there contemplating where we are at, a Japanese nurse comes in to check on

Nan. I haven't met her before. Her name is Kuro. She is middle-aged and pleasant and of course very polite. Her English is good enough, but she speaks in bursts and measures and with a quite strong accent. She asks about what has happened to Nan and what she did before she became ill. When she hears Nan was an artist, she responds that she too likes to paint in her spare time.

'I had some friends back in Japan,' Kuro volunteers. 'The woman had a very bad accident, and she was left with brain damage. She was like a two-year-old child mentally after that. People think that that's not good quality of life for someone to be like that. But she knew them, and she was still the person they loved. They all believed it was giving her a "second life". I thought so too.'

A 'second life' I think to myself. If Nan comes through this in whatever capacity, it will be like she has been given a second chance, or a 'second life'. This strikes a chord and sticks with me.

David is talking to a nurse
He wants to get lunch and a Coke

A few more days into her 'second life', Nan is in the princess chair again. Getting her into that for a period each day has become a routine by now. Routine is a good thing. It helps establish normality and provides markers in our days. Nan is getting a routine of moving from the bed to the chair, and back again.

Nan is appearing a little more alert. She's not reaching out or turning around, she just looks more with it. She seems to be focusing on her surrounds and not only those immediately close to her like my hand or the bed sheet.

It's approaching lunchtime and a friendly young Asian nurse is in Nan's room with us. She tells us her name is Kim and seems to want to chat. I ask where she is from, and she asks me to guess. I look at her appearance and she has a squarish jaw, more in keeping with many Japanese. However, it's her name that makes me plunge.

'Korean', I say.

'Yes. How did you know? No one ever guesses.' She's very surprised.

'Well, I've travelled a lot through Asia, but actually it was your name.'

She seems amazed, but I didn't think it was that amazing. She changes the topic to ask me if I'm going to have lunch soon.

'Yes,' I respond.

'What will you have?'

'Well, probably just a sandwich. Maybe chicken and avocado. I have that a lot.'

'What will you have to drink?' she asks.

I'm surprised she needs this much detail, but I answer anyway. 'A Coke.' All my life I have drunk Coca Cola. Never Diet Coke, I didn't like the taste. Some brief flirtations with Coke Zero and Coke No Sugar, but again, I could taste the difference, and I thought they might be causing me some gut issues. My romance is with the real thing: Coke Classic. People like to lecture me that it's bad for me and I should give it up. Too much sugar, too much caffeine. Too much taste and enjoyment I say. I have a long-established routine of a Coke with my lunch.

'Got to have my Coke for lunch, haven't I Nanny?' I add and look over to Nan.

Nan is looking at me and nods in furious agreement. Her eyebrows are raised in full cooperative support as she does this. I nearly fall off my chair.

'Did you see that?' I ask the nurse, making sure I'm not dreaming.

'Yes.' Kim is wide-eyed and her mouth has dropped too. Totally amazed. I am sure she's reflecting my own awe.

We both keep staring at Nan, wondering what will happen next. I ask her to nod again, but she doesn't. We ask her to poke out her tongue, but she doesn't. It seems it was a fleeting moment of engagement and understanding. I feel the routine of getting her up each day is making her more alert. She knows my routine. I drink Coke every day and I love it. She knew that and still knows it. Routine gives us and those around us something to latch onto; reliable life rafts to cling to.

'Can you please make sure everyone knows what just happened? The doctors, the other nurses?' I ask Kim.

It's Kim's turn to nod. She is still staring at Nan wondering what might happen next.

'Yes, I will,' she replies and heads out of the room.

After some time of smothering Nanette with affection, I leave to get my sandwich and my Coke. I try to ring Jill but can't get an answer so I reluctantly call Joan instead. This is too big an event not to share.

'Are you sure?' she responds sceptically to my account.

'There was a nurse with me, and she saw it too.'

I'm not going to have this excitement ruined. This is a real step. Nan is awake. She was following the conversation and participated with her own response when she was addressed. At the right moment too! She is still with us is what it means. Not a lot of indication before this, but she IS still with us. She isn't ready to talk and still has the trache in her throat anyway which would have made it difficult, if not impossible. So, a nod will more than suffice.

Things are starting to happen. Nan's limbs were lighter, she pulled the feeding tube from her nose, her eyes are now open for most of the day and then the nod. The feeding tube was replaced by a PEG into her stomach, but the tracheostomy is still in place in Nan's throat.

Julie, the clinical nurse and Claire the physio come in to see us one afternoon in Nan's room. They want to take Nan's trache out. They think it's time. For me it's another daunting step. Of course, I want the thing out of her throat and for Nan to be able to breathe naturally, but what if she can't?

Julie begins explaining the process by which the trache would be removed. There is a balloon of fluid that keeps the airways open, and the balloon will be deflated slowly. It sounds simple but the question will be whether Nan starts to breathe naturally through her nose and mouth and whether her airways remain open. Julie and Claire reassure me that if things don't work out successfully, it is simple to reinstate the trache. The risk is understood and manageable. We all know we must try, but it's another worrying step.

Julie gives me clear direction to not be around for the process. I am happy for that. I don't want to watch.

The next day at 2pm, Julie and Claire both arrive, and I disappear to leave them to do their thing. I take with me high hopes of returning to find Nan without a tracheostomy. I feel confident about it and make my way downstairs.

There are two nice women with me
'Nan, we want to take the tube out of your throat,' they say
They are playing with the thing
It's tickling and scratching me
It makes me cough
I can't stop coughing
It is so uncomfortable
They look worried
They feel bad that they made me cough and they stop
'I'm sorry, Nan,' one of them says
It's OK, I know they are nice

It's Julie that breaks the bad news to me when I return an hour or so later. Nan went into a coughing fit when they tried to remove the trache. Their view was that the gradual deflation of the balloon was irritating Nan.

They have already devised a new approach. They want to quickly deflate and instantly remove the trache. Have it all over in a matter of seconds. They also tell me they will arrange for a doctor to be there as well just in case. I am very encouraged to know that it is Raju from intensive care who they will seek. He remains in godlike territory to me since the day Nan first squeezed his hand.

So, the second attempt is set for the next afternoon. When the time comes and I see Claire, Julie and Raju arrive, I'm a little lost for words speaking to him, which is unlike me.

'I'm glad you're here, Raju,' I say to him. It is all I can get out. I wish them well and then retreat out to the local café again.

There are two nice women with me
And an Indian man too
'Nan, we want to take the tube out of your throat', they say
I want it out too
One of them reaches forward and pulls it out
I feel the air come through my mouth and nose
It's good to have that tube out
The people look happy
'Well done, Nan', they say

Only about twenty minutes has elapsed since I left them when my phone rings.

'David, it's Julie here. The trache is out and Nan is breathing well. She's been breathing without it for about fifteen minutes now.'

'Oh Julie, that is such good news. I can't thank you enough.'

I can hear she is happy on the other end. She knows this is a big deal. Removal of the trache gives Nan a greater chance of rehabilitation if we get that far. After we hang up, I feel a massive weight is lifted. I walk to the counter, pay for my Coke and go back to Nan.

When I get to her room that afternoon, she is sound asleep and looking the most peaceful and relaxed I have seen her since this all started. She is breathing peacefully and regularly. She wears an angelic disposition as she lays there. There is a bandage across her throat where the trache was; I'm told the site will quickly seal up again. I sit there for quite some time enjoying every one of her beautiful and natural breaths, riding the crest of her inhales like a mindfulness zealot. Wondering at the miracle of that simple act of breathing.

When Julie and Claire drop in soon after, I continue my inadequate expressions of gratitude and praise. I draw their attention to how peaceful and happy Nan looks. That thing must have been irritating, I say to them. How can you thank people that do things like this? We can at least try, even if we seem a little goofy and gushy in the process. They would know how much joy they brought even if they modestly don't show it.

I am sitting quietly with Nan as she sleeps. It's early evening, around 5pm. I sense there is someone behind me. I assume it's a nurse but wonder why she is stationary. I turn around and see it's not one, but two women. On first glance, I mistake them for nuns, but then realise it is two Islamic women in full length garb and hijabs. It's like an apparition and I pinch myself to make sure it's happening.

'Hello David,' says Rania and I'm jolted to my senses.

'Rania, so nice to see you. How are you?' I respond. I am surprised, but very happy to see her.

'I'm good, David. This is my friend. We thought we would come and visit you and see how Nanette is.'

'That is so kind of you, Rania. Nan is better than when I last saw you, that's for sure. She's been awake a lot. They've taken out the trache. A few days ago, she nodded in response to a question I asked. But she's not really interacting otherwise. I think she is showing some positive signs.'

'David, that is wonderful news. We have been praying for you and we have something for you.'

Rania produces an envelope and hands it to me. Inside is a narrow piece of green fabric with a gold leaf pattern. It is wrapped in soft tissue paper.

'David, this is from a very holy site in Iraq, and it was blessed by a very holy man. Would you like it? We hope that it helps Nanette.'

'Thank you so much Rania. Of course I want it. It's so kind of you.'

We talk a little about Rania's husband. He is making progress and they will soon leave the hospital. I'm happy for her. They are good people and I'm very touched by their kindness.

As they leave, Rania asks me to bury the cloth should I not want it any longer. I know I will always want it, and I still have it.

When they leave, I take the cloth from its wrapping, sit it on the chest of my sleeping darling and say a prayer for her.

THE MIRACLE OF ST GEORGE

October 2014 is delivering small but positive outcomes. Nan is hanging in there. We have no new setbacks. Good things are happening slowly. Prospects seem a little brighter, especially when compared with late August and most of September of that year which were no doubt the darkest days of both of our lives to that point.

Saturday 18 October 2014 remains the most profound day of my life. The day I witnessed what some would describe as a miracle. Others might attribute the events of that day to medical science, to luck, or even to the power of love or perseverance. All of those factors no doubt contributed.

Sydney experienced torrential downpours in the week leading up to that day. I am drenched to the skin just crossing the hundred metres or so from the St George entrance to Bezzina House across the road.

Patrick had visited again the previous evening and witnessed his own small miracle. We were sitting with Nan and talking but then decided to go and get dinner. She was awake but unresponsive as we sat there. As I was readying myself to leave, I noticed Nan's head a bit slumped over and reached across to straighten her a little on the bed.

I had a small bolster which I was putting under her pillow to keep her head in a good position.

As I reached across Nan to adjust her, she puckered up and kissed me. Patrick saw it happen and was stunned. He wore the same look that Kim from Korea had: wide-eyed and open-mouthed. Patrick was soon leaning over wanting a kiss too, and Nan obliged. We both felt that our day had been made.

Some years later, the Radio National program *Life Matters* ran a competition called 'The Kiss'. They asked people to send in accounts of their most memorable kiss. I wrote this one up, sent it in and promptly forgot about it until a woman I knew told me she heard it read out on air. I didn't win the competition, but it was certainly a memorable kiss.

On Saturday, I spend the day with Nan as usual. She hasn't been waking until mid-afternoons. It is a long wait each day to see her eventually open her eyes; there haven't been enough days of consciousness to assume it would just happen. The nurses think it is because her sleep cycle is out of phase having been in a coma for most of two months.

When she does wake, she seems to be focused on me and raises her eyebrows as if to say hello. Maybe I am guilty of interpreting that eyebrow raise in the way I want to see it. As she lay in the bed, her head is slightly elevated for safety reasons. I reach for her hand and hold it. I am regularly prompting her and trying to get a response.

'Nanny, will you poke your tongue out for me? Poke your tongue out lovey.'

I have asked this question so many times each day without receiving any response, so my expectations are low. This time though, I notice some movement of Nan's mouth, a little like she is chewing gum and trying not to be noticed.

'Poke your tongue out, Nanny,' I prompt her again.

More of that little movement and then she opens her mouth as if she is going to say something. Her mouth opens, then closes and then opens again, like it is a struggle to do so. I can see her willing herself. I could see her tongue. Her mouth stayed open in an 'O' shape. Then her tongue comes forward slightly. The anticipation is unbearable. It isn't yet at the point where I think she is doing what I asked. A little more, and then it is definitely poking out from her mouth. It is slow, like a turtle emerging tentatively from its shell.

'Good work Nanny. Well done.' She pulls her tongue back in.

'Can you do it again please? Poke out your tongue.'

This time, having done it once, it happens more smoothly and more promptly, but it is still quite a slow process. She repeats it. There is no mistake. I decide to ask her to do some other things.

'Can you give me a thumbs up?' She slowly raises her right thumb.

'Can you point at me?' She points her index finger towards me.

'Can you point to yourself?' She curls her hand and index finger around to point at herself.

'Can you touch your nose darling?' She slowly brings her index finger up and touches her nose.

'Can you touch your chin sweetheart?' Her finger goes down to her chin.

The whole time she is wearing an expression like a young and very well-behaved child eager to please a schoolteacher. Waiting for the next test and really wanting to do well. I decide to see how she goes with her legs.

'Can you wiggle your foot or your toes, Nanny?' She wiggles her right foot. Her left foot and side are completely knocked out by the stroke.

'Can you lift your knee?' Up goes her right knee. Quite quickly, in fact.

Holy hell, I'm thinking to myself. I can't believe this. I need to get the nurse. I need someone else to see it, but I must see something else first.

'Can you nod your head darling?' She gives a little nod.

'Can you shake it to say no, Nanny?' A little shake.

I reach forward and clutch her shoulders. I kiss her on the forehead and go out to look for Ping who is nursing her this afternoon. I can't locate her so I go back to Nan, ring the nurse buzzer, grab Nan's hand, and sit down again. I can't resist another request.

'Nanny, can you squeeze my hand please?' She does that too. I am hopeful that Ping will arrive soon, and that Nan won't lose focus in the meantime. Ping arrives after a few minutes.

'Ping,' I say urgently. 'Nan is responding. Watch this.' I go through several commands again, including the tongue poke, finger points, thumbs ups and head nods. Nanny nails them all in front of Ping.

'What do you think, Ping?'

Ping is nodding and looking from Nan to me and back again. She doesn't gush with excitement like I did. I guess nursing in a ward like this you get to see it all. But she does respond. She speaks in a very measured fashion.

'That is really very good Nan. Very good David.' Off she then goes to attend to her other tasks.

I look at Nanny. I know I am simultaneously crying and laughing. At the outer end of emotional extremes where those two reactions met. After nearly two months, Nan is awake and responding. It means she understands and can process. Some of the things Andrew said she would be able to do if she woke.

'I'm so proud of you darling,' I say. 'It's so good to have you back.'

I don't want to overwork Nan, but I can't help throwing her some more commands every now and then to make sure she is still there. She is. It isn't fleeting like the head nod.

After some time together, I need to let the family know what has happened. I ring Jill and let her have the good news. I preface it by telling her that the nurse had also experienced this and there is no doubt what has gone on.

'She's responding Jill, to virtually every command I could throw at her that she could respond to without talking.'

I hear Jill gasp at the news. She knows I wouldn't be imagining it or telling her anything untrue. I repeat that Nan has successfully responded in front of Ping as well.

'That is so wonderful, David.'

'It really is incredible to see. Can you let Joan know please? I don't want to talk to her. This is too special to have ruined. It might be good for you to come up again when you can. I don't know whether she will hold onto this. It's impossible to tell.'

We hang up. I ring Patrick and tell him the good news as well. He tells me he will be back in a couple of days. I also shoot some texts out to my own siblings.

It is by now approaching dinner. It is Saturday night. I am alone, but I decide to eat at the Italian place nearby where Jill and I had sometimes bought pizzas. As I walk up, I recognise two of the younger doctors from intensive care having dinner there as well. I can't help myself and walk over to them.

'Hi there,' I say. 'Do you remember me? I'm Nanette's husband. The most amazing thing has just happened. She is awake and responding to commands.' I gush on about her achievements that afternoon and that the nurse had witnessed it. They both smile happily and nod. They don't say much. I apologise for interrupting them and tell them I just had to say something. I then leave them alone and go in and order a veal scaloppini in celebration of Nan's mighty achievements.

I take a table outside. The weather is very mild and after being in the hospital all day, I want to take in some fresh air. To take deep and beautiful gulps of oxygen to help fuel and maintain the high I am experiencing. I must have looked like I was on something to any passer-by. Or trying to sell something. Nobody sits alone beaming like that, bidding hello to strangers as they pass.

Soon after I sit down, I notice a tall, slim man in blue scrubs approaching. I recognise it is Stuart, another one of the neurosurgery registrars. He is British and would be late twenties or early thirties I guess. I had only met him since Nan moved to the neurosurgery ward, but he was very kind and very nice. I could tell he was compassionate. He could see what we were going through. He had a nice bedside manner when he dealt with Nan and was respectful when he spoke with me. We lock eyes as he approaches, and I stand up to tell him what has happened.

'She's responding Stuart. Virtually everything I could think of to ask, she did successfully this afternoon. It's the most amazing thing.'

'Really?' he says. 'I'm going to the hospital now. I'll go and see her myself.'

'OK great. I hope she is still responding when you get there.'

Stuart continues up the hill towards the hospital and I resume my seat. My veal is served, and I tuck into it. One of my favourite meals. Tender veal in a mushroom sauce. It is quite succulent, but every aspect of life feels that way right now.

A tall young man in blue comes to my bed
'Hi Nan, I'm Stuart, one of the doctors here,' he says
'Can you poke out your tongue for me?'
I do it
He asks me to do other things and I do those too
He stands back and smiles and nods
'Well done, Nan,' he says

I've just finished my meal when I notice Stuart approaching from the direction of the hospital. He comes to my table, beaming.

'David, I've been to see Nan. She responded to me the same way.'

'She did, Stuart?'

'Yes, she did. I am very happy for you.'

'Thanks Stuart. It's hard to believe after almost two months.'

'Enjoy it!' he says. Stuart shakes my hand and goes on his way.

I sit down at my table again. I need to savour the moment a little longer. It is like a scene in a movie, one you wouldn't expect to experience in everyday life.

I feel like I am a first-time father; Nanny is born again. I want to light and share some cigars in celebration.

As I sit there, I wonder what is still in front of us. Too much has happened to naively think that everything will be OK now. Nan is paralysed down the left side. She is incontinent. As Andrew had indicated, life will be very different.

But there is so much to be positive about. Nan heard, understood and responded appropriately. It seemed that she could see, having pointed at me and then herself. The advice that I had been given was that stroke victims gained most improvements in the first six to twelve months afterwards. By the two-year mark, it was reasonable to assume all gains had been realised. So, there is reason to hope for more improvements yet.

I am a little reluctant to return to the hospital. I don't want to encounter anything that will take away from this incredible high. It is time though, so I pay the bill and go back to Nan. She is asleep again and I think it best to leave her be. I return to Bezzina House and turn in.

The next day I am hopeful of more positive developments. Again, it takes Nan a long time to wake. It is close to 4pm when she does. It is frustrating and disappointing to wait that long, but when she wakes, she is still responsive. She has clung on to her achievements from the previous day.

The following day is a Monday, and being a weekday, there is more of a buzz around the hospital with the return of more staff after the weekend. Good things might happen slowly, but it seems good news can travel quite quickly in a hospital.

While standing in the corridor waiting to go into Nan's room, a young woman approaches me. She introduces herself as Alessia, and says she is an occupational therapist. She wants to spend some time with Nan and asks whether that will be OK. I didn't really know what an occupational therapist did, and Alessia explains that they work with patients to help them regain the skills they need to live their lives. I'm paraphrasing there, and I guess it varies depending on the situation.

I say it will be OK and sometime later when I am sitting with Nan, Alessia comes in and introduces herself, maintaining good eye contact with Nan. She wants to get some idea of where she is at and what her needs might be now that she has regained consciousness. Nan remains silent of course while Alessia speaks, but when she asks Nan if it will be OK to proceed, Nan raises her eyebrows and gives a little nod.

'Nan, I'm going to give you something now, and I want you to show me how to hold it and what you would do with it.'

Alessia hands a pen to Nan. She deliberately gives it to her the wrong way round, with the nib facing away. Nan takes the pen and instantly manipulates it into the writing position. Then, while correctly holding the pen, she makes a writing gesture with it. I can see Alessia is very impressed. Nan keeps pretending to write.

'How was that Alessia?' I ask, beaming with pride like a pain-in-the-arse parent waiting for their child to be lauded.

Alessia shakes her head and smiles and says slowly and very deliberately. 'That … was so … excellent …'

Alessia and I look at each other. We don't really need to say anything more. Nan's response has pretty much given her what she needs for now. Unfortunately, neither of us has any paper to enable Nan to write something, but that could come later.

Alessia gives Nan a few other basic tests. She asks her to demonstrate what a hairbrush is for; she also presents her with two objects and asks her to pick out the larger one. Nan got some but not all correct, but clearly Alessia has seen enough with the pen to be satisfied.

Over the next few days, whenever Nan is out of bed, I give her a pen and the writing pad I bought a week or two before. I am hopeful that if she isn't yet able to verbalise anything, she might be able to write me a message explaining how she is or what she is experiencing. She is fine holding the pen each time but when given the pad she just seems to scribble. Every now and then she will break out of the repetitive scribbling into an extended line but even they look very shaky. I encourage her to write a few alphabetical characters or her name, but nothing is working yet.

At this point, she is still silent and I try to get her to say a few things. She seems to understand what I am asking her but isn't quite able to get anything out. She is trying though and that is both thrilling and troubling to see. Such a highly intelligent person. So incredibly literate over the course of her life. Someone whose written skills and vocabulary are really second to no one I have ever met. Yet here she is struggling to either speak or write a solitary word.

I decide to keep it simple and ask her to repeat things – asking her to say her name or to say mine. She seems to have trouble engaging her breath, vocal cords, lips and tongue at the same time. As the week progresses, she improves. If I ask her to say her name, I can see her mouth the word 'Nan', but nothing comes out. Same with mine, 'Dave' but mouthed only. No sound.

Eventually this develops into a whisper, and sometimes if she catches her breath at the right time, a fully-sounded word. But it is a surprise when everything engages properly.

She begins trying to talk in sentences, but it is garbled and hard to understand. Sometimes a word stands out but those around it are indecipherable. I have never tried to lip read, but it is now essential to grasp what she is trying to say. The good thing is that if she is asked to repeat what she has said, she will try again. It might take three or four attempts to get the gist. Sometimes I still can't get it and then sometimes I can, and it doesn't really make sense.

It is better if she is responding directly to questions. That at least means that both the topic and the range of likely answers are understood.

Later in the week, Claire the physiotherapist organises a session with Nan. She comes armed with a couple of assistants, two young women in their early twenties. I ask if it would be OK to stay and Claire is fine with that.

The team gathers around Nan, and they use a hoist and sling to get her up from the bed. Rather than tilt-tabling on this occasion, Claire decides to sit Nan on the edge of the bed with a team member either side.

All three young women are so kind to Nan. This seems to be a very special thing for them as well. To see someone coming out of a long coma and a very large brain injury. Someone who is clearly very loved. Someone who most people thought had absolutely no chance is now embarking on her 'second life'. Nan is now responding and that is incredible.

She seems to be coming forward quickly. Less than a week ago, she had hardly responded. Now she can get a few words out and is attempting to form sentences. It's like a dam breaking: a few small leaks becoming larger cracks, letting more out.

As the team works with her, Nanny's big beautiful blue eyes are wide open with child-like wonder at the situation she is in. *How could anyone not love her?* I think to myself. I am so proud to see her trying. So thrilled when she reaches forward to take something on request. Or hands it back again when asked. She is doing so well, and she is being cheered and encouraged by the team every time she does. But suddenly she starts to tire. Her attention is waning. They tell me fatigue is a big issue for people with brain injuries.

As Nan seems to have consumed the last of her energy for the day and looks to be visibly slumping, I sit down next to her on the bed, team members on the other side and behind her. I put my arm around her. Christ, I love her so much.

When she sees me, her eyes light up again. Because I am a lot bigger, she tries to straighten herself up to get closer to my height.

'She knows who you are,' I hear one of the team say.

'Who am I Nanny?' I ask her.

'David,' she responds in a whispered tone.

'You're making yourself tall there, Nanny,' I say. 'How tall are you?'

'Five feet and half an inch,' comes out softly, but audibly and clearly.

That half an inch was always something of great pride to Nan. Still a matter of great pride! The team reacts with a combined cheer and big laugh at that beautiful response. It is such a joyous and precious moment in my life. I will never forget it.

It is time to finish the session. Nan is spent. The team puts her comfortably back to bed. Claire tells me afterwards that they hope to get Nan accepted into a rehabilitation hospital. I hate the thought of her leaving the good care of St George. Claire explains that given the size of her injury, she needs a long period of hospitalisation and would best benefit from rehabilitation via physiotherapy, occupational therapy and speech pathology. A rehab hospital is the place where that kind of support is best provided rather than an acute hospital like St George.

I tell Claire we have an apartment in Melbourne and that it would be better if we could seek a place down there for longer term care.

'There are several rehab hospitals there, David. One of them is Caulfield. They have just spent tens of millions on a brand-new acquired brain injury clinic. It is the best facility in Australia.'

Those words resonate strongly with me. Where else would I want Nan other than the best place available?

* * *

It is good to see Jill again. She returns the day after the physiotherapy session and can see Nan's responses for herself. As a teacher and mother of two, she very naturally transitions her interaction. She is comfortable, kind and encouraging.

With Nan sitting out of bed, I hand her the writing pad and pen to see what will happen. I feel a bit self-conscious about that since I had already been accused by Joan of thinking I was a doctor. I just want the best for Nan. I am sitting there all day with her, why not use the time effectively? I also want Jill to see things for herself as well so she can take back first-hand accounts to Albury.

Nan takes the pen and begins scribbling on the page. For a minute or so we let her go, wondering if she is in the process of creating an artwork or a picture that will convey something important to us. Eventually, it becomes clear that it is just scribbling. She is scribbling quite compulsively. I put my hand on hers to stop and speak to her.

'Nan, can you write your name?'

She raises her eyebrows in acknowledgement and writes something that looks quite close.

'Jill, I think that's a capital N and it looks like a small n on the end.' In between the two Ns it might be an 'a', but there is scribble around it as well. If we showed it to someone else, they would struggle to interpret it.

'Yes, I think so too,' Jill responds. 'Try it again, Nan. Write your name,' Jill says.

This time, there is a much stronger capital 'N'. There are two other characters. They are an 'a' and an 'n'. I hold the pad up for Jill to see more clearly. We look at each other. There is no doubt she has just written her name.

I still have that book now. On the cover I wrote 'Nanette's written responses' and the word 'Sacred'. I am looking at the page she wrote on that day in front of Jill and me. I dated it 24/10/14 at the time. There is scribble on other parts of the page. Elsewhere, there look to be attempts to formulate some English characters. A capital 'E' stands out. Some lines drawn in parallel to each other. There is a string of 'xxxxxxxx'. Were they kisses to us? I don't know but they look like it.

On the page opposite, also dated from the same day, is where we asked her to write Nanette. She has written it as 'nannette'. Next to that she has made another attempt at 'Nan'.

Johnny the neurosurgery registrar comes into the room not long after this while doing rounds. We show him the pad that Nan has written in. He looks at it, and it is his turn to have his mind blown. Last time I saw Johnny, he was with Sayeed. Nan was still unconscious, and they were clearly wondering what to do. Now she is awake, and she has written her name.

Johnny looks at Nan and then at Jill and I and says, 'Whatever you are doing, keep doing it.' He then adds with a smile, 'she looks like she could do with a haircut.'

Her hair is an absolute mess. Nan normally had a haircut every four weeks. She has plenty of hair and it is fast-growing. It is now ten weeks or so since she had a clip. One night after that, a nurse saw to Nan's hairdressing needs and I arrived to find her with short greying hair. I had always loved her long dark locks, but to my surprise, the new cut really suited her.

That evening, feeling elated and even some measure of relief, I decide to attend a concert at Sydney Opera House. Jazz guitarist and composer Pat Metheny is in town. I am quite a fan and had purchased tickets to see him this tour in Melbourne. Frank and I were scheduled to go together but when Nan became ill, Frank's son Alex went in my place.

Nan and I first saw Metheny live in 1985. It was an incredible show. We sat in the third row of the Comedy Theatre in Melbourne and were blown away by the musicianship and the compositions. It was a two-and-a-half-hour assault on our senses that left me completely spellbound and unable to think about anything else for days.

This time, I managed to secure a ticket and am seated at the side of the stage of the Opera House Concert Hall. It's not a great position to take in a show. The performers are oriented towards the audience in front of them and it's more like you are witnessing rather than participating in a concert event. The backdrop of the events of the last two months is also impossible to ignore and override in my mind. I reflect on Nan's progress of the last few weeks and where she has come from. I think about her writing her name and telling us her height and of her much improved and consistent responsiveness generally.

I can't enjoy the concert. I know that some of the best musicians in the world are on stage. Metheny, Antonio Sanchez on drums, and the mighty Chris Potter on saxophone. I know that they are brilliant. I know Jill is just over the road from the hospital staying in Bezzina House. None of that matters. I can't properly focus on the show, and I feel anxious about being even thirty minutes away from Nan.

Over the next couple of days while Jill is there, Nan delivers some more writing for us. She writes the name of our hometown Albury and its postcode. She wrote 26440 instead of 2640. She writes Jill's and Bruce's names. In both cases, the first names are written relatively clearly, and the surnames are not. She writes her mum's name. In that case, her first name is not clear, but the surname 'Parker' is. She attempted to write our surname Hoysted. The gist is there, with some characters clearer than others, but it would be difficult for someone else to interpret.

We have some visits from rehabilitation doctors. They are assessing Nan to determine if she can go to a rehab hospital or be sent immediately to aged care. My experience with the medical profession to date has been overwhelmingly positive. People doing everything possible to bring Nan forward.

I am somewhat flattened therefore by my initial exposures to rehab doctors. I had expected optimistic people who drove hard for improvement. Instead, I found pessimistic, negative people painting very bleak pictures. Despite that, Nan is given the OK to go to rehab. I know that people like Julie and Claire are thrilled with that outcome. I know we are all thrilled to find out that Caulfield Hospital has accepted Nan as well.

Plans are made to transfer her by air ambulance from Sydney to Melbourne. This is scheduled for 29 October. I arranged my own private flight and Frank had my car delivered to me in Melbourne by his friend KC.

On our last two evenings at St George, Nan is remarkably alert and interactive. On the first of those evenings, I use my iPad to access

Coronation Street and play it for Nan. She is a big fan and has watched it each night since we had a long stay in England in 2004. After twenty minutes or so, Nan indicates she has had enough so I turn it off.

Nan then has a coughing fit and becomes quite agitated. She complains of noise and then a pain in the back of her head. She waves her hand down in front of herself.

'What are you doing Nanny?' I ask.

'Drawing a blind down on him,' she replies.

'There is no one else here Nanny. You know that don't you?'

'Yes,' she says somewhat unconvincingly.

She then seems to think I have had an anaesthetic. I explain to her she is in hospital in Sydney, but we will soon be transferred to Melbourne.

'I'm going to need to go over this house very thoroughly,' she says.

I remind her she is in a hospital in Sydney.

'When I look at you, I can only think about the cost,' she says.

I notice she is looking downwards as I stand in front of the bed.

'What are you looking at, Nanny?' I ask.

'Your fly.'

I laugh at that, and she gives a cheeky half grin, but I am a little alarmed at what I am hearing. On the positive side of things, she is very conversational.

I locate Stuart in one of the corridors and tell him Nan is starting to say some odd things. I also ask him if he could have a look at her ears given she complained of noise.

When I tell Stuart the things she said, he says he will reduce the level of amantadine as that may be making her hallucinate. I thank him and go back to Nan who is quite fidgety. I get her attention and talk to her, and she seems to focus and remain attentive.

'I love you,' I tell her. I am tearing up again. 'I am so glad to have you back. I will not be working again. I'm only going to look after you. It will be you and me and the cat.'

Nan doesn't really make any response until the night afterwards at a similar time, around 6pm. She is smiling at me. She then says some things to me that are even more sacred than our exchange of wedding vows.

'You're a perfect husband'
'You told me you would stop work and look after me. Just you, me and the cat.'
'I really did!' David replies.' 'I guess I'm obliged now Nanny!'

I am far from perfect. There is no such thing. But that is the most perfect thing anyone has ever said to me in my life. It is also the last time I experienced Nan recalling a new memory a day later. Her memory is now permanently affected by the stroke and everything that happened after that.

PART TWO

CAULFIELD

Only once the plane pops through the cloud cover and begins its cruise bathed in brilliant sunshine am I able to relax a little and reflect. A lot has happened in the two months since I was last airborne and howled all the way from Albury to Sydney.

I wasn't sure I would see the day when Nan would leave St George alive. I felt like we were criminals who had slipped out of the reach of the law on a charge that should have stuck. Our departure happened quickly, and there was no time to express our gratitude or say goodbye to the many people who had done so much for Nan. I wonder what our experience will be like at Caulfield. At least now there is a place for hope.

I also wonder where Nan is at that instant. Somewhere further ahead on the same flight path I expect, perhaps even landed in Melbourne by now. Did she appreciate she was flying, or did she sleep through the whole thing?

After disembarking in Melbourne and making my way to baggage collection, my mobile starts to ring. I thought it would be family but the 'No caller ID' message is an instant giveaway.

'Hello. Is that David Hoysted?' asks a young male voice.

'Yes.'

'I'm one of the doctors at Caulfield Hospital. We have Nanette here and she is not well. She has very high blood pressure. We are doing our best to get it under control.'

'I'm on my way. I've just landed. I will be there as soon as I can. What is her blood pressure?'

'It's 250/150,' he responds.

'Jesus.'

'Yes, it's very high,' the doctor confirms.

Caufield Hospital is on a large parcel of land. There are a lot of older buildings, their differing architectures indicating they were built generations apart.

My taxi drops me at what looks like the entrance gate, but it turns out to be two hundred metres from the entrance I need. I feel frustrated having to backtrack to get to Nan.

When I eventually find the hospital reception, they advise Nan is in ward Rehab B. I'm instructed on how to get there, 'via the breezeway', whatever that is.

It's a long walk after multiple taxis and a flight, and the knowledge that Nan is not doing well. She remains tantalisingly out of my reach. I find the 'breezeway'. It is well named. It is wide and little more than a covered walkway. It and the buildings around it are probably Second World War vintage, constructed to process returned injured servicemen.

I step off the concrete of the breezeway into the ward and onto an obviously false floor, my footsteps booming as I walk down the harshly lit hallway. I find the nurses' station and a common area where some wheelchair-bound patients and their family members are seated in front of a large TV. One of the nurses directs me back to a room next to the entrance to the ward. I hurry to find Nan in the bed and a young male doctor attending to her.

'Hi Nanny,' I say to Nan and kiss her. She raises her eyebrows and opens her eyes wide with surprise and kisses me back. As she does so, she silently mouths a 'Hi' in return. Her hand stays on my arm. I turn to the young doctor.

'I'm David. Nan's husband.'

'Hi. We spoke on the phone,' he replies. 'We have her blood pressure back to a better level. We have been trying to speak further to St George as well. We suspect she didn't get her medication this morning before she left.'

'Oh,' I respond, not quite believing it. I didn't want to think anything negative about St George.

'We have been reviewing her medication needs. Do you know anything about the amantadine? Can you tell me what she has that for?'

'My understanding is it is some kind of stimulant they were using to help her wake from the coma.'

'We don't have that available here. It's typically in tablet form which is a problem to administer with a PEG. We are trying to sort something out,' he goes on.

'At St George, they melted the tablets down and mixed them with water,' I offer. I can't really suggest anything more than that.

The doctor leaves soon after and I sit next to Nan holding her hand. She is looking hard to her right, so I move to that side of the bed to make eye contact. A younger woman in her twenties soon enters the room and posts a schedule above the bed.

'This is Nan's therapy schedule,' she tells us.

It has a list of her activities by day for the forthcoming week. There are other notices posted above her bed. 'Nil by mouth', 'non-verbal', 'falls risk', and another with her doctor's name.

The non-verbal sign pisses me off. That isn't right, she is talking. Sometimes it comes out clearly and sometimes a bit garbled. Just take the time to understand her. I hope they can bring her forward.

A nice male nurse named Matthew comes in and introduces himself. He is looking after Nan. He made a point of talking to us both, getting over to Nan's right and into her field of vision to make clear eye contact and engage her. He already appreciates the communication challenges.

Some therapists arrive and introduce themselves. A physio, an occupational therapist and a speech pathologist walk into the room. Separately. A dietician also comes to ensure Nan's PEG feed is properly in place. They are all young women in their twenties and thirties. The speech therapist is quite pregnant.

One by one, I ask each of them if it will be OK for me to attend the therapy sessions with Nan and one by one, they agree. No sessions are scheduled for a day or two. I ask when I would see the doctor Nan is under, and they tell me Friday. It is only Wednesday.

Nan seems comfortable and unbothered despite the scare, but they don't call high blood pressure 'a silent killer' for nothing. There aren't any symptoms. I imagine it creeping away stealthily in the background, as insidious as a corporate frenemy, smashing constantly against the blood vessels in her brain, trying to find another weak point.

It was a big adjustment when Nan changed wards within St George. This time we changed not only hospitals, but states as well. This obviously is not the shiny new Acquired Brain Injury (ABI) facility I heard about. The buildings are ancient, yet despite their age, have stubbornly maintained a temporary feel about them.

'What is this ward?' I ask the day's nurse in charge when she drops by. She is a tall, middle-aged Chinese woman. 'I was expecting we would be admitted to the new ABI unit.'

'This is a neuro rehab ward. This is where we have traditionally treated stroke patients like Nan. The ABI unit is very new, and they are still staffing up and getting started.'

'Will we be transferred there soon? Isn't that where we should be?'

'The treatment and therapy would be the same here or there,' she replies and moves on.

I turn my attention back to Nan. Her head and gaze are persistently turned to her right. She is stroking and crunching up the sheets of the bed. I gently place my hands on either side of her face and turn her back to look at me. We make eye contact and I give her a kiss.

'God you are gorgeous,' I tell her. She raises her eyebrows to receive the compliment but says nothing back. She goes on playing with the sheets.

I must accept the change. We have moved. Nan is in a new hospital, and they seem to be attentive. There is no choice. It's another stage and hopefully we will see more recovery from Nan.

'I better go back to our flat now and have my dinner, Nanny. I will see you tomorrow,' I tell her. She raises her eyebrows and gives a little nod of acknowledgement.

I walk back to the front of the hospital and call a taxi. While I am waiting, my phone rings and it's Joan. I let her know we are both at Caulfield and what had happened with Nan's blood pressure, or what I know of it anyway. She wants to know that they are looking after her properly.

'Yes, they seem to be very attentive,' I say.

'We are all counting on you now, David. It's up to you,' is her response.

I am not sure what to make of that. All I can do is be there for Nanette, look after her and look out for her.

'I will do whatever I can, Joan.'

I had no real idea what happened in a rehab hospital, but quickly a routine falls into place. A combination of allied health treatments under the oversight of rehabilitation consultants and other doctors who manage the medical needs of the patient. Of course, it's the nurses that keep things going, attending to patients' medication and personal needs throughout the day and night.

Each morning the nurses arrive to give Nan her bed bath and change her diaper, or pad, as they call it. Nan can't turn herself, or sit up, so it is a two-person job, the nurses rolling her to one side and then the other to pull out the old pad and insert a new one beneath her.

One holds her on her side while the other conducts the personal care clean, front and back. It is a labour-intensive exercise in an already busy ward, and timing depends on there being two nurses available.

After we have been there a few weeks, I begin volunteering to help in place of one of the nurses. I am there all day and happy to share the load rather than exit the room and walk aimlessly around the ward killing time. I leave the cleaning aspect to the nurse, but take my place on the other side and help roll her or hold her while she is cleaned, and push the old pad out and the new one in.

It's amazing how quickly you get used to something like this. I thought about pre-stroke Nan being so self-conscious about her body and bodily functions. She wouldn't even fart in front of me and wasn't comfortable being seen naked, yet here I was, helping clean up after her. Post-stroke Nan never seemed bothered at all by any of this.

After the clean, we hoist her out into a wheelchair for a few hours, put her back to bed at lunch time for a rest, and then get her up again for a few more hours mid-afternoon until early evening. I always leave the operation of the hoist controls to the nurse, but help get Nan into the harness, into the hoist and then into the wheelchair.

Her first day in a wheelchair, a nurse encourages me to take her outside for some sunshine and fresh air. I am anxious about taking her out of the ward, but at least at Caulfield, everything is flat, and I don't have to negotiate lifts or much other traffic.

'How do you like this Nanny?' I prompt her.

'Good,' she mouths inaudibly, nodding as she said it and her eyebrows going up.

It isn't long before the sunshine and warmth on her face lulls her off to sleep. The first time outside together in more than two months and I am struck by how pale she is. Ghostly, sickly white. I know it is an indication of what she has already been through more than the lack of exposure to sunlight.

I am conscious of passers-by looking at her, and eventually that and the anxiety of being away from the ward win, and I gently turn her around and roll her back down to the relative safety of the ward again.

The rehab consultant arrives as expected on Friday. Her name is Julia. Forty-something, slim and bespectacled. I tell her our story. She tells me she did a short stint somewhere near our hometown earlier in her career. Small world sometimes.

She begins a full examination of Nan, focusing particularly on her left side which is immobilised by the stroke. She checks the range of movement of Nan's left leg and foot and left arm, hand, and fingers. Nan's left foot is starting to point downwards. Her tendons are shortening. Her left hand has closed quite tightly as well. These things happen because Nan isn't moving her left side anymore. Spasticity is setting in.

Julia recommends some Botox shots to try and release the tightness. I thought Botox was only for the cosmetic ruination of the once beautiful sourpusses of South Yarra. Apparently, it can deliver something more worthwhile than competitive vanity. I wonder if it is safe, but after Julia takes me through the risks it seems the odds of a problem are low. She will bring it with her in the following week.

'Julia, one of the doctors mentioned that you are having some issues sourcing the amantadine that Nan has been on. Have you been able to obtain it? Is she back on it?' I decide to ask.

'We aren't prepared to administer that drug in that manner. The dosages can't be guaranteed that way. We have withdrawn it,' Julia explains.

'Oh. Do you think she can do without it? She seems fine.'

'It's hard to know what it has been doing for her but it's not an approach we use.'

Nan lays there quietly during this exchange and the whole time Julia examines her. She responds as best she can when asked to, but otherwise lays there, seemingly listening and taking it in.

When Julia leaves, I sit on Nan's bed against her. It's hard for me to resist touching her. I've nearly lost her, but I have her back. I want contact. I just want to hug her and keep her with me.

'You're going to have some Botox, Nan. You, with your youthful skin. You certainly don't need it for your face you beautiful thing.'

'I do,' she manages to whisper back.

'Where do you need it?' I challenge her.

She slowly brings her fingers to her face and makes some gentle pats at the corner of her eyes.

'You do not,' I laugh. 'How did you get to be so gorgeous?' I ask her in complete wonder.

'Good genes,' she whispers back deadpan and with the timing of a comedian.

The therapy sessions are normally timed for an hour first thing in the morning, or mid-afternoon, after her lunch time rest. I like physiotherapy from the outset because it is stimulating for Nan both mentally and physically. Our physiotherapist is Rosie, a slim late-twenties brunette.

Initially, we do a couple of physio sessions in Nan's room while she lays, or we sit her upright on the bed. As in Sydney, I am immensely proud when she successfully completes a stretching or reaching task, or receives a ball or passes it back to me. She is trying so hard, and it is so hard for her.

Rosie is keen to progress and so by the start of the second week, the sessions are relocated to new, purpose-built gymnasiums in the main building at Caulfield. There is one larger gym where several other patients and their therapists would be working out, and next to that, a smaller, quieter one where distractions are minimised for neuro patients like Nan. We can close out the rest of the world in there and conduct the physio session in silence.

Nan is very sleepy in the mornings, and some sessions she isn't up for anything much. We would get her cleaned, into the chair and over to the gym or ready for an occupational therapy session only to see her fade quickly. It was obvious she was tuning out and not paying attention. Sometimes I would be talking with Rosie and realise she had quickly fallen back into an exhausted sleep. It's one thing to encourage and even push a patient along the path to recovery, but it's another thing when that patient has a severe brain injury and is experiencing heavy fatigue. In these cases, it is best to let her rest.

The therapy sessions are only conducted on weekdays and the therapists' commitments to other patients mean there isn't the ability to reschedule if Nan is too sleepy on the day. That can leave a lot of free time within the week and particularly on weekends. It is frustrating. She is brighter by mid-afternoon but that is after therapy has concluded for the day. It seems Nan's body clock is out.

I decided to do what I could during these idle times and took a trip to a local Officeworks to buy some stationery: colouring pencils, pads, crayons and a whiteboard and markers. I prompt Nan to practice writing our names and her family's names and addresses. I ask her to write 'Melbourne' or 'Caulfield Hospital' to try and orient her. She writes these out in a shaky hand but on one occasion writes 'right paddock'. I guess she may have been experiencing some word confusion or substitution between 'paddock' and Caul-'field'.

After a week at Caulfield, I notice changes in Nan. It isn't just the morning therapy sessions where she is not responding well. Her handwriting is losing its shape. Characters have transformed into illegible lines and hieroglyphic-like markings. Her writing and symbols are becoming smaller, and it has become impossible to decipher the words. Over the next few days, that degenerates further into repetitive scribbling. She scratches back and forth with the pen, over and over the same spots on the page.

Her responsiveness has dried up too. I can no longer get her to follow the simple commands like poking her tongue out, pointing at me, touching her nose, or giving me a thumbs up. Occasionally I get one of these back successfully, but it is after a lot of attempts.

Equally concerning is that her speech and head nods and other interactions and gestures have also left her. Her voice had been soft, but she was previously getting words and sentences out. Now her speech and even any attempt to speak are gone altogether.

Nan is unresponsive and mute again. This is such a setback. Someone said it would be three steps forward and two steps back, but this was three forward and three back. Things get even worse when Nan starts making what I can best describe as a long and low-sounding, combined groan and grunt noise. It starts with an mmm and then ends with an exhaled uhh or ahh. 'Mmmmuhhh'. It is the kind of sound an animal might emit. She just keeps doing it. She builds up with each one getting louder and longer. It is all she can do. I hate listening to it. I can't stop her or settle her. Once she starts, it often goes on for twenty minutes or until she falls asleep. I can't distract her from it no matter what I do.

It is both distressing and infuriating to listen to. I am concerned she has taken a backward step and that the hospital will decide she isn't worth the effort and evict us. What hope would she have if she is turned over to a nursing home now? She has only been in Caulfield for such a short time that they mustn't appreciate how far she has come forward against impossible odds. I know from a scan of the other patients in the thirty-bed ward that Nan is in easily the most challenging situation. Most other patients are mobile. Those that aren't, look much more interactive and are probably able to at least make some of their own decisions.

I can't help suspecting that the change in Nan is due to the withdrawal of amantadine. I only know the drug is a stimulant and that the doctors at St George believed it had helped Nan and other patients as well. The timing seems too coincidental.

I begin alerting nurses and the therapists to the changes I am seeing in Nan. By the time Julia next arrives she is already aware of my concerns. She is only a few steps into the room when I blurt out what I am thinking.

'Julia, Nan isn't responding now. Is it because she's not getting amantadine?' I ask anxiously.

'David, it might be that Nan has suffered a new setback of some sort. We will do some brain scans, X-rays and blood tests to see if anything else is going on.'

Shit. I had convinced myself it was because the drug was withdrawn. I sit at Nan's side holding her hand and stroking her hair while Julia goes about prepping the Botox injections. She will focus more on Nan's left hand which is now quite stiffly closed and painful for her if I open it.

Julia draws up the Botox, finds several points in her hand and wrist and carefully injects small quantities there. It takes maybe fifteen minutes and then Julia gathers her things and leaves, advising she will arrange for the tests to be done for Nan.

Over the next week, the hospital conducts the tests. Nan's situation is unchanged. She is still not responding to commands and not talking or communicating. She continues to make eye contact and hold my hand, but that is about the limit of it.

Pathologists arrive to extract blood for analysis and Nan is taken for a brain scan as well as chest and abdominal X-rays. They also test her urine to see if there is a urinary tract infection (UTI).

The hospital team is exploring what might have set Nan back cognitively: the brain scan is looking for a new stroke, the chest X-ray checking for pneumonia, the abdominal X-ray checking for constipation. Any of these conditions or a UTI could apparently affect her cognition.

I haven't had a UTI or pneumonia and not even much constipation in my adult life, but I'm sceptical that any of these caused the issue. I am concerned about the brain scan though.

Fortunately, the results are returned quickly. The good news is no change was found in the brain scan; in other words, no new stroke. That's a relief. There is also no pneumonia found on the chest X-ray. Also a relief, but there hadn't been anything to suggest that might be the case.

The bowel scan shows some constipation, so the team give Nan extra medication to fix it. It might take a few days. The blood tests and urinary test didn't produce anything remarkable, so it's a matter of waiting until the constipation is sorted.

There is no improvement in Nan's responsiveness or interaction at all after the constipation is addressed. She is still mute except for the groan/grunt which kicks in each day.

When I next see Julia, it is in the ward hallway. She is doing rounds and a pharmacist is with her. I tell her that there is no improvement in Nan's condition, but she is still reluctant to reintroduce amantadine for Nan.

As I'm talking with Julia, it seems the pharmacist is looking at me in a contemptuous fashion. I remain pleasant but I can't help assuming she is the one who raised the concern on amantadine. I don't have that direct exchange and she remains silent during the discussion. I may be wrong, but I felt in receipt of a death stare, and it wasn't fleeting.

I leave the conversation having got nowhere, and privately fume about it for days. I sit with Nan all day long, holding her hand, asking for responses and getting nothing. The grunt/groan kicks in regularly and I sometimes leave the ward so I don't hear it. I feel very disloyal doing that, but it is too much.

They did their tests and effectively proved nothing. As I've been told, I'm not a doctor, but I don't need to be. Isn't the timing a little too coincidental? Doesn't it make sense? What is there to lose? My beautiful wife was interacting and responding and now she isn't. This is such a setback, and it seems to me that anything is worth a try.

I can't sit idly by and do nothing. I decide to ring St George and ask them about it. I call the neurosurgery department and eventually get a call back from Johnny the neurosurgery registrar.

I tell him that Caulfield has withdrawn amantadine and Nan has become unresponsive. They have conducted tests and not found any other reason for her decline. I'm privately hoping St George would somehow get involved to advocate. His response is surprising.

'Well, I'm sorry to hear that, David. We thought of Nanette as a real success story. As far as amantadine goes, I would say if she's off the drug, then leave her off it. I mean, in terms of our usage of it, it would be really too much to describe that as off-label.'

'You mean it's quite experimental?' I ask.

'Yes, it really is. There haven't been enough trials to validate its usage. I suggest you give her more time and see whether she comes forward again.'

'OK. It's just so frustrating. She was doing well and now we have this setback. It's hard for me to believe that this is not related to the withdrawal of the drug. The timing seems too coincidental.'

'I know,' he says and then he too uses the three steps forward and two steps back saying. Seems to be a well-known dance routine for recovery from brain injuries.

So, I need to play a waiting game. I am not good at that, sitting in a hospital ward day after day, seeing my wife unable to interact anymore. I begin googling amantadine to see what I can find. There is plenty about its history. It was developed as an anti-viral drug and is sometimes used to assist with movement disorders from Parkinson's and other conditions. There isn't much else about its neuro-stimulant properties or use for brain haemorrhage sufferers, but there was one study published in the U.S. where it had been analysed for that.

I find the details of the doctor on the publication and send him an email. I tell him what has happened to Nan and that amantadine has been used and then withdrawn. I want to know if it is safe to use. I think it is a long shot.

To my surprise, the doctor writes back overnight. He suggests that if she is impacted by withdrawing the drug, then get her back on it. At various intervals, it is worth weaning her off it again but reintroduce it if she goes backwards. Then he says that she can stay on the drug indefinitely if she needs to.

I wonder what to do with this information. It gives me some hope, but I don't think it will carry a lot of weight at Caulfield. There is then the problem of how to get the drug into Nan given the PEG. There was mention in the google searches that it is available in a syrup form. I talk to my sister Christine about it all, and she suggests I contact a compounding pharmacy. She has some experience with them seeking a medication for one of her Scottish terriers. I find one not far from the hospital.

The pharmacist there says he will be able to make something but needs to know the concentration of the active ingredient so it can be properly dosed. I have no idea. He tells me to ask the hospital about it.

I feel this is a potential solution to try. Why isn't the contemptuous pharmacist doing this investigation? It isn't up to me, but I can't help myself. We have lost four weeks with Nan being unresponsive. Therapy sessions have stopped. The only thing I can do is walk her in the wheelchair round and round the hospital. We cover kilometres daily, up and down the long corridors, out into the open if the weather allows, and out to a rotunda in the front garden.

Jill is visiting for a couple of days and happens to be there when Julia comes in with a cardiac registrar filling in for the ward, and the junior doctor, Veronica. I go straight to the point.

'Julia, it's been four weeks. Nan is still unresponsive. You did all your tests. You haven't found anything that has caused her this setback. I want her back on amantadine. This is no life for her. Whatever risk is perceived, it is worth it.' I then tell her of my communication with the doctor in the U.S. and locating a compounding pharmacist.

I felt I had done the wrong thing by doing that, but there is no complaint from the doctors. It seems Julia is now more willing to try it and the hospital has been doing its own investigations.

'David, there are legal aspects we will have to work through for this.'

'Bring whatever documents you need signed and I will sign them, right now,' I reply.

'We would have to get all of that made up.'

'OK. I want her back on that drug please.'

'As for sourcing the medication, the hospital has its own suppliers, and we would operate through those.'

'OK. How quickly can you get it? This guy could have it for us in a matter of days.'

'We will come back to you on that.'

We have agreed to get Nan back onto amantadine. I am relieved but worried that if it's reintroduced and there is no improvement, then what?

The next day, Veronica advises that the liquid form of amantadine has been ordered from the U.S. I was disappointed, thinking it might take another month to get here.

'No, it will be flown out. We will have it within a week.'

'Fantastic. Thanks very much.'

I wait a few days and check in with the nurses to see if the drug has arrived. It hasn't but shouldn't be long. There has been no change in Nan. She is still unresponsive.

Five or six days after the discussion with the doctors, I walk in and sit next to Nan. She instantly looks more alert.

'Hi Nanny,' I say to Nan and kiss her. She kisses me back. I decide to prompt her to poke out her tongue, give me a thumbs up, lift her leg, touch my nose, and touch hers. Every one of the commands she executes instantly and perfectly. I race out of the room to find the nurses at the station. There are three of them standing there.

'If the amantadine hasn't yet arrived, then don't put her on it when it does. Nan is responding well again,' I blurt out.

'The drug arrived last night, and we gave her a dose then and another one this morning,' responds the nurse in charge.

NOT A SILVER BULLET

It is a great relief that Nan is responding and interacting again. I suspected the withdrawal of the drug was the problem but that wasn't a certainty until it was reintroduced.

I understood the concern of the medical team. Medical practice in the western world is conservative, and generally that's a good thing. It isn't typically the role of hospital doctors to experiment. That's for laboratories and universities. When there are new drugs, they need to be properly evaluated for their efficacy and safety.

But Nan took a huge backward step without amantadine and bounced back when she received it again. Her life prospects weren't great post-stroke. She needed it to have any quality of life.

I demonstrate Nan's renewed interaction whenever I can to anyone who will listen. There is a nice rehab registrar there called Olivia. When she comes in one morning soon after amantadine was reinstated, Nan is in the wheelchair and quite responsive. It's an opportunity for one of the medicos to see it first-hand. While Olivia is watching, I show Nan four coloured pencils and ask her to pick one of an identified colour. She does that successfully several times. Olivia is impressed but then asks if Nan can perform two or three step commands. This proves beyond her, but Olivia is positive about what she has seen anyway.

The medical staff remain concerned though, and more than once I am told that Nan will not remain on amantadine. I don't know why amantadine helps her. I don't know why doctors at St George and other hospitals overseas decided to try it in cases like Nan's. I don't need to understand any of that. I was desperate after the drug was taken away, and fearful that it would be taken away again. I know it made a difference. A critical difference. If she had not been on that drug, she may never have woken from her coma and never have responded nor interacted in any way.

I knew amantadine was used for Parkinson's patients. I also knew Nan's stroke had originated in a part of her brain affected by Parkinson's disease. When she developed a peculiar habit of rubbing her thumb repeatedly against the tips of her fingers, I made a simplistic connection and speculated this may be the 'pill rolling tremor' associated with Parkinson's that I had read about. I flagged it to several doctors, and they conceded it looked that way. I privately hoped this could be a justification to keep Nan on amantadine. She might have Parkinson's symptoms, or a condition known as Parkinsonism, where you have the symptoms and not the disease. When I look back on it now, I'm a little embarrassed that I tried to diagnose medical situations, but I was desperate on her behalf, and Nan couldn't argue for herself. Her speech was limited, and she didn't volunteer what was wrong, so I had to guess, and I had to advocate for her.

Richard is a very senior neurologist who oversees the neuro patients in Rehab B. He visits the ward once a week and reviews new cases or new needs. He is highly regarded by the medical team at Caulfield. One senior rehab consultant told me he is one of the world's leading neurologists.

Richard is in his sixties. Tall, bespectacled, and a man of few words. Something about him reminds me of photos of the great composer and conductor, Gustav Mahler.

Richard has a lot of patients to see at Caulfield, so access to him is limited. I am sitting with Nan one day when he comes in and asks how she is going. I tell him she is doing a lot better since amantadine was reintroduced. I also lament that the other medical staff were keen to remove it again. I describe to him what happened when it was stopped. I also ask him to look at what Nan is doing with her fingers.

'Is that a tremor, Richard?' I ask him while pointing to Nan's fidgeting right hand.

He studies it hard and immediately conducts some diagnostic steps. He asks Nan to take a pencil with her hand and then put her hand back in her lap. As she does what she's asked, the 'tremor' stops.

'Well, it certainly looks like a tremor,' Richard says, 'but it is interruptible, so it's not that. Patients with injuries like she has can develop habits like this and I think that's what this most likely is.'

'Richard, why does amantadine help her? Does she have Parkinson's symptoms and is the drug addressing those?' I ask. I know what outcome I want and am trying to find a way to get there.

'I think it is giving her energy.' Then after a pause he adds: 'I'm happy to give the OK for her to stay on amantadine.'

That is good news. 'Do you use it for other patients like Nan?' I ask.

'I use it for some patients who have MS.'

'It has really helped her a lot. It makes a huge difference.'

'It's not a silver bullet though,' Richard says. I don't quite understand what he means by that. I don't expect the drug will reverse the brain damage Nan had sustained from the stroke, but whether it is energy-giving or whatever it is doing, it is giving her some quality of life.

With that caution, Richard is off. Gustav Mahler has other complicated works to conduct. Medical prescriptions are his compositions to help broken brains play a little more in concert with others. Neurology is a difficult and imperfect science.

* * *

Nan's therapy sessions can restart. Physio with Rosie and occupational therapy with a new therapist, Eloise. Eloise is a tall, pretty, blonde girl from Tasmania. She seems to instantly take a liking to Nan and Nan responds well to her. She speaks to Nan in an enthusiastic and very animated way, and I notice that her voice with a higher pitch and melodic variation is cutting through with Nan.

OT, along with physio, means two kinds of therapies that elicit good interaction from Nan, but it depends on how she is on the day and the timing of the session. She is still very sleepy in the mornings and often through until after lunch.

We are struggling by comparison to get any successful speech therapy happening. The sessions were initially scheduled for mornings, but strangely, when Nan did happen to be awake for speech therapy, they focused completely on her ability to swallow and eat. I understand the desire to get her eating again, but I am more concerned by her speech. I think good communication is far more important. Her voice remains very soft, and she isn't reliably engaging her breath and vocal cords at the right time to clearly get her words out. There are also some struggles in articulation with her lips, so that sometimes there is enough sound but it isn't clear, and we often have to ask Nan to repeat herself.

I am curious to find out why Nan is so tired in the mornings, so one evening, I decide to stay beyond visitors' hours. I want to see what time she drops off to sleep.

I sit on her left. The impact of the stroke means she can't see out the left side of either eye, so I am out of her sight. I don't want to be a distraction, so I remain quiet. I force myself not to touch her.

Nan is initially quite alert, but I notice as it approaches 9pm, she is getting sleepy. She drops off to sleep soon after, and her head moves back to the centre to face forward in a more natural position than she has been maintaining. After a few minutes, I begin quietly gathering my things, planning to make a silent exit, but she suddenly wakes again. She must have been asleep no more than a few minutes.

She immediately turns to her right and starts fidgeting with the sheets and blankets around her. She bends her right leg at the knee and seems to be reaching her leg and arm outwards as though she is trying to get out of the bed. I walk around to her right side and catch her attention. When she sees me, she looks surprised as if caught out. She focuses and reaches out to me.

'Come on now, you need to go to sleep,' I urge her.

She is becoming more alert, as though she has woken first thing in the morning after a good night. She turns her head and eyes harder to her right, pushing her head into the pillow and opening her eyes wide. The fidgeting with the sheets gains in intensity as does her intention to move her one good leg.

I can't leave her like this, so I sit down on her right side and hold her hand hoping that will help her settle. There is only a momentary pause. I place my hand on her forehead in a further attempt to calm her. She feels warm and by the light from the hallway, she looks flushed. I grab a paper towel, fold and wet it and put it on her forehead to keep her cool. She seems to like that but is still drawn to her right and the towel keeps falling off.

An hour passes, and then another. It is after 11pm. I am tired. I have been there since 9.30am myself. I decide to try wetting another towel and placing it over her eyes. With her sight cut off, her distraction to her right abates and her head drifts back towards the centre again. After fifteen minutes or so, she goes to sleep. I wait another ten or fifteen and decide I need to go for my own rest.

It is approaching midnight when I arrive home. I go straight to bed, anxious about what had gone on that evening. The next day, Nan is sleepy through the morning, but I think I have a better understanding of why.

The next evening is no better. The same pattern kicks in. Nan is even more wound up. I went to have dinner while they put her back to bed and when I return to check on her, she is fidgeting. She seems to be conversing with someone she believes is there. I can't make out what she is saying.

'Nanny, who are you talking to?' I ask. She doesn't respond to me.

'Nan, is there someone else in this room besides you and me?'

'Yes.'

'Who is it?'

'There is a little boy.'

'Where is he?'

'Just there,' she indicates to her right in the corner of the room. There is no one there. She restarts her conversation with him. I still can't make it out. She is certainly very sped up. Going fast. Talking and fidgeting. I try the wet paper towel to settle her, but she is too wound up for that.

I don't know what to do. I sit again to her left out of her view, my head in my hands, crunched up into a foetal position. Is this what life will be now? I feel helpless. Again, I can't leave her like this, but I don't seem to be able to settle her no matter what I do.

Suddenly, I have an inspiration. I grab my iPad and open the books app. Before Nan became ill, I had downloaded a copy of *Winnie the Pooh*. I hadn't read it as a child. Nan was mortified about that. She had loved those written stories since her own childhood. She had read everything. She still loved Pooh.

I open the first page and start reading. I have Nan's attention. She is listening. I keep going and going. She is so wide-eyed as I read to her. Her little mouth opens into a smile with excitement. I really feel she is living the story in her own way. Completely caught up in it. Perhaps she is visualising the characters: Pooh, Piglet, Owl. She maintains that look of childlike wonder as I continue to read. It is after 11pm. Then after twelve. She is becoming settled. I am becoming exhausted.

Eventually she goes to sleep, and I go home. This time it is approaching 1am when I get there. I met the night shift nurses who started their shifts at 11pm. What a life they led, I thought. But now I was there for most of a day and an afternoon shift myself.

The next morning, I ask to see one of the doctors. Veronica the junior doctor arrives, and I reluctantly confess what had gone on the last couple of evenings. I knew amantadine was the likely cause given the experience we had at St George.

'Well, I can reduce the dosage,' offers Veronica. I am not sure what to do but think that is worth a try. I wondered if Nan would lose her interaction again with less of the drug.

'How much is she on, and what's a normal dosage of amantadine?' I ask.

'She's on 150mg twice a day. That's the normal dosage. If you like, I can cut out the evening dose and see how she goes?'

'OK,' I say, happy that an answer is offered. I go away feeling a little lighter. Veronica didn't give me a hard time about the drug. She didn't suggest taking it away. I guess by then, Richard might have thrown his support behind it, and I doubt anyone is really going to argue the toss with him.

The reduction in dosage doesn't seem to affect Nan's interaction, nor has it settled her sleeplessness. The pattern of the last couple of evenings continues. I keep reading. All the way through *Winnie the Pooh* and then into and through *Wind in the Willows*. I am amused by that book and its characters, particularly *Toad*. Once finished, I start it again and reread it from the beginning. Nan doesn't complain. She lays there each evening, eyes wide and listening to the story. It settles her from the fidgeting and eventually she drops off to sleep.

For three weeks or so, this is how we spend the evenings. It is tiring for us both. After a couple of weeks, I convert to a talking book version of *Wind in the Willows*. I made myself redundant, replaced by technology. I don't much like the voice of the narrator, but Nan doesn't seem to mind.

After some time at each revised dose of amantadine, the dosage needs to be further adjusted and I talk again with Veronica or one of the other doctors. To 100mg, then sixty, then fifty, then thirty, then back up to fifty again when we think thirty is too low. If Nan seems too agitated at night-time, I agree with the nurses to withhold the drug the next morning. There is no clear path through this. I am starting to appreciate what Richard meant by amantadine not being a silver bullet. Without it, I know Nan won't interact or talk or have any quality of life. With it there is agitation and sleeplessness at night.

* * *

During the days, the therapy sessions continue. They are retimed to late mornings and afternoons when Nan might be more alert.

In the physio sessions, Rosie works on Nan's awareness of her left side. The stroke on the right side of her brain has not only impacted her ability to move her left limbs, but also resulted in left side neglect; Nan seems unaware of the left side of her body. Her vision is lost on the left side of both eyes as well.

Rosie passes a ball to Nan from her left and asks her to give it to me on the right. Then she takes it back again from me and hands it to Rosie on the left. Nan moves slowly from side to side, balancing the ball against her chest, using her one mobile hand underneath it. Her mouth forms an 'O' shape, her eyebrows lift, her face reflecting the great concentration and focus this is taking to achieve.

Rosie encourages Nan to reach around and find her and touch her, again prompting her from the left-hand side.

'Nan, touch my nose,' she urges. 'Good, now turn to the other side and touch David on the nose as well.' Nan turns to her right and does the same to me. Again, Nan's movements are slow and careful, as if moving underwater or trying to find her way in the dark.

Sometimes Nan is asked to use her right hand and arm to lift her left upwards from its stationary position in her lap to as high as she can go. This is a lot of physical effort for her.

There are other exercises aimed at improving Nan's balance and strengthening her core. Using a hoist, we transfer her from the wheelchair to the edge of a workout bench where we help her stay upright while she sits without the support of the chair. If we don't sit either side of her, she will topple over, unable to right herself. All these tasks would once have been simple for Nan but are now tiring for her.

Rosie is concerned about the tendons in Nan's left leg shortening through lack of usage. Her left foot is more stiffly pointing downwards, so Rosie wants to try some load-bearing activities to bring it back to its correct position.

Nan is strapped into a standing machine which lifts her out of her chair and into a more upright position, meaning she is almost standing, and her weight is borne by her feet. We try a tilt table for the same purpose, Nan's feet resting on the plate at the bottom while the angle of the tilt is raised, and she can bear more of, but not all her weight.

Eventually, Rosie and Tim from the orthotics department decide that a plaster cast should be made for Nan's left foot and lower leg to hold it in a better position throughout the day and night.

Unfortunately, a regular but involuntary stretching and contracting of Nan's leg set in, causing friction against the cast and a deep pressure sore on her lower leg. The cast must be removed. The nursing team at Caulfield is worried about this becoming a source of infection and they bandage it and apply disinfectant creams and review it daily.

It takes a long time to heal over. It looks like it would be painful but there is never any indication from Nan. I don't know if she can't feel it given it is on her impacted leg, or if she just doesn't volunteer that it is hurting. Hopefully not the latter.

In the OT sessions, Eloise encourages Nan to perform some daily personal care tasks such as brushing her hair or applying lipstick. Knowing Nan had been an artist, she also starts her on some colouring and drawing using crayons or pencils.

There are cognitive tasks involving playing cards or geometric blocks of different shapes and sizes. Eloise deals the cards out and Nan selects pairs when they are presented. The cards must be placed properly into Nan's field of view on the table before her.

With the blocks, Nan might be asked to select the red ones or the rectangular ones. She is generally quite successful at these except when her attention is waning.

'Na-a-an,' Eloise expresses in a kindly singsong, mock-exasperated manner that sometimes, but not always, snaps Nan back to attention.

Eloise has a young trainee working with her. Her name is Simone and she takes Nan's OT sessions if Eloise is busy. After her first meeting with Nan, I encourage Nan to wave goodbye to her and Eloise. Nan has a variety of waves to show off.

The first is done with her fingers wiggling a 'goodbye'. The second is really the 'royal wave': fingers extended upwards, and the wave performed by repeatedly moving the hand backwards and forwards in a sideways motion from the wrist. The third is like the royal wave at a tremor-like speed. As Nan moves through her repertoire, Simone is very amused and laughs happily in appreciation. Every time we see her afterwards, we get Nan to run her repertoire for Simone's approval.

When weekends come and there is no scheduled therapy, I sometimes take Nan to a meeting room with a whiteboard in the newer part of the hospital. There is no one around and it is quiet.

Speech pathology remains a frustration, with the continued focus on eating. I try to make up some basic word games to get Nan thinking and saying things out loud. I came up with one where I would ask her to give me a word starting with each of the letters of the alphabet.

'Nan, can you give me a word starting with an A?' I ask. 'I'll write it up on the board.'

'Anaconda,' she responds to my surprise. Not exactly a simplistic word. There is still plenty of information stored in that big but injured brain.

'Great. Can you give me a word starting with a B?' I prompt as I write 'Anaconda' on the whiteboard.

'Breakfast,' she replies softly but without any hesitation.

'A word starting with C?'

'Cool.'

'D.'

'Dinner.'

'E?'

'Extra.'

'Can I have an F word, Nanny,' I absentmindedly ask as I write 'Extra' on the board. This time, there is a hesitation from her. I turn around. I can see a little smile starting to form on her face. I know what is coming. I laugh as well.

'Come on then, what's your F word?'

Her smile is becoming a broad smirk. She gives a little giggle and then, 'Fuck 'em all, big and small,' she blurts out and bursts into a cheeky giggle. That does me in too. Gold. Still has her sense of humour. God, I love her.

When we both recover from the F word, I ask her a couple more and then she begins to tire, so I take her out and wheel her around our loop of the hospital a couple of times before making our way back to her room in the ward.

We have had a few co-tenants in the other bed in Nan's room. Cheryl, Nan's current roommate, is a woman in her sixties dealing with pancreatic cancer. We talked quite a bit and she had also lived in Albury for a time earlier in her life. She is something of a staff favourite and I can see why. Despite her own serious battle, she is kind and compassionate. She knows what is going on in our evenings and she looks at me with concern when I arrive each morning.

'Hello Nan,' she says kindly when we come back into the room. It surprises Nan and she looks around to Cheryl and emits a soft and slow 'Hi' and a nod with her eyebrows raised. I explain we have just been out for a walk.

I preferred Nan being in her own room, but I like sharing with Cheryl. We talk about what happened to Nan and the town of Albury which she remembers very fondly. Nan would be listening but not participating. I never really understood why Cheryl was in a neuro rehab ward. It may just have been that a bed came up here. She was waiting for a transfer to a hospital on the peninsula, so we only shared for a week or two. I was disappointed when the time came for her to move on.

When Cheryl leaves, her bed is taken by Roger, who I initially guess to be well into his seventies. I found out later that he was much younger than that. Roger is suffering from some form of dementia. Something makes me wonder if he had been homeless. He didn't seem to communicate and had very few visitors. The hospital staff help him out of bed each morning and sit him in the chair. He stays there all day except for toilet and shower visits. Roger is lost in his own world.

One day I walk into the room and find Roger in tears. I call the staff to attend to him and go back to my focus on Nan. It is impossible to ignore though and sad to observe. He can't communicate his distress as the nurses do their best to console him. He just becomes more and more upset. Something has tripped off in his mind.

By comparison, his demeanour is completely calm, maybe distracted, as he sits there one other day covered in his own excrement. I notice a smell and look over. It is all over his hands, on his pyjamas and in his hair. I go to the hallway and catch Debbie's attention.

'Deb, I'm sorry to tell you this, but I think Roger needs a clean-up,' I say to her apologetically.

'OH ROGER, NO!' she exclaims loudly when she sees him. She grabs another nurse and they hurry him out of his pyjamas and into a shower. It isn't a high point of their working careers, but they do their job and treat him kindly and respectfully.

Debbie is one of my favourite nurses, but they are all good at Caulfield. Christine, Matthew, Cherry, Rose, Glenda, the four Russian women who are cool but capable. Debbie is about fifty and has short brown hair. She only works weekends. We talked on a few occasions about the tragedy that had beset Nan and me.

'David, the other nurses were saying you are a good husband supporting Nan so much. I told them it's not so much a statement about you as a statement about her. What a great wife and person Nan must have been,' Debbie said one evening. I loved that and I'm sure it gave the other nurses pause to reflect on the Nan that wasn't revealed to them at the time.

* * *

Despite the word game, writing exercises and other therapy Nan is doing, I haven't seen any evidence that she can read. She had been such an avid reader before she became ill, but any time I show her a book or whiteboard with text on it, I can't get her to say a word or read a sentence back to me.

Walking our laps on another Sunday, there aren't many other people around. We stop at the hospital entrance where there are some comfortable chairs, and I can sit down and rest with her. There is a quite large, clearly written sign on the wall:

Patients and Visitors may enjoy
their refreshments in this area
but please place your cups
in the bins provided.

I decide to wheel Nan up in front of it as close as possible. 'Nanny, can you read this sign back to me?' I ask her as I point to it. She looks up at the sign and then softly says 'this, your cups provided.'

I am disappointed, wondering what she is seeing or thinking until I spot those words in a narrow cluster to the bottom right of the sign. I turn her chair slightly more to the left, walk up to the sign and point to each word from the beginning of the notice.

'Nan, can you read the sign while I point to each of the words?' I conduct her through it, and she reads it properly when prompted. Her vision and left neglect meant she had been looking to the lower-right of the sign and likely every other piece of text we had shown her previously. This gives me hope that with the right support, Nan might be able to read again.

MERRY CHRISTMAS, NANNY

'How long have I been an invalid?' Nan asks suddenly. It's a Sunday. We are in the hospital gym hitting a balloon back and forth to each other. The slow passage of the balloon gives Nan time to sight it and hit it back to me. Rallying like this seems to hold her concentration. She keeps trying, her competitive, fighting spirit clearly on display. But the fact she is still alive is the best possible evidence of that.

We are taking a break. She is looking down at herself thoughtfully, but actually, she has risen to the surface and popped her head up to take things in. She initiated the question. I hadn't prompted her. She looks up at me, waiting for my answer.

It is three months or so since the stroke. I had wondered when the time would come to explain what happened. She hasn't asked before this. I hesitate, fearful of what I need to say.

'Nanny, about three months ago, you had a stroke. We are in Caulfield Hospital in Melbourne. It's a rehab hospital. You are doing really well.'

I see my words sink in with her and her sweet, innocent little face fall. She understands it. A few more seconds pass and then she bursts into tears. She can't get any words out. The tears are too overwhelming. I put my arm around her shoulder, trying to hug her as best I can, but the wheelchair is such an obstacle to work around. If it's not the chair, it's the bed. I can never quite get close enough.

'Nanny, you have come so far. We were in Sydney at a hospital there, but you may not remember it. It was very worrying then. Now you are in rehab. I'm here with you and I always will be. I talk to your mum and Jill every day. Everyone loves you and cares about you and has been so worried about you. We all want you to get better now.'

I am walking a tightrope. I don't know if I have said the wrong things or the right things. I told her what happened. I'm hoping she doesn't ask about Hester our Labrador. I don't want to tell her about Hester as well. She keeps crying, and I keep consoling. Hugging her, kissing her, loving her. After a couple of minutes, she stops, and I look at her waiting for what comes next.

Nothing does. She settles and looks calm again. It seems to have passed. I'm expecting another outburst of tears, but it doesn't come. After a couple of minutes, I ask if she is OK. She gives her usual eyebrow raise and nod. I don't need to be told that twice and don't want to pry any further.

Looking around, I decide that some quoit throwing might be a good distraction for her. She liked quoits on family occasions like Christmas. I was terrible at it, Nan much better. I grab the pin and the hoops and set the pin in front of Nan, a little over a metre away.

'OK Nanny, time to throw some quoits. See how you go,' I tell her. I hand one of the quoits to her and she grasps it and takes aim. She is focusing intently on the pin, holding the quoit up in front of her. She stays in that position.

'Throw it Nanny,' I urge her. She does a series of short practice back lifts, simulating the first part of the throw, but doesn't quite let go. She stops again with the quoit held up.

'Throw it,' I urge again, but a bit more strongly, and she does, but misses.

We move through the set of six a few times. I bring the pin closer and Nan lands a few successfully around it. I congratulate her each time. She doesn't really show any emotion for her success. Standing there watching her throw, I reflect on the recent conversation with the rehab doctors and start to fume. It keeps coming back to me like trauma.

'David, we've decided that if Nan was to have a major life-threatening event like a heart attack or another bleed, we wouldn't try to revive her, nor would we send her to the Alfred for treatment,' they told me one morning during rounds. It didn't quite make sense to me at the time. I had assumed that decisions to treat were made by the family as had been the case with my aunt some years earlier. Perhaps it was just their recommendation, I decided.

I clarified it a few days later with Olivia, who told me that the laws had changed in Victoria, and the medical team had the call. I was horrified. How could they think that way? How could a medical team be given that right? They didn't know Nan. Their exposure to her was limited to a weekly review or at times when there was a problem. I felt like the deck was stacked against her. It was deeply hurtful. They didn't value my darling's life. She had come so far; she was trying so hard and she was so loved.

'Well, if you people won't revive her, make sure you are out of my way, because I will be trying to,' I said firmly back to Olivia. Her only response was a look of grave concern.

Nan's father Bob's death to a heart attack fifteen years before started to weigh heavily on me. I wondered whether she could have a heart condition as well. There had been no indication though. Hopefully she had Joan's heart.

I talked about hereditary medical conditions with Nan's uncle Ken and his wife Glenda when they visited Nan at Caulfield. I hadn't seen them since Bob's funeral, but I recognised Ken through his resemblance to his brother.

Nan was having a particularly sleepy day and didn't wake while they were there. As we watched her sleep, I told them what had happened. Then Ken filled out some history about his and Bob's mother (Nan's grandmother) Rena.

Rena suffered a series of strokes from around the same age as Nan is now. She wound up in a wheelchair and passed away in her sixties. Her husband Percy died suddenly days later. Nan viewed it romantically; Percy had died of a broken heart. He gave Nan a book in the days between his wife's and his own passing, and something Nan detected in his demeanour made her think he had decided his time was up too.

I had heard that story previously but didn't know that Rena had a sister who also died of a stroke in her mid-fifties. It happened while she was at the hairdressers. Family history and genes weren't on Nanny's side.

Nan seems to have had enough quoit throwing, so I take her back to her room for a rest in bed.

* * *

After Nan read the sign at the entrance to the hospital, we work on her reading in the OT sessions. She can read individual words back. We write them in large characters on an exercise book but need to hold them over to her right for her to locate them. We can't get her reading full sentences or paragraphs given her sight and concentration challenges. I begin dictating a daily diary to her to try and aid her memory and comprehension of where we are and what is happening. A few simple sentences each time:

> *My name is Nanette Hoysted. I am here with my husband David. We are at Caulfield Hospital in Melbourne. The date is 5 December 2014. Today we had a physio session.*

Nan writes this out in a scratchy hand on either the whiteboard or a pad. She always starts at the far-right side of any available space. Even if there is a sentence to be written, she begins at the edge of the surface and almost immediately runs out of space and moves down a line. I direct her over to the left, but once she concludes the first line, she starts the next indented to the right of the previous one.

Given her artistic background, we encourage Nan to draw or colour as much as possible. On one occasion, she draws a cartoon-like, but characterful outline of a horse that she then labels 'Ginger'. Ginger was owned by a friend of Nan's, and I rode him when I went riding with her. Ginger had been deceased for decades, so it is curious that she chose his name and not one of her own horses. In Nan's drawing, Ginger is saddled, ready to go.

With Eloise, she creates a pen drawing of a man's face in profile. It is labelled 'side on, my darling.' I think it is me.

Most fascinating are the drawings where the figures are distorted in a Picasso-like fashion. Men's heads sitting either atop or in front of legs. No torsos. Sometimes she draws faces featuring noses and mouths more prominently. The lips are precisely drawn.

There is also a vase of flowers. The vase looks a little like a face with a nose. Two stems with flowers rise out from the vase. The flowers look like hands with fingers.

* * *

I'm updating Jill and Joan on the latest and they both tell me that they are coming to visit Nan. Joan hasn't seen Nan since she became ill. It will be good for them both I hope, but I'm anxious about it given the things that were said when we were in Sydney.

Joan is legally blind and hasn't driven for years. Frank and Jill are bringing her down from Albury. They arrive late morning and come into Nan's room. We say hello. I detect a cool attitude from Joan, but she's civil at least. I don't care. She and Nanette are very close. I want her to be with Nan.

Nan is still in bed. I direct Joan and her guide dog Peggy around to Nan's right side to get into her field of view and place a chair underneath her so she can sit down.

'Hello Nan,' says Joan and then gives her a kiss on the cheek. Nan isn't awake long and is looking sleepy but sparks when she hears Joan's voice. They are holding hands and I can see the bond between them. The presence of anyone else in the room is lost on them. They are just looking at each other.

Jill and Frank are talking to me about their trip and I'm talking to them about the hospital. That's good because it allows Joan to talk to Nan without being overheard. I'm watching anxiously. I can't quite hear what Joan says, but see Nan give her usual eyebrow raise and nod.

There is a lull in the conversations, and I hear Joan ask if they are looking after her properly. Nan nods. Joan is finding that it's a one-sided discussion that she needs to lead. Nan doesn't initiate. As the pause continues, and everyone is watching, I jump in.

'Yes, they are doing a good job here. They are very attentive. All the nurses are experienced and professional. The therapists are great. I was a bit worried about the ancient building when I saw it, and that this wasn't the ABI unit, but after having been here for a month, I wouldn't want her to move.'

'Don't you think she should be in that new specialist unit they promised?' Joan asks.

'They are only getting that started and I was told the care would be no different there. They also told me they are having a challenge keeping young mobile guys with head injuries out of other patients' rooms. That convinced me she should stay here,' I respond.

'Oh, we don't want that,' Joan replies emphatically.

We continue talking. I tell them what I can about the therapy and the medical help. We get through to lunch and Jill and Frank go to buy some sandwiches. Joan and I keep maintaining the conversation with Nan looking on and listening until they return.

We eat our sandwiches and I ask some nurses if they can put Nan into the wheelchair so we can take her out. We wait in the breezeway while they do that and then when Nan is ready, we take her in the wheelchair out into the fresh air. I'm pushing the chair and Joan is holding onto it too for guidance. Peggy is happily following along on the end of the lead, her tail wagging.

We make our way to the rotunda. It's early December by this and it's a beautiful sunny afternoon. Melbourne is mostly crap in the mornings, but afternoons are sometimes sunny. Mostly they are crap too. It's like living in the U.K.

We are sitting in the rotunda as a family again. Nan, Joan, Jill, Frank, Peggy the guide dog and me. By this stage, we are all more relaxed and comfortable. It has gone better than I expected. I was initially reluctant to say anything for fear of criticism, but that didn't happen so I am more comfortable and talk a lot about what has been going on.

Everyone is engaging with Nan, asking her things and telling her things. She's responding as best she can. Her voice is soft and sometimes the words are too blurry, so we ask her to repeat them, which she does.

Peggy is a little unsettled. More a pet than a guide dog, unlike her predecessor Isla, but she is a beautiful companion and we take every opportunity to move her close to Nan. Nan reaches out and pats Peggy and rubs her neck and feels her body. She is clearly still a dog lover. Peggy is an attention lover and happily wags her tail, moving in and around us all. She's a golden Labrador like Hester. They used to swim together. I'm hoping it doesn't prompt a question about Hester. It doesn't.

Suddenly, Nan bursts into tears again. I go to comfort her. There didn't seem to be any conversational prompt that would have upset her. I don't think it was anything to do with Peggy nor associated memory of Hester. I tell them that Nan has been quite teary on a couple of occasions. It's normally hard to understand why. The tears overwhelm her, and she can't get control to tell us what she's thinking without more tears. Asking her to explain makes it worse. By the time she settles, it seems forgotten about as though it didn't happen.

Joan takes this in her stride, and I'm impressed. She's older and has had exposure to strokes. Nan's grandmother for one. I tell them the doctors call it lability, meaning a changeable emotional state. It's a common thing after strokes.

We had a pleasant time there but eventually they need to leave to return to Albury. It's a three-and-a-half-hour drive. We take Nan back to the room and I walk them out to their car. In a private moment, Joan tells me I'm doing a very good job. It feels awkward to be complimented for looking after Nan. I tell her I would do anything for her. Of course I would.

Once they've set out for the long ride home, I'm sad to see them go and to be left alone again.

A week or two later, Jill returns with her daughter Lucy. Lucy lives in Melbourne, and with Christmas approaching, she and Jill are having a shopping day. Lucy and Nan had always had a close relationship. Nan was her confidante and buddy. Age difference didn't seem to matter. Nan was fun and youthful. They would stir and tease each other. Only a month before the stroke it was Nan's birthday and I have a photo of the two of them together, smiling for the camera. Lucy, tall and blonde towering over her diminutive and dark-haired aunt.

They encounter Nan at her best. The most animated and interactive she has been since the stroke. She is clearly uplifted by having them there. She is keen to chat. Her speech is hard to understand, but her enthusiasm is not. We don't need great verbal skills to communicate. She's with her sister and her niece!

We walk her around the hospital and take a few stops in quiet places. Her voice is soft. She is non-stop, excitedly talking like nothing has happened. I look at the three of them and think it's like old times except we are at Caulfield Hospital and Nan is in a wheelchair.

We walk and stop at the entrance to the hospital because there are chairs there. I'm showing Jill the sign that Nan had read.

'Oh Nan,' Lucy bursts out loudly and into laughter.

'What?' I ask.

'She said she hates going to the toilet in public.'

We are all laughing at the suggestion. Nan is innocently affirming that she does hate that. I'm wondering what her experience is as she sits there at the public entrance. I can't resist her and give her a cuddle and a kiss, even if she is going to the toilet.

When it's time to leave, Jill looks at me and smiles and shakes her head in disbelief at the afternoon they have had. Lucy and Nan are still teasing and stirring each other. Nan's energy is still up. As they are about to leave, Lucy walks over and whispers one last tease in Nan's ear and then turns to go. Out of nowhere, Nan flips Lucy the bird. It's a fitting send-off. She extends her right arm and hand up as high as I have seen her since before the stroke. She holds her hand with the extended middle finger proudly to make sure Lucy doesn't miss it. Lucy responds with the same gesture and then Nan does it again. There is much laughter, and we christen the gesture 'The Lucy Wave'.

* * *

I am more comfortable operating the wheelchair, but Rosie suggests we practice some more difficult challenges like moving over grass or down a couple of steps. We put Nan in the chair and head out along the breezeway to a parking area nearby.

It's a Monday morning in December and the weather is suddenly much warmer. Humid, the temperature is probably only high twenties. I'm feeling hot and I'm sweating. I notice Nan's cheeks are flushed. She is low on energy today. We don't spend long out before we decide it's too hot and instead go to the quiet gym where we will put Nan on the tilt table for a body stretch.

After only ten or fifteen minutes of tilting, we think she's had enough, so we cut the session short and take her back to her room and to bed.

Back in the room, Nan is looking poorly.

'I think we will get her straight back into bed, David,' Rosie suggests, and is about to get the hoist, when Nan starts shaking violently. Her eyes roll back, and she slumps in the chair. The shaking is powerful. Even I know what's happening, and I've never witnessed a seizure before. It's horrible. I see a brief look of panic on Rosie's face then she marches to the wall and slams the 'Emergency' button. Within seconds, the room is flooding with people. Doctors, nurses, Nan, Rosie, me.

I'm freaking out. I don't know what to do. I'm sure I'm going to lose her. How can she survive this? Her body is convulsing as though it's possessed. Surely, she must be, because she can't move like this under her own steam or volition now.

They get her onto the bed somehow and a team of doctors I have never seen before is preparing to administer clonazepam.

'Be careful. Only one or two drops,' I hear the guy taking the lead tell the one measuring out the drug.

It's put on or under her tongue and they stand back waiting for it to take effect. Within a minute, Nan starts to settle. The shaking stops and she seems asleep or gone. She is still breathing though. Breathing deeply, as that beautiful and powerful tranquilizer wraps its protective, motherly arms around Nan's ailing brain, fending off the uprising.

Her eyes are still rolled back. The doctors remain, standing and observing. After a few minutes, they visibly relax. That should be a cue to me to do the same, but I can't take it. After everything that she's been through and her state of fragility, I can't believe Nan can survive or bounce back from this. After more time, Nan opens her eyes again.

'Nanny, are you OK? Can you hear me?' I plead.

There is no response from her. She is looking through me or

around me, not at me. Her waking is enough for the medical team, and they pack up their trolley and leave the room. It's just Nan and me. I'm waiting, needing some kind of response.

Rosie is busying herself writing a report. She needs to make an account of what has gone on given there has been a code blue. That's what they call this. She asks me some factual question and I answer it distractedly.

'I should have said something. I could see she was flushed. We shouldn't have tilted her,' I begin my Catholic act of contrition to Rosie.

'We weren't to know this would happen, David.'

Eventually, Nan's responsiveness returns. Thumb raises, tongue pokes, nods, and so on. She is wiped out, so we leave her in bed for the rest of the day. The seizure must have been exhausting and the sedative as well.

By the next morning though, she seems like nothing has happened. The doctors decide Nan needs the preferred anti-seizure medication: Keppra. She was on it immediately after the bleed, but it was taken away when there was no evidence of seizures. There is evidence now.

* * *

Nan is in good spirits, seemingly unaffected by the seizure when her family next returns. It's just before Christmas and Joan, Jill and Frank, and Bruce and Joanne come bearing gifts. There are several items of clothing for Nan: nighties, a sun hat and a Woody doll from *Toy Story*. Nan is a big fan of *Toy Story*.

'He's beautiful!' Nan exclaims, quite loudly for her. She is wearing the hat and clutching Woody to her face to hug him. Her excitement and enthusiasm are real.

This is what matters to Nan: being surrounded by her family. That's when she was happiest pre-stroke and now post-stroke too. She is interacting well again. It's good. This is the first time Bruce and Jo have seen her since St George when she was just opening her eyes and unresponsive. The difference is obvious to them.

It's a nice day, but I know that their visit means they won't be here on Christmas Day. We haven't had a Christmas without our extended family or families since we met.

When the day comes, it's Nan and I in the hospital ward. A lot of other patients have been allowed to go home for the day. Melbourne isn't home for us.

'Merry Christmas, Nanny,' I say when I arrive that morning, kissing her on the cheek. I have a few things for her as well: some more clothes, some perfume, some stencils and other drawing aids to use. Gift giving unlike our usual Christmas extravagance. That doesn't seem necessary or appropriate now.

Nan opens her eyes and mouth wide and quietly responds, 'Merry Christmas.' Then she tells me she hasn't got anything for me. What an innocent angel. Not aware of the day or time. Not fully appreciative of her predicament. Living in the moment. Christmas was a big deal for her, so for a few seconds she is feeling remorseful about her oversight. It's funny, sad, and beautiful all at the same time.

She seems to be doing OK, given a couple of days beforehand Veronica advised she had a chest infection. Pneumonia in other words. Veronica must have seen my reaction because she was quick to add that it was very treatable, and they had already started a course of antibiotics.

Twice a day, the nurses put a nebuliser mask onto Nan and administer a drug to help ease her chest congestion. That's exactly how she is when I arrive on Boxing Day morning. Nan is on her right side, mask on and very alert. The nebuliser is hissing away as I bid her good morning. She is quick to respond with a good morning as well, her voice somehow amplified yet muffled by the mask. I sit down and hold her hand.

Within seconds a large vomit projects from Nan into the mask.

It is a shock but having seen Rosie recently go for the 'Emergency' button, this time I do too. I anxiously sit back down in front of Nan and ask if she is OK. In the panic, I don't think to take the vomit-filled mask off her.

'Yes, are you OK?' Nan responds back anxiously. The look of panic on my face had worried her and her first concern was for me, not her.

'Yes sweetheart, I'm fine,' I'm stupidly responding as one of the Russian nurses rushes in, sees the problem, takes the mask off Nan and sits her upright. She is quickly followed by a team of doctors and their trolley and other nurses. They begin going over Nan and establishing what has happened.

A competent young doctor named Riana seems to be in charge and I'm impressed by her thoroughness. They take Nan's vitals, give her something for nausea and order the usual brain and bowel scans and chest X-ray to check on the pneumonia and check on her brain. I'm taking it in and realise there are four doctors in the room. They respond incredibly quickly to an emergency here. Combined with the high quality of everyday medical support, nursing and therapists, it's very reassuring. We are in the right place. The old buildings don't mean anything. It's the quality of care that matters.

The bad news is that Nan has had two new strokes. Apparently, they are small, and they are infarcts, not bleeds. Some doctors I haven't seen before break the news that afternoon. Somehow, they know the newly identified strokes have not just happened. I don't know how they know that, but they know. I'm told the strokes probably happened the day of the seizure. The seizure was a response to the two new strokes, not the other way around.

This is deflating news and I feel very despondent for a few hours. As the afternoon wears on, I realise I haven't detected any change in Nan since the strokes occurred.

We've been in Caulfield two months. The first month was a write-off without amantadine. After its reintroduction, we saw significant steps forward again in her interaction. Now strokes, a seizure and pneumonia. Yet, she is still here. She is strong.

The course of antibiotics is finished, and an X-ray confirms her lungs are clear again. She has beaten the pneumonia.

* * *

It's another Sunday, so we are doing our own rounds of the hospital corridors, out to the rotunda and some time in the empty gym. I want to buy a newspaper, so I push Nan just into the little convenience shop and make my way to the counter. As I'm paying the volunteer, I hear the call from behind me.

'Dave,' her voice is strong and clear. It's as it was, not the soft blurry murmur it's become. She's calling me. Calling me back in time to when she was well. That's where I'm transported to in my own mind. I'm taken back to our house in Albury. Imagining Nan calling out to me from downstairs.

'Yes Nanny?' I ask her. She looks at me like she wants to say something but can't quite think what it was. I pull the chair out of the shop.

'You champion Nanny,' I tell her as I push the wheelchair on through the corridors. Once cruise level is achieved, I keep one hand on the chair and put the other on Nan's shoulder. She reaches back and puts her good hand on mine. She leaves it there as we roll.

Moments like these are precious. Precious time with your great love; interaction and closeness no matter the circumstances. That's when time should stand still. That's what heaven or an afterlife should be like.

THE SHUNT

Driving to Caulfield, I'm thinking about Nan's forthcoming MRI. It will be her first since the radiologist at St George reported she might have a tumour. That was discounted by the neurosurgery registrar there. I am hopeful he was correct, but a lingering doubt remains. I've been trying to put it out of my mind ever since.

I arrive at Rehab B, hit the green button to enter, and as I'm making my way through the door, I hear a patient call out in distress. I only catch a hint of the sound before the noise of the door and the ruminations of my own mind drown it out. Once the door closes behind me, I become aware that it wasn't a short solitary shout. It's a continuous, doleful wail. It's loud and coming from the other end of the ward. I am in the midst of my own distress, grief, and trauma but I can't imagine what it takes to unleash like that in a public place, oblivious to or not caring whether anyone else is listening.

And then it hits me. It's not some random patient. It's Nan. How can she be so loud? Her speaking voice is a murmur, but her wail overwhelms all other sound in the ward.

I race to her bedside. The distress is written all over her face and her tears are streaming wildly.

'Nanny, Nanny, Nanny,' I call to her to try and bring her back from this. I'm hugging her and holding her hands and arms now. No one else has come to her aid. Why have they let her go on like this? It must be upsetting for the other patients as well.

'Whatever is wrong Nanny?' I plead with her, but her only response is more wailing. She can't possibly get the words out and any prompting makes it worse. It's the anguish and despair of my plane trip to Sydney, or her own the night her father lay on the kitchen floor dying of a heart attack while I tried to revive him. It's like an outpouring of all the sadness the world has ever experienced. It's an anguish not restrained by inhibitions.

The only solution I can offer is physical comfort. Hugging, stroking, kissing, wiping the tears from her face. This is her third outburst but definitely the worst. There are more before a young and kindly psychiatric registrar arrives a few days later to see how she can help. Her questions bring more tears from Nan but no real explanation.

'Nan, have you been feeling sad or depressed?' was all it took for her to start. Again, there could be no consoling despite much trying, and after some follow up research for PEG-friendly anti-depressants, the registrar prescribes sertraline.

It's a week or so before the drug is started and then several weeks from there before it will take full effect. There are more outbursts and I'm worried about the possibility of another the day of our ambulance ride to The Alfred Hospital for Nan's MRI.

Two patients are loaded. Nan and a bald man in his fifties, who is unaccompanied and lies on his stretcher staring into space. He seems unaware of his surrounds. No one tries to communicate with him, and he is motionless.

We are taken to a transit lounge. To call it a lounge is flattering. It's not at all comfortable. Nan and other patients lay on hospital beds. I'm on an uncomfortable chair at her side, holding her hand through the sidebar. We wait for some hours before a porter arrives to take Nan for the MRI. He wheels her at almost reckless speed the entire length of the hospital. I struggle to keep up.

When we arrive at the radiology department, we wait some more before the MRI is conducted, then wait for another porter to take us back to the transit lounge.

By that stage, it is five hours since we set out from Caulfield. Jill arrives to accompany Nan back so that I can attend a meeting with NSW Trustees and Guardians where they award me a financial management order for Nan (because we didn't have Powers of Attorney in place). They tell me I will need to report our expenditure each year, and that significant decisions like where Nan lives, or disposal of property or other assets in Nan's name require their approval. Government overcompensating for the worst of society by placing imposts on all of society, even in harrowing times.

There were no outbursts from Nan that day and there is no tumour. The cocky young neurosurgery registrar was right. That's a day of good news. There is more news too. The neurosurgeons at The Alfred want to insert a shunt into Nan's brain to alleviate hydrocephalus.

A few weeks later, we repeat the trip to The Alfred to attend a neurosurgery clinic. We meet Michael, another neurosurgery registrar. He's tall, bearded, and balding with glasses. He hasn't met Nan in person, has only seen her scans and is keen to examine her. He asks for some background about Nan and what has happened, so I give my usual speech about her intelligence and artistic talent, what happened with the stroke and what has gone on since. Nan lies there distractedly looking to her right as we talk.

Michael turns his focus back to Nan and asks her to do some cognitive tests, including following a small torchlight with her gaze. She loses sight of it as he moves left of the mid-point of her face. He then checks her limbs for movement.

'Her left side is not working at all,' I interject, but he continues asking Nan to try and move each of her limbs to see for himself. When he's done, it's time to explain his thinking and he addresses both of us as he speaks.

'The MRI showed that Nan has hydrocephalus. Do you know what that is?'

'Water on the brain I think it's called, but I don't know what it is,' I respond.

'It's a build-up of cerebrospinal fluid in the ventricles of her brain. The ventricles are the cavities in the centre of the brain. The damage caused by Nan's bleed means not enough fluid is getting away and the ventricles have become enlarged which is placing pressure on her brain.'

'How serious is it and what can you do about it?' I ask, feeling uneasy.

'It's definitely serious if left untreated. She will deteriorate further unless we do something. In terms of treatment, the normal solution is to insert a brain shunt which will drain away the excess fluid into her abdomen,' Michael explains.

I ask what a brain shunt is, and he draws a picture that looks like a gun with tubing on the end. They insert the barrel of the gun into the ventricle. It acts as a valve which only drains fluid away when pressure goes above a certain level. It drains the fluid down into the abdomen where it is reabsorbed. There is much I want to ask about this. Won't it cause brain damage when they put it in? Will it drain away too much fluid? What are the risks?

He explains that they can push the shunt gently into the brain and find a path through with the sections of the brain parting around it. They don't need to break through brain tissue to do it. I'm amazed by that. The valve will ensure that it doesn't over-drain. The risks are the usual of any surgery: further stroking, infection, death, and so on. The other is that the shunt can become blocked, and they must replace it.

'David, this procedure has the potential to bring her forward,' Michael adds. 'Patients with hydrocephalus typically suffer cognitive decline. The shunt won't help with her walking or limb mobility, but there is a chance she can come forward cognitively.'

That's a big upside and not to be ignored, but the prospect of any surgery for Nan is scary. I tell Michael of the recent strokes, seizure and pneumonia. I'm feeling punch-drunk from new and serious issues after the initial onslaught. Like Cassius Clay has had his way with me.

After more discussion that she will deteriorate without this treatment, I sign the consent form after Michael assures me that we can still pull out at any time.

I'm not comfortable with the idea of Nan having more surgery and I decide to get a few opinions on this. I start with Julia, the rehab consultant back at Caulfield. I tell her about the meeting with the neurosurgeons and their recommendation to install the shunt.

'What do you think Julia? Will it bring her forward? Is it worth the risk?'

'That's very difficult to say, David. No one can be sure. It's not a guarantee.'

When I talk to Jill about it, I try and remain positive that the surgery might help Nan, but I also tell her of my concerns. Jill knows of schoolchildren who had shunts installed and recovered well.

'I don't know, Jill. She's just had a seizure and new strokes. I think it's a big risk and while this mightn't be a big deal for people in otherwise good health, any surgery is a big deal for Nan, particularly any brain surgery. I also think there are positive signs in her recovery. Other than those events, she seems to be coming forward, even if it is slow.'

Jill doesn't push a view one way or the other. She lets me use her as a sounding board, talking out both points of view. She knows I will likely have an opinion expressed by Joan and that in the end I will need to come to my own conclusion.

When I talk to Joan, she is clear on her view and less accepting of Nan's progress.

'Of course she should have the surgery, David. She has no life the way she is now,' she says. I find this hard to hear. I am grateful for still having Nan and any improvement she has made.

But I need the opinion of the one who matters the most in this: Nan. Before her stroke, she was highly intelligent and highly creative, but she had simple needs. She was generous and kind. Stable, not demanding of attention, nor difficult. She certainly had strong views and could argue them very well, but she was no seeker of the limelight. She lived a simple life: her husband, her mother and family, her pets, her art, her house. She loved reading, cooking and decorating. My once boss and still friend Jonathan, described her as 'self-contained'. Apt for Nan.

Now, she is a beautiful being with the innocence of a very young child. She doesn't ask for anything, doesn't initiate. All decisions each day are made for her: when to get up, what therapy she will have, what treatments, whether we will go outside, what clothes the nurses will put on her, whether she will do some writing, some colouring or drawing. The only obstacle she puts up to suggestion is fatigue. She willingly accepts if she can. She is compliant and does her best. Paradoxically, she is more self-contained and completely dependent on others at the same time.

There are days when she pops her head out of her shell, tortoise-like and says: 'How long have I been an invalid?' Or at another time of self-reflection when she suddenly proffered, 'With all the drugs I'm on I should probably be dead.' I didn't see that coming and pushed it away, telling her they were just working things out for her, helping her get well. But these occasions are goldilocks moments when everything is just right with Nan.

I don't want to play God. Agreeing to brain surgery is a big decision to make for another person. When Nan was unconscious at St George, the decisions were either necessary to save her life or clearly on the path out of intensive care treatments towards recovery. Now that she has achieved a degree of stability and some progress, I fear that this is taking a big risk with her again.

I will have to make the decision and it is most likely just to follow the neurosurgery team's recommendation, but I want to elicit some consent or indication from Nan. I'm concerned that any discussion of the surgery might provoke another reaction of extreme distress.

Nan is in the wheelchair and I'm pushing her around the ample grounds and gardens of Caulfield. It's a sunny but comfortable day in March, and it's late in the afternoon.

'Nanny, we have to make a decision on whether you have this shunt installed in your brain,' I announce while watching for her reaction. 'I'm not sure what to do. I'm not sure what's right. The neurosurgeons think we should do it.'

'I have complete confidence in whatever you decide,' she responds.

Given where she came from, that shows progress. I can only interpret it as Nan comprehending the situation, and her response the closest thing to a consent I am likely to receive.

* * *

In parallel to contemplating the surgery, Rosie and I want to take Nan to our apartment for a trip. We'd thought about it for a while, and I had even taken measurements of door widths at home to check wheelchair accessibility, but when Nan suffered the seizure, the plan was put on hold. Rosie sought and was given medical approval for Nan to travel. We are required to carry clonazepam with us in case Nan should have another seizure. Perish the thought.

The trip will be a chance for Nan to be in more familiar surroundings and out of the hospital. Her things, her place. Not really her home, but her Melbourne home. Eloise decides she will come with us, and I let Jill know and she and Frank plan a trip to Melbourne to coincide with the visit. The team schedule a break from therapy for Nan, so the day won't be too much for her.

Rosie booked a wheelchair taxi and we set out after lunch. She's lifted into the van and secured, and we head off on the eight-kilometre trip. Nan, Rosie, Eloise, and me.

When we arrive at our apartment, Jill and Frank are there to greet her and we wheel her in. Once inside, we move into the lounge. Nan sits there wide-eyed, taking it in. It is clear things are registering with her. She looks quite stunned to be back in surroundings so familiar to her. We position the wheelchair to show her some of our artworks.

'Who did this one, Nanny?' I ask her.

'Me,' she says softly.

'Where are we lovey?'

'Home.'

From there we move Nan into the kitchen and point to the many small ornaments she has placed on the top shelf. She again looks overawed, but there are no tears. I can't be sure exactly what her experience is, but she knows where she is. It looks like surprise, bordering on shock. I think we have uncovered a forgotten memory of Nan's.

We do a pass into and out of the bedroom which requires some tricky manoeuvring of the wheelchair and then it is time to return to the hospital. Rosie had pre-booked the wheelchair taxi. While on the front footpath waiting, Liz, our neighbour from upstairs, arrives home and walks right up close to Nan to talk with her. I can't hear what they are saying, but I'm touched to watch it. Liz and her husband Rick and the other neighbours here have known how difficult things have been.

We load Nan into the taxi, and I say goodbye to Jill.

'That was so great to see her here, David,' she says looking happy.

'Didn't think I'd see it, Jill. A special thing to do. We will do it again.'

When we get Nan back to the hospital and into bed again, I thank Rosie and Eloise profusely. It was a beautiful experience. I'm certain it was profound for Nan and very touching for me as well.

* * *

I accepted the recommendation of the neurosurgeons to insert the shunt. They are the experts. I guess to do otherwise would have been playing God, but they are deciding based on a scan and limited examination of Nan. They haven't lived the last six months. They don't love her like I do. She is a patient, one of many. There is some hope of improvement for Nan, and if the surgery isn't performed, we are advised she will deteriorate. That's what makes the decision.

On the day we are scheduled for the transfer to The Alfred, I arrive at Caulfield at 7am. The nurses have Nan cleaned, medicated and ready to go. Just before the patient transfer team arrives to collect us, Nan has another emotional outburst. I don't know what has set her off, but she is loud, and I can't settle her. The crying continues as she is rolled through the ward on a trolley. Everyone is looking. I can only walk by her side, stroking her face and arms and trying to calm her. Once we are out in the cool, fresh morning air, she settles again. The change in atmosphere must have distracted her.

When Nan is settled in the neurosurgery ward at The Alfred, I ask for some time with Michael. I tell him I'm still very concerned about the surgery. We spend a lengthy period discussing it further. He shows me the scans they took of Nan and enlarges the images. He shows me the edge of the ventricles and points to a series of highlighted dots.

'David, you can still pull out if you want, but those dots are the cerebrospinal fluid already leaking into Nan's brain. This is a problem now.'

There really is no choice, so I tell him to go ahead. The surgery is set for two days after that, and when the day comes, I'm there earlier than usual to escort Nan to the theatre. The doctors have stopped some of her medications, like aspirin which had been introduced after the recent infarct strokes to keep her blood thin. They also stopped amantadine again.

I kiss Nan goodbye at the entrance to the surgical theatre, look longingly as they wheel my darling off, then walk out of the hospital to sit in Fawkner Park while I wait. It should only be an hour or two.

It's April in Melbourne and quite chilly in the park. The decision has been made and there is no turning back. I start to feel hopeful. I want her to 'come forward' somehow from this surgery. Perhaps she will be less sleepy, or more interactive. Maybe her short-term memory will be repaired. Able to make her own decisions. Joke more, anger more, put me in my place, initiate things, watch TV, set goals, and create art. The physical impairments matter less than these possibilities. I start imagining that Nan begins making such an improvement that with help, she can live with me again.

But I'm getting ahead of myself. I don't know if any of that is possible, and there is still the fear of how she will get through the surgery.

A little earlier than the expected time, I return to the neurosurgery ward in case they finished early. There is no sign of Nan of course and nothing to do in a hospital ward without her there. I find an empty waiting room and sit in there, staring at the walls. Someone has left a newspaper from the day before, but it takes me about a minute to flick through it and half-read one article.

I know not to worry when the expected time has been and gone. I know the patient doesn't necessarily go straight to surgery from the moment they enter the theatre rooms. But she's an hour overdue and I am worrying. I find a nurse and ask if she has any update. She checks the screen and finds that Nan is still in surgery. I ask if it says how long she has been in there but it's difficult to know.

I text and call family and friends to let them know she's not back yet as a way of killing time but want to keep the phone line generally open. After double the expected time my phone rings and it's Michael.

'David, the surgery is done, and it has gone well, but we had some trouble waking her up afterwards.'

'So, is she awake Michael?' I ask.

'Yes, she's in recovery and they will bring her back to the ward after some observation.'

'Thanks a lot Michael, I'm very relieved.'

I think Michael is too. I could sense that struggling to wake her had troubled him. Any form of sedation seems to knock Nan for six. After a nurse gave her a double-dose of Endone to settle her one day, I couldn't wake her. I asked Julia to come. She applied some pain pressure to Nan's chest and to my relief, she stirred and woke.

When Nan is finally returned to the neurosurgery ward, I'm there to see her. She's asleep. Her hair has been shaved behind her left ear and there is a long line of staples to seal the cut closed. There is a swelling nearby like a slightly smaller squash ball.

When she does wake, she is wilder than I have seen her. There is a suspicious and angry look on her face and at one point she tells me to 'get away' when I try to interact with her. I was probing for an improvement. Hopefully this isn't the new Nan, or the real post-stroke Nan previously suppressed by hydrocephalus.

Carl is one of the nurses in charge of the neurosurgery ward. He is an enormous, bald British man with a pleasant, kind manner. He tells me it is probably a reaction to some of the drugs they would have used during the surgery.

Her 'Nangry' demeanour was temporary, and she returned to her sweet and gentle self by the next morning. She isn't talking though, and her interaction is limited. She needs a few days to recover from the surgery according to the team, but there is no improvement after those few days have passed.

Nor is there any improvement after a week either. I am flagging concerns to the team there: nurses, junior doctors, and registrars. I haven't met the consultant before or since the surgery. No one seems to know what to think. They try a new scan to ensure nothing new has gone wrong. They can't see anything on that.

Nan is moved from the two-person post-surgical room to her own room in the ward and I feel we are out of sight and out of mind. It's rare that I even see, let alone get any time with Michael. He isn't on the ward much.

It's nearly two weeks since the surgery and no improvement. They want to send Nan back to Caulfield to 'continue her recovery'. I'm unhappy about that but eventually become resigned to it and decide she might be better there in the hands of the full team and receiving some therapy again.

When we return to Caulfield, Rosie has left for maternity leave. One of the last things she organised was a new wheelchair for Nan which I purchased. It is a red and black tilt-in-space chair. It's narrower, sized for her and lighter for me to push. It has a special headrest with an adjustable sidearm on her right to support her head and discourage her from looking to the side so much.

Rosie is replaced by Val who had taken Nan for some sessions before this and established an instant connection with her. Val is so engaging for both Nan and me and Nan responds very well to Val's strong and animated voice. Val is always trying something. She's terrific.

Riana assumed the registrar role in the ward in the New Year. On our return, I tell her what went on at The Alfred. Soon after, she asks to meet with me to discuss the latest scan. We sit outside in the sunshine while we talk.

'David, Nan's latest scan shows a new stroke,' Riana carefully informs me after some initial small talk.

'What? There hasn't been any new scan since we were there.'

'It seems to be where the shunt was inserted. It's on the radiologist's report.' Riana hands me the text and points to the relevant wording. It's another blow from Cassius but this one is saddening. Clearly, we, or I have made the wrong decision in going ahead with the surgery. We should have left things alone. Should have done no harm.

'They must have known about this. They didn't tell me about it. Nobody raised this,' I said to Riana.

I wonder if this is the cause of Nan's poorer interaction and lack of speech. When I ask Riana about it, she can't be sure. Eventually, my sadness is turning into anger and fury. Not at Riana, but she is there as the unfortunate conduit.

'Riana, I want a meeting with the head of neurosurgery. Let him know I want an explanation of why no one told me about this in the two weeks we were there in the ward. We have been sent back here without any explanation.'

Within a week I have an appointment at a neurosurgery clinic. It's with Charles, the consultant who led the operation and an American registrar who I had met in the ward. After very brief formalities are exchanged, Charles wisely cuts straight to the chase.

'We know you want to discuss the radiologist's report on Nanette's scan.'

'I definitely do. I've been told that she's suffered an additional stroke. No one here said anything about that.'

'We don't believe that the mark on the scan is a stroke.'

'You don't? What is it then?'

'Sometimes when we install a shunt, there is bruising of the brain like this at the point where it is inserted.'

'Bruising? The brain can be bruised? Why hasn't the radiologist reported it this way?'

'Yes, it does bruise. As for the radiologist's report, depending on who the radiologist is, they may not have seen this kind of thing before.'

My anger is dissipating quickly, but I still don't know what the bruising means.

'It must have looked like we were keeping information from you?' Charles asks. He's smart to call out the issues so quickly and address them. You would expect a neurosurgeon to be smart, but it doesn't mean they are adept at communication. Charles is proving to be.

'That's exactly how it looked,' I say. 'No one said anything about a stroke or bruising or anything showing on a scan. Will the bruising heal up? Is it brain damage? Nanette hasn't bounced back to where she was before the surgery.'

'The bruising will heal just like any bruising does. It's not brain damage. As for why she hasn't bounced back yet, that's harder to say. Any surgery for someone in Nanette's condition is a significant ordeal. It's been three weeks since the surgery. Let's see how she is after a couple of months.'

In that short conversation, Charles has taken away my anger, and left me still with some hope she will improve again.

'There was the possibility that this surgery would bring her forward. Do you think that's still possible? Her short-term memory isn't working. If she could regain that, it would be a huge help.'

'It's hard to know. Only time will tell.' Charles then hesitates a little before proceeding. 'As for memory, Nanette's brain has shrunk because of the bleed she suffered. Memory and other cognitive functions are more difficult because of this.'

My internal organs drop with this news. Her brain has shrunk? Isn't that what happens with dementia patients? I don't ask him these questions. I can't bring myself to. I don't want to know the answer. I think that's why he hesitated and that's what he's telling me. I leave it alone.

There isn't much more we can cover, but I want to ask about amantadine.

'Should we restart amantadine? She's still off that and has been since before the surgery.'

'Give it a few more weeks. It would be better to give her the chance to make any improvement that she can naturally.'

A couple more weeks elapse and there is still no improvement. Nan is still not speaking. We have a visit from Richard the neurologist. He seems to have more time to talk this day.

'Richard, how do we know that this shunt is even working? She isn't doing as well as before it was inserted.'

Richard reaches forward to Nan's head and pushes down on the small squash ball underneath her skin. Once he lets it go, I see it instantly inflate again.

'Well, that's what's supposed to happen. The shunt is working,' he reports back.

'They thought there was some chance that she would come forward through this. She isn't even where she was before the surgery.'

'Any gains she was going to make should be evident by now,' Richard says gently but clearly, watching me as he speaks to make sure I understand him. He's the one to listen to, I decide. I think he's head and shoulders above anyone else in understanding Nan's condition. He is not pussy-footing around with what needs to be said. His level of experience and understanding enables him to be more certain.

Six weeks go by since the surgery and Nan is stable. She understands when we speak to her, and can participate in some therapy, but she is not speaking. It's been long enough so I ask the doctors to put her back on amantadine again. After a few days back on the drug, her interaction improves and her limited speech returns. It seems amantadine was the missing ingredient again.

Unfortunately, there is no cognitive improvement from installing the shunt. It's extremely disappointing. Nan put through more surgery. All that worry. All that hope. No obvious benefit. The only comfort to be taken is that it has perhaps alleviated Nan's hydrocephalus and reduced the pressure on her brain. I must accept that most of the time people are operated on, it is to fix something or take a problem away. This is another of those. But there had been hope of something more.

* * *

It's June 2015, six months since Nan had pneumonia and the two new strokes. Before then, the nurses were feeding her yoghurt which has the right thickness for a patient with swallowing difficulties. All her nutritional needs are being met by the PEG. The pneumonia was assumed to be from aspiration: breathing food or liquid into the lungs. The PEG was suspected to be the culprit, but as a precaution, the limited feeding by mouth was also stopped.

Leonie, one of the speech pathologists, keeps advocating that eating would improve Nan's quality of life. She suggests Nan can undergo a test called a video fluoroscope, which is a live or moving X-ray to enable an assessment of her swallowing capability. A doctor and other staff will be on hand if there are problems.

I agree to try it, so we make another trip to The Alfred, this time to one of the radiology departments where we are taken into a room full of X-ray equipment.

I am sent into the control room where I can view the X-ray on a screen along with the doctor and technician. It is fascinating to witness the X-ray vision of Nan's head and throat as she is fed a barium-infused liquid. It is clear she is swallowing well, even to me; the highlighted barium is passing quickly down her oesophagus into her stomach.

Leonie and the doctors declare it is safe for Nan to eat again and she is started on some yoghurt and pureed food. Leonie pushes me to feed her with a teaspoon portion each mouthful, to watch for Nan's swallow and then to check her mouth is emptied before the next spoonful.

Initially it is a very slow process; around thirty minutes to get through a tub of yoghurt. Often Nan doesn't want the whole tub. She hasn't been eating much for nearly a year, and she tires halfway through. There is no opportunity yet to add the pureed food. She likes the yoghurt. It is tasty and goes down well.

* * *

Nan has been at Caulfield for almost eight months, and the hospital says it's time for her to leave. There is nothing more they can do. I've resisted two previous exit dates, but I don't think I can conscionably build a defence this time. I am out of reasons and I know the hospital has done everything they could.

Richard arrives one afternoon with a team in tow. A pharmacist who has been on the ward since New Year and who is personable (unlike her death-stare-wielding predecessor), a younger female trainee doctor with red hair, and a couple of others I don't know. No doubt it was a good learning experience to do rounds with Richard.

When Richard asks how Nan is doing, I answer, 'About the same.' I then notice him pause and hesitate for a minute.

'It's a shame,' he says, 'but eventually people here will take hard decisions to make beds available to others.' He says it in his usual calm and factual manner.

'I don't care about anyone else in the world needing a bed, Richard. Where were the beds in this state when Nanette desperately needed one? They were occupied by people with the flu. Who gave one up then? We had to go to Sydney and Nan lost a lot of time,' I say this with more than a little bitterness but without any anger directed at Richard.

I know he is telling me her time is up here. It isn't his job to do that. It is a show of compassion on his part, and I probably seem like I'm shooting the messenger. Most doctors become doctors because they want to help. I am sure that never really goes away and there are many cases they would find personally confronting, wanting to do or offer more, not wanting to turn off the care tap.

We stand there looking at each other, nodding and raising eyebrows like guys do when they don't know what to say next. It isn't a confrontation. It is an exchange of perspectives and in his case a perspective that we both understand but probably neither of us agrees with. He pauses a little longer and then he and the team leave. That was the last time he reviewed Nan at Caulfield, but certainly not the last time she would be under his care.

Soon after that, the message is formally conveyed that Nan will be leaving. She will move to a transition to care program at a nursing home; a thirteen-week period during which the patient and their family determine the permanent home, either in a nursing home, or for those lucky enough, back home.

When Riana stops to talk on a Saturday evening, it's just after I've witnessed a female patient harassing the nurses for Valium. She's wearing a neck brace and her voice is deep and coarse. Her face looks hardened by addiction. She's been begging for Valium all day, complaining of headaches or whatever.

'So, you are off soon?' Riana says.

'Yes, we are Riana. Thanks for your good care.'

'Are you feeling ready to go?'

'No, I'm not, but I guess we have no choice now.' Then, after an uncomfortable pause, I can't help saying what I say next.

'It's such a shame Riana, that a beautiful person like Nanette, who has been selfless and only done good in her life, hasn't done drugs or lived a dangerous lifestyle, has something like this happen to her. It's a disgrace that she can't stay here in the care of a wonderful facility when this is the kind of care she needs. Instead, we get pushed out to make room for ice addicts and young guys who are the victims of their own reckless behaviour. We've paid our taxes. We've paid more than our share but that means nothing. Despite her goodness, she is not valued any more than anyone else. In fact, she is valued less because of her condition. She's not considered worth it. That's social justice for you.'

I apologised then for being so harsh in my assessment, but it's what I felt and what I still feel.

The day before we leave Caulfield, we have a nice visit from Jill and Lucy, and Lucy arrives with her ragdoll cat, Henry. She pulls Henry out of his cage and sits him on Nan's bed. Nan the animal lover is of course fascinated, and pats Henry constantly. Henry the ragdoll is relaxed despite being in a hospital ward. When the visit is over, Jill wishes us luck for the transfer to the nursing home.

I was dreading the day that we must leave, and when it comes, it is sad. Eight months in Caulfield. One by one, beautiful people who have looked after Nan come to say goodbye and good luck. Nurses, therapists, some hospital porters. Several of them hug Nan. They have a bond with her and are sad to see her leave. They know she is precious, and that she is loved. Adored in fact. They can see why. They know her needs are high, and they would keep her if they could.

Nan accepts their wishes with her innocent eyes wide and eyebrows up. I'm fighting back tears the whole time. I haven't been that emotional in public since this all began, but I can't help it. Our gratitude is so great, and the parting is so sad. The transport team arrives and loads Nan onto a stretcher. We head out of Rehab B and out of Caulfield.

AGED CARE

Two years are like any other day in a nursing home. Except the days when things go wrong. We've had a few of those. There have been good moments too. It's April 2017 now.

'Hello, come here, help me,' the old Laotian woman calls out to me as I walk past. She's starting early. Her son hasn't arrived. She's in her wheelchair at the doorway to her room, calling out to passers-by or to no one when there is no one there. She's been like this for the eighteen months she's been here in the nursing home. We arrived a few months before that. I ignore her and keep walking.

'You no good,' I hear her say to me when I pass.

'Boy, come here,' an impatient crone snaps at me from her doorway on the other side of Nan's room.

'I don't work here,' I snap back at her short-temperedly.

'Aaaah,' she snarls and waves me away with her hand. Too late, I'm already gone. She doesn't care what I'm dealing with. She would happily enslave me, along with all the paid care staff if she could.

I enter Nan's room and slam the heavy fire door behind me to shut them both out of earshot, and my mind. I go to Nan's bedside. She is laying there and sleeping peacefully, so I buzz for the Personal Care Assistants to come and get her up.

I look around her room. I decorated it as best I could with her ornaments and her art in an attempt to make it familiar. Nan loved collecting trinkets, decorative items and ornamental birds: a magpie, a kookaburra, a seagull. A cat figurine as well. I added her horse-riding helmet and crop too; riding and horses were so significant to her, and I hoped these might help orient her somehow. Make her feel like Nan.

I brought in three of her artworks. Most notably, the last significant one she did before she became ill. It's a linocut and she spent three weeks carving out the pattern before she was ready to print it onto paper. Three weeks or so after finishing, she had the stroke. I can't get past it now. I showed it to Deb, a psychiatrist we met at Caulfield and who still oversees Nan.

'Don't you think this looks like the surface of a brain, Deb?' I asked her.

'It does. And what are those red splashes?' she quickly observed.

'I don't know, but given the bleed in her brain, I see them as blood. It's completely eerie, but I think it's one of her best works. It's powerful. She never talked about the brain though.'

Returning to the sleeping Nan, it's time to get her up.

'Good morning, Nanny,' I say and kiss her. She wakes quite quickly, opening her beautiful blue eyes and wishing me good morning too. She's on her back as usual, propped up and wedged into the large triangular pillow. The PEG feed for the evening is complete, so I turn it off and detach the tubing from her and throw out the used feeding bag and cabling, clamping the PEG closed when done.

The PCAs arrive with the hoist in its trolley, and they attach it to the ceiling, put the sling under Nan and lift her out of bed on her way to the commode chair. They tear away her pad and place a pan under her to catch her liquid bowel output while she is suspended.

Swinging in mid-air, Nan looks at me, raises her eyebrows and gives me one of her little waves before they plonk her down on the commode. It makes us all smile as the carers roll her over to the toilet.

'David, will you watch her while we attend to others?' one of them asks me.

'Yes, I'll buzz you when we are done.'

This is the morning ritual and it's repeated in the evening when she goes back to bed. Time on the toilet twice a day, and I'm checking to ensure she is having a bowel movement. This is the routine ever since the gastroenterologist found she had an anal fissure. I can't rely on the facility to ensure she is regular, even though they are supposed to.

Nan was crying a lot, without warning and at seemingly odd times. I couldn't get her to say what the problem was. I thought it was the continuation of the emotional issues she had at Caulfield, but Sidhur, an observant PCA, noticed the tears coincided with her bowel movements. We opened her pad one evening and found blood around a firm stool. I reported it to Nan's doctor, Patricia. The gastroenterologist prescribed Movicol twice daily to keep her loose and regular. It made her very loose, but that's better than her not going.

I'm looking at Nanny from her room. She's not concentrating on her poo. She's fiddling with the toilet paper. Patting her hand under it, watching the unrolled part ripple to the floor.

'Do your poo, Nanny,' I call to her. She nods, but within seconds, starts fiddling with the paper again.

After twenty or thirty minutes, I check the contents of the toilet bowl, confirm with Nan that she is finished, then call the PCAs to shower her.

I go downstairs to the café for a Coke and a break while they do that, brushing off the calls of the Laotian woman, the crone, and any other demented folk on my way out. This is supposed to be a high care floor, not a dementia ward, but over time, they have placed more and more demented residents here. The small dementia ward is full, so they jam them in here, not wanting to lose out on finances.

It's literally a madhouse and it's hard to take. They've changed the circumstances around Nan's (and therefore my) residency, but I learned long ago not to trust them nor expect them to do the right thing in any way. Management that is. The nurses and care staff do their best and are kind and good. The management doesn't care.

When Nan is showered and dressed, they put her into her wheelchair, and I return to her room to be with her. She's normally sleepy then, and I let her rest while I download the video recording I made of her overnight to my laptop. I've been doing that for a few months. She is still sleepy in the mornings, and I no longer think it is amantadine keeping her awake. I'm worried she could be having seizures overnight.

There have been more seizures since Caulfield, one soon after arriving when Nan was in her wheelchair. The seizure caused her to slide out of the chair onto the floor. I hit the buzzer, ran to alert the nurse when she didn't come at the speed of Caulfield, then back to Nan. When the nurse arrived, she gave her clonazepam and then the PCAs put her into her bed where she recovered and began responding again. Like the occasion at Caulfield, it was frightening to witness. I felt an exhaustion afterwards as though I'd had the seizure myself, or that someone had pointed a gun at me. Effectively that's what was happening. When Nan is under threat, I feel it too.

There was another seizure one Friday afternoon when Patricia and Angela, the registered nurse, were in the room with us. We were talking and I noticed Nan's eyes start to roll back.

'She's having a seizure,' I interrupted.

Nan began shaking and Angela ran to get some oxygen. I reached for the clonazepam which I kept locked in Nan's bedside table. Under Patricia's watchful eye, I dispensed a couple of drops into a plastic spoon and placed it on Nan's tongue.

The seizure was long, and we could only wait. Angela noticed Nan had stopped breathing, so she put the oxygen mask on her and turned on the tank.

When Nan came round and became responsive, Patricia said she should go into hospital. She had a couple of nights in there and the usual scans and tests. A neurologist told me there had been no change in her brain, and that he would lift the Keppra level further.

'Do you know why she seizes?' he asked me.

'I guess because of the haemorrhage she had.'

'Yes. The damage from the haemorrhage and other strokes and even the shunt all cause interruptions to the electrical flow in her brain.'

'Is it possible to get her to the point where she won't?'

'Yes, it's a matter of getting the medication right.'

My night video surveillance did find another seizure and when I showed it to Patricia, she lifted Nan's Keppra further again. I still record to keep an eye on her. I review the videos on high speed the next morning. I notice that Nan seemed to be stirring every few minutes throughout the night. She would keep waking short of breath, gasping for air at times.

'Does this look like sleep apnoea Pat?' I asked.

'It does. I'll give Nan a referral to a respiratory doctor I know for his view. He will likely organise a sleep study to be done.'

I didn't know much about apnoea, but of course better sleeping would improve her overall health and comfort. Now though, she is asleep again, so I let her recover from the toileting, showering, dressing and interrupted sleep while I review last night's video.

The video shows the usual sleep/wake pattern happening for Nan. Around 1am, two African women come into the room to check and change her pad. I can see Nan is awake and they are smiling and having quite a conversation with her. I decide to watch the video at normal speed to listen to the audio. They are looking at the bedside table photo of the two of us from thirty years before. The day after our wedding.

'David was punching above his weight to marry you, Nan,' one of them muses.

'Wasn't she beautiful?' the other responds.

'She still is,' I say out loud with a smile watching the video.

Nan is nodding to them in cooperative appreciation, and I laugh at the compliment to her and ridicule of me. There is nothing else noteworthy on the video, so I delete it from my laptop.

If the weather is good, I take Nan out for some sunshine before lunch. We either sit in the beautiful grounds of the nursing home or make our way to Fawkner Park. Most days I take her to the hall where there is a piano and I practise a bit while she sits and listens.

'How was that Nanny?' I sometimes ask her after playing a jazz standard.

'Very nice,' she answers in her near whisper.

I didn't play for fifteen months after Nan had the first stroke. I couldn't enjoy it, and I had no interest. My concentration was elsewhere, and I felt short of time. Now things were more stable and the nursing manager, on hearing that I played, encouraged me to use their piano.

It's a Kawai of similar size to my own but a little older and it's in a large hall with a peaked roof that the facility uses for functions and funerals of residents. The piano sounds good in there. Once I started playing again, I kept going and practised everyday both there and at home.

After we'd been there a year, I organised a gig one Sunday afternoon in the hall. I played with friends I met at a music course, and we did a ninety-minute set in front of fifty or sixty residents and family members.

Nan was there just over my right shoulder like my good angel while I played. I kept taking little glances at her to check she was OK and whether she was tuned in. I could see her eyes wide and little mouth open. She looked like the most well-behaved child being very grown up at an adult event. I so hoped she wouldn't have a seizure during the show.

From the first song, one old girl from the dementia ward was up and dancing to the music. She was pushing ninety, if not already there, and was really busting some moves. It was a great afternoon and we had positive feedback and encouragement to do it again. Nan said she liked it too when I asked, but she wouldn't remember it now.

It's lunch time and one of the PCAs delivers the two trays of food, one for Nan and one for me. It's a Tuesday, so I know it will be a roast. The last few were pork, lamb and beef, so it will be chicken again today. I spoon-feed Nan lunch and dinner every day. Her meal is pureed because her swallowing was compromised by the stroke.

Soon after the video fluoroscopy, I was feeding Nan yoghurt and some Sustagen. We tried drinks that were thickened with a solution to make them easier to swallow. If it wasn't thick enough, it went down the wrong way and made Nan cough and splutter. The thickening solution added an unpleasant taste and texture to water and Nan didn't like it much, so water doses were provided either by myself or the nurses via the PEG. Nan did enjoy some cups of thickened tea though. She had always loved her tea and it was good to see her doing that again.

A speech pathologist visiting at the time suggested I try baby foods in squeezable tubes. I found a range of elaborately flavoured varieties at the local supermarket. I tried them myself and they were tasty, particularly roast lamb with mint.

'Yum, this is delicious,' Nan exclaimed when she tasted it herself. Leonie at Caulfield was right. Enjoying food does add to quality of life.

The chef of the nursing home said they could provide pureed food for Nan, so we moved from baby food to pureed meats and vegetables that I served her in teaspoon-sized chunks. As she ate more, her endurance for eating improved, and we were able to reduce but not eliminate the dependence on the PEG. She now consumes whole meals for lunch and dinner and clearly enjoys them.

After lunch, I buzz the carers to put Nan back to bed for a couple of hours' rest. Two lovely Nepalese girls arrive. There are three of them working regularly on our floor now. They are the pick of the PCA crop. They are very kind and very reliable and have learned Nan's routine and needs. The situation has improved on what it was.

Early on, I counted nineteen different carers attending to Nan within a week, and that didn't include night shift because I wasn't there. There was no continuity, and I was constantly explaining her needs to the carers, some of them not paying much attention. I would return to the room to find her badly positioned in bed or in the chair and I'd have to explain Nan's routine virtually every day.

Between that and serious medication mishaps, I got fed up and wrote a letter to the chairman of the board of the nursing home. I'd had enough dealings at that stage with the management to know they would ignore me. I received a letter back in the chairman's name (that I am sure was written by senior management) which denied all my concerns and insisted that a good job was being done. They hadn't bothered to address anything I raised. 'Move along people, nothing to see here' I imagine Barbrady on South Park saying.

The medication mishaps occurred when Angela was off the ward, assigned to other duties. Several casual and agency nurses were floated in to cover for her.

One evening, I found Nan very agitated and unsettled. She looked flushed, was fidgeting excessively and talking constantly, but her speech was hard to follow. I knew something was wrong and decided to take her blood pressure. I had purchased my own machine soon after she was admitted to the nursing home.

Nan's blood pressure was back at normal levels after good management by Caulfield and St George. The reading I found that evening was far from normal though. Her heart was racing at 130 beats per minute and her blood pressure was high. No wonder she seemed unsettled and agitated.

I reported it to the evening nurse and following my gut, asked to look at her medication chart. I was shocked by what I found. Metoprolol, one of her critical BP medications (and one she was on an unusually high dose of) had been stopped. In addition to that, her Keppra (to manage seizures) had been missed on several days.

I contacted Patricia who corrected the charts and then I had a meeting with the site manager and nursing manager about the mistakes made. They were very apologetic. They were nice people and doing the best they could, but they had limited resources. They were trying to give Angela some rotation in her duties, but in the end, as I pointed out to them, Nan's life had been endangered.

They decided to put all of Nan's meds and med charts under lock and key in her room. They gave me a key so I could ensure the meds were given and recorded properly. I shouldn't have to do that, but it meant I knew what was going on.

So, there I am. Regularly checking Nan's blood pressure, video recording her at night, reviewing her medication charts to ensure the correct meds are given, and checking her bowel output in the toilet twice per day. Feeding her, speaking for her, and watching out for problems. When casual nurses are on duty, I often help them navigate the workings of the PEG and explain the medication and how it is to be given. Sometimes it's easier if I give Nan the medication for them while they just tick it off.

It's a seven-day-a-week job. There are no days off unless I'm sick and that hasn't happened yet, but it will, and I worry about Nan's care if I'm not there. If regular nurses like Angela and Maureen are working, then it will be OK. But some days they are not there, and other days they are busy dealing with a lot of other residents and their problems. They might have multiple residents become ill and need hospital admission. People die in these places all the time. The nurses' phone is always ringing; family members wanting to check on their 'loved one', or give some special direction. Or perhaps it is a visitor wanting to get into the premises and the nurse needs to open the security gate that management installed to make sure no one is using their precious car parks.

To the facility, I am a carer. A gap-filler to cover the shortcomings in the care they deliver to a person with high needs. Actually, I'm not sure they care too much about whether the gap is filled or not.

I view it as being Nan's other half. I am her voice, her advocate. I am the surrogate for that part of Nan's brain knocked out by the stroke. We married for better or for worse, in sickness and in health. This is the worse and sickness bit.

Does it sound like I'm doing too much? Or perhaps I'm just a control freak in action? Bullshit. Tell me it isn't necessary given our experience to date. Who will do these things if I don't? Our time in the facility has shown that I can't rely on them to look after her properly. Yes, her needs are high, but so are the fees and so, I am sure, are the salaries of senior management.

Nan's afternoon rest is between 1pm and 3pm. It's a chance for me to take a break and I sometimes go home for a nap or to play piano if I have the energy. If I'm concerned about Nan, then I will stay in her room with her while she rests.

I'm back to prompt the carers to get her up again at three. Some don't need the prompt. The routine is better understood now but early on, if I was late to get back, Nan would often still be in bed. If I wasn't there to look after her, they would forget her and leave her there all day like they do with other residents who don't have anyone to represent them. Or they might stick her in the lounge room with half a dozen demented old girls, all of them on different planets, and subject her to hideous Andre Rieu DVDs played at deafening volume. I'm sure that prancing prat has caused many a resident to give up the ghost. Nan would hate it, and I didn't want her becoming a newly discovered orbit in the solar system of dementia.

By 5pm, it's time to feed Nan her dinner. At six she has her medication and then she has another stint on the toilet before being put to bed again around 7pm. I stay with her until eight to ensure she is settled. If there are problems, I stay longer. I have nothing waiting for me at home other than much-needed rest.

* * *

I try to make a life for us, despite our premature sentence to a nursing home. I say 'we' because it is both of us. I can't put Nan in my car and take her anywhere, but I can take her out in the wheelchair. We have covered many kilometres, and I know every bump on every footpath in the area. Melbourne's penchant for cobblestones is a pain in the arse for anyone commanding a wheelchair.

Sometimes I take her to our apartment. It's a fifteen-minute walk, but a little longer if I'm pushing Nan in the chair. Last time I did it, I wheeled her up to the front gate and then asked, 'Where are we Nanny?'

'Home,' she again said without hesitation. Just like that time with the team from Caulfield.

I pushed her inside and let her take in the surroundings. The place is filled with our regular furnishings and artworks from Albury. I sold our Albury house to pay for the bond after Nan moved into the nursing home. NSW Trustees and Guardians insisted I get their approval on the price paid and two real estate agents' written estimations of value. For Christ's sake. It was Albury I was selling in, not one of the capital cities. It is a buyer's market there.

Nan was looking around the apartment. She was fascinated by our cat who ran underneath her wheelchair and sat on a desk behind her. Nan tried to reach her, and when the cat ran off, she called 'Beryl, Beryl, Beryl' in the strongest voice I had heard her use since the day she called me in the convenience shop.

On our next visit to the neurology clinic, I reported it to Richard. I was hoping for something insightful or inspirational from him.

'What did the cat do?' he responded with a smirk. Reportedly one of the biggest neurology guns in the business, and he's curious about what the fucking cat did!

'Nothing. She's a cat and not a very cooperative one,' I responded with a laugh.

I'd never seen him laugh before and I didn't expect him to take the piss like that. Pretty good. Pretty humanising. I doubt he has a very funny job all up, dealing with people with brain injuries and brain diseases.

Two days a week, Val the physio from Caulfield visits to deliver therapy for Nan. I look forward to it. Val has the voice and manner for cutting through to Nan and getting her attention, and Nan sometimes remembers her name when she arrives. We conduct the sessions in Nan's room with Nan either in her wheelchair, on the bed, or sitting on the edge of the bed. I am Val's physio assistant, supporting Nan while Val attends to her left leg, foot, hand, and arm. A few weeks back we were helping Nan roll to her left side.

'I'm getting a new car,' Nan suddenly announced to us.

'Are you just?' Val responded with enthusiasm and a laugh.

'I didn't know this. What kind of car are you getting?' I asked.

'A Toyota,' Nan insisted. Val and I looked at each other, amused. We started rolling Nan to her left and I was over on that side.

'Reach over to touch David's face,' encouraged Val.

As she rolled, Nan made a fist and started to smirk. She was moving in slow motion as we rolled and pulled her over. She pretended to hit me on the chin with the fist. We were all amused. So, she did it again a few times.

There are some good activities like craft and cooking conducted by the lifestyle team at the nursing home. They are nice people doing nice things for residents. It's a challenge to admit Nan to some classes based on timing. They are often too early in the morning or straight after lunch when she is back in bed.

One day a week, the cooking class is run by Karen. Four women attend including Nan. We all sit around the table. I put Nan next to Pat. Pat has advanced Parkinson's disease and is in a wheelchair as well. Despite her challenges, she is a pleasant sweetheart, and she kindly reaches out her shaking hand to Nan, and they sit holding hands until they have to perform a task. I look at Karen who is melting at the site of Nan and Pat holding hands.

Across from Pat sits her BFF, Zelma. Zelma is ninety, good-hearted, quick with a smile and quick to take the piss. I was told she could be pretty tough. I haven't seen it. Next to Zelma is Mavis who is sweet too but extremely deaf. She laughs beautifully though when she gets it, and she laughs at herself when she doesn't.

We are making cupcakes. Karen calls the shots, and everyone does something. In goes the flour and sugar and whatever else you use to cook cakes. Love, I think it is. Then the pan comes over to Nan for a stir. We give her some milk and she pours that in first. She concentrates hard as she lifts the milk to the pan. She was such a phenomenal cook before illness, there must be something familiar in this for her. She happily takes the wooden spoon and does her best stirring the mixture. Around she goes a few times. She's done her part, but she can't do any of the eating because of her swallowing issues. So just like in better times, she's cooking purely for my benefit. I down plenty of the vanilla cupcakes afterwards and they are really good thanks to Nan and the other ladies' efforts.

Every Tuesday morning, a retired couple, Bob and Barb, bring in their two beautiful Australian Shepherds, Raji and Gemma. They take the dogs to visit residents who are dog lovers. I quickly made sure Nan was added to their list, and then acquired some packets of Schmackos for Nan to reward the dogs with.

Raji can be encouraged onto Nan's lap, well, half of him anyway, and she gladly rubs him all over. Bob and Barb are as regular as clockwork and attend every week barring ill health, or scheduled trips away. Even days when Nan is at her worst; after one of her many urinary tract infections, or barely conscious because of sleeping issues, she will stir to greet and pat Raji and Gemma. Dogs and humans have a special bond.

There are many other kind souls in a place like this. The nurses, the lifestyle team, the PCAs, or Marion the cleaner, a woman of Indian descent who works hard on our floor, five days a week, with little or no acknowledgement. I know she gives our room special attention to clean up after Nan's bowel accidents. Marion sees me there every day. On the rare occasions when Marion is not working, the standard of cleanliness drops quickly. I think about that story of JFK visiting NASA and the janitor who said he was 'helping put a man on the moon'. Marion is helping me look after Nan.

'Good morning, Nan,' she always says with a genuine and loving smile.

Last Christmas I found a gift of chocolates for Nan that Marion had left along with a nice card. I didn't have the heart to tell her that Nan wouldn't be able to eat them because of her swallowing issues. I ate them anyway, so they didn't go to waste.

Carole is a New Zealander, aged close to seventy. She is in the lifestyle team but also doubles as a carer for extra money. She has knee issues and a husband with a dodgy heart. Her life is tough, and money is short, but every Christmas and Easter she buys gifts for a lot of residents. She loves Nan and hugs her and kisses her when she sees her. I love to see that. She sees Nan react with joy. She sees into Nan's soul. She sees what a beautiful person she was and still is.

At a recent Sunday afternoon concert in the common lounge, some old guy with a guitar and harmonica is playing even older songs. He isn't Neil Young. While I am out for a break, Carole kidnaps Nan and brings her to the 'gig'. I walk in to see the last half-hour and sit behind Nan. Carole is leading the sing-along and moving from resident to resident to encourage them and add to their experience.

She dances over to Nan, grabs her two hands and swings them with the music, singing to her and placing her face close to Nan's. She kisses her on the cheeks. Nan is beaming. Her eyes are wide, her cheeks popping with colour and excitement. She is glowing. Carole has made something magical happen. She has reached in and pulled Nan's beautiful soul to the surface for all to see. She's still a gorgeous human being. A life of quality with quality of life. The doctors at St George somehow brought her back from the brink or beyond, but Carole has elevated Nan's inner beauty to the surface. But I'm sure it was only me and Carole watching and noticing in that room.

This is what Nan's second life looks like. And mine. The full extent of her recovery is now known. This is the best she will be both physically and mentally. The two years after the stroke where recovery and improvement can still be achieved have passed. I'm not going to get her home. I sometimes contemplate having her there with me for a night and arranging carers to come in, but then I think about if something goes wrong, or we have another hospital admission for a UTI, or a seizure, and it seems too risky and too hard.

Every day, regardless of the day of the week, or the month, or season of the year, is largely the same. The days might be punctuated by special visits such as Jill and Frank and Joan, my sisters, or long-term friends, but mostly our world is now made up of the people in the nursing home and the things that happen there. Nan experiences those visits 'in the moment' but doesn't recall them for long. No more than thirty minutes or so. Sometimes even less than that.

It's too early in life for this to happen. 'No one wants to go into a nursing home, even when they are older,' said my school friend John, who became a doctor. It's particularly the case in your fifties. It's way too early. Who would have thought it was even possible?

It's a life of contradictions. It is often boring. But then the awful alternative is that when it's not boring it's frightening, because it means something has gone wrong, and Nan is admitted to hospital. I wonder how long I will have her and how long things will be like this, but I certainly don't want to lose her. I just wish there was a way for things to be better for her. I don't want it to be over. I'm committed to the cause. I'll be here for her as long as I can have her, and I hope it's a long time.

Even if it is boring, it doesn't mean that the worry and stress go away. There have been plenty of shocks. Strokes, seizures, and then sudden vomits always set my mind wondering if there has been another bleed. It is best to appreciate boring as beautiful because the alternative is awful. Strange how both boredom and stress can be coresident.

Yes, I want it to be a long time, but I don't want her to suffer. It has been a hard road for her, but she is stable now. I believe she is comfortable. She has me and her family. She is loved. Her life is very much reduced from what it was, but I strongly believe that while there is stability, then time together and love mean there is still quality of life for Nan. She can still derive pleasure. She can still be content. Still feel connected to people. Still feel calm, relaxed, happy even.

I love her more than ever, but she is different to the Nan I first loved. Another contradiction. Innocent, childlike, completely dependent, precious. Much diminished mentally and physically. Still Nan though. Still my wife.

I don't want to lose her. I think about my own quality of life. I am living in a nursing home too. I don't sleep there at night, but I spend virtually all my waking hours there. My quality of life is better because I have Nan, but I have so much less of her. The relationship largely goes the one way now. She can't help that, but I can't deny it is hard, and it is lonely.

Nan is unable to give back like she always did in the past. We can't converse like we did. We can't be physical like we were. The list of things we can do or places we can go is much-reduced. She can't detect my emotional needs and salve them like she would. We can't live together like we had. But she still gives in the way that she can. She gives back by simply being there. By being Nan. By trying her best.

'Who is caring for the carer?' well-meaning family and friends would say, trying to encourage that I take some time off. They want me to try and live a life and not just be focused on caring for Nan. They are considerate things to raise. Jill rings every day. I hear from others less often. No one else is here though. Who is caring for the carer? In reality, and practically, nobody much. I understand people have their own lives to live and different priorities. I appreciate that if it was someone else, I wouldn't do any more. But this is a battle for Nan and me. And it requires all the effort we can muster to throw at it.

SLEEP THERAPIES

Fawkner Park is a refuge from the nursing home when the sights, sounds and smells become too much. When we need fresh air, to feel the sun beating on us or just to be free of institutionalised life and its overwhelming sameness.

It's a large green expanse that sits in South Yarra. There are half a dozen sporting grounds and as many tennis courts, where I later took lessons and played social games. Elms and Moreton Bay figs line the many paths that cross.

Before Nan became ill, we often took Hester into Fawkner for a stretch in the off-lead area. I crossed the park every day on my way to the nursing home, and I took Nan there regularly. I knew Nan loved Fawkner too. If it was winter, I wrapped her up as tight as a bug in her mohair rug. If it was warm and sunny, I put the oil skin cap that she bought in Windsor on her head.

Sometimes we crossed the entire park to our apartment. The first time was with Michelle, an OT from Caulfield's community team. It seemed a long way to stray from safety then, but with time, that distance became shorter and easier to negotiate.

Most times, Fawkner itself was the destination. A couple of park benches were my favourites. I rolled Nan to one end and tilted her chair backwards, then took my place on the bench next to her. We sat like that many times and for many hours, soaking up the sun and watching passers-by.

On weekends, no matter the season, the park was filled with competitive sport. Cricket in the summer, and football, soccer, and softball in the winter. Tennis all year round.

Large congregations of dog owners and their dogs often met in the middle of the sporting grounds. The owners would chat and socialise while their dogs did the same.

Dog walkers sometimes passed us with four to six dogs of all shapes and sizes, happily out with their pack for exercise. One Sunday morning, I noticed a woman walking a pack of four, including a gigantic Bernese Mountain Dog. She saw me with Nan and brought the dogs over. The mountain dog's name was Axel and the walker kindly angled him in close, so Nan had access to his massive, bear-like head. Axel lapped up much rubbing and patting while the walker, who also worked as a nurse, asked me what had happened to Nan.

It is in Fawkner another Sunday morning, when the Nan of old emerges again. We stopped at a park bench in the area we used to take Hester for her run around. Nan is sitting in her chair and looking at me intently.

'Don't you be mucking around with anyone,' she suddenly says.

It takes me by surprise. It comes from nowhere, like the other occasions. I was only describing how nice the park is.

'I won't lovey,' I respond, perhaps not very convincingly.

'You'd better not,' she fires back quite sternly. It is with the conviction of the Nan of old, not at all like the Nan she has become. It leaves me wondering what is coming next. I don't have to wonder for long.

'Where's the dog?' she asks.

I pause, not knowing what I should say. Nan is staring at me, waiting for my answer. There is no doubt now, at this moment, she is 'back in town'.

'She's not here,' I say, hoping that will be the end of it.

'Where is she?' Nan demands.

I have to answer her. She is so determined. She wants to know.

'Nanny, we don't have Hester anymore. She passed away a couple of years ago, while you were in hospital in Sydney.'

I think Nan is scowling at me. I can see she is angry for maybe the only time since her first stroke.

'You are an awful person to say that. How could you say that?'

'It's true, lovey. She had a stroke. She was old. Do you remember? I wouldn't say something like that just to be mean.'

Nan begins crying, there in Fawkner Park, not far from our apartment. What can I do? I decide it is getting close to lunch and we should go back to the nursing home. I turn the chair around and begin rolling her. The crying settles and she is fine again. She'd popped up and then popped back. There was no more questioning about Hester or of me.

* * *

I need to tell more of this last year before I relate what happened with the sleep doctor and Nan's sleep apnoea. This period started badly and finished terribly. I feel guilty about something, but it's not what you might suspect.

When people tell me I should live my life, I know they mean well. They think meeting up with friends or going to concerts, movies, football or other sources of entertainment will make life better. Realistically, it's hard to schedule things with much certainty. I had a ticket to see a modern American jazz piano trio called 'The Bad Plus', but Nan was having an unsettled evening and I didn't feel comfortable leaving her alone and didn't go. I worry about her when I am away from her.

Anyway, it's not doing things or going places that I miss. It's Nan's company. My best friend. Our conversations. Her presence with me as we stare at the TV at night. Sharing our views. Collaborative bagging of celebrities or politicians. Winding each other up. Her next to me when I go to bed or wake at night. Her companionship. The reassurance that she is there with me and for me. She can't be any of that now to the extent that she was. That's what I miss.

I met a woman. She is a pharmacist and works near Nan's nursing home. I often purchase things from her pharmacy for Nan and me. She was friendly and we talked on a few occasions. She's of Vietnamese descent but has spent her whole life in Melbourne. She is engaging and attractive. Her name is Miranda. I told her what was going on with Nan during one of our conversations. I even talked about our experience with amantadine given she is a pharmacist. She was sympathetic and nice to talk to.

I bumped into her one day outside of the pharmacy and she was keen to talk. She told me about her weekend. She recently split up with her partner and he returned to her apartment late at night and smashed her car with a brick. It frightened her and she showed me photos of the damage he had done. She called the police and gave a statement. A restraining order was imposed to prevent the guy going near her.

As we talked and she got it off her chest, I gave a sympathetic ear. I felt us making eye contact. She needed to get back to her work and as I was bidding her farewell, I told her I was sorry for the drama she was dealing with.

'I know a bit about drama,' I added.

'I know you do,' she said and moved closer. She reached forward, grasped my arm, and began stroking it while she smiled and maintained eye contact. I was surprised and aroused as she continued stroking me.

I couldn't stop thinking about her, but it didn't change what I did for Nan or how I felt about her in any way. I continued my routine and my affection for her as I had.

I bumped into Miranda soon after that and asked for her number. I called a couple of days later and had a long talk and agreed to meet for a drink Sunday evening.

When it came to the evening, she asked if we could postpone. On the next scheduled date, she rang and asked whether we were to meet that day or the next.

'Today,' I said, feeling miffed at a second cancellation, but trying not to show it.

'Oh, I've made a mistake and got things mixed up. I'm heading to Mum's for dinner now. Let's make another time,' she answered quite flippantly.

'OK,' I said, and we agreed to meet the following Sunday.

I was disappointed, and I should have opted out after two cancellations, but I was hooked. I couldn't believe I was trying to date a woman while I was caring for Nan, but the pull was suddenly strong. It had come out of nowhere. I hadn't even considered anything like this.

I went to bed at the usual 10.30pm or so, Saturday evening. Things seemed stable with Nan, and I was hopeful of finally meeting Miranda the next day.

Through the fog of a deep sleep, I heard my phone ringing. I awoke in a panic. It must be the nursing home. There must be something wrong with Nan. I found my phone and flipped open the cover. It was Miranda calling at this hour!

'Miranda?' I asked. 'What's up? I thought it was the nursing home ringing, and something was wrong with Nanette.' I was pissed off and made little attempt to disguise it.

'I'm sorry to call at this hour David, but I think my ex-partner might be outside my apartment. I didn't know who else to call and I know you are nearby.'

'Call the police,' I said, feeling more than a little irritated. I looked at the time. It was 1.30am.

'I'm sorry. I will do that,' she said, and we hung up.

I couldn't get back to sleep and after ten minutes or so I rang her back and told her I would drive over and check if there was anyone around.

I pulled some clothes on. It was 2am and I was feeling anxious when I got there. I didn't want to confront this guy. According to Miranda, he was six foot five, and the photographs of her car showed he had a temper problem.

There was no sign of anyone. I drove around a couple of times to make sure and then rang to tell her. She was grateful for the reassurance, and I went home and back to bed, where I struggled to return to sleep.

Next day, she cancelled again, claiming she was tired from the worry of the night before. Not a great excuse given she had woken me for help. A few days later, I waited for her after work, and she told me she had decided she didn't want to date me now. She looked uncomfortable and made some excuse; she was waiting to meet a 'much older gentleman' who would be able to advise her on her problems with her ex. I felt suspicious of what she was up to. She seemed caught out.

I let her go and went back to Nan feeling quite crushed. I moped around for weeks over it. I hadn't felt this way since I was a teenager. I had been with Nan since my early twenties. I was lucky to have had a great partner all that time and never wanted anyone else.

A couple of weeks later, Miranda texted me again to suggest we get together. Suspiciously, I agreed, and she did the same thing, cancelling last minute. I initially thought she might be struggling with my situation, or her own recent relationship, but really, she was just playing with me. I don't know what possessed her to do that.

Next time I saw her, she began flirting and telling me how good I looked, but I let it go. The pattern and intent was now very clear, and I had had enough time to get over her. When I reflected on the 1.30am call that night, I had serious doubts that anything she said was legitimate.

I'd been hurt, but she had awakened me to the idea of being with a woman in a more mutual relationship again. I knew I would stick by Nan. I wasn't going to abandon her. I loved her as much as ever. I had a confidential talk to a couple of doctors about it. One of them said he had heard of carers divorcing their partners so they could get on with their own lives. I was horrified at the suggestion. There was no way I was doing anything like that. Either I would find someone who was comfortable with my relationship and life with Nanette, or I would stay alone.

How could I say I still loved Nan and at the same time want a girlfriend? Isn't this just what all philanderers would maintain? The nature of my relationship with Nan had changed in the two years of her illness and it was clear it was a permanent change. I felt and acted more like a parent than a partner now. I was spending seven days a week as Nan's carer and then going home at night to no one. 'Who is caring for the carer?' people asked, or 'There are two people whose lives are affected by this.' 'This might go on for twenty years' I was told. Nan had reached stability. I might not outlive her. As I said, I didn't want to lose her, but I needed something more too.

I decided to try dating apps. I created a Tinder profile and had some chats with women. Many of them bailed as soon as they found out my situation with Nanette. I did meet a few women in person, and either they wouldn't proceed because I was still with Nan, or I became uncomfortable about it. One woman arrived to meet me and within one minute announced she 'had considered my situation and couldn't be my lover, because she was a strong believer in solidarity with the sisterhood.' Oh God. I wasn't attracted to her in person when we met anyway.

I realised I didn't want to be pulled in two different directions.

I didn't want a relationship where someone would expect more of me than I could give or pull me towards them at the expense of my commitment to Nan. Yes, I wanted to have my cake and eat it too. I wanted a relationship on my terms. Spend the day with Nan and the evening with someone else. A girlfriend but no more than that. A relationship where the woman understood and accepted that I was married and caring for my wife. I would not and could not be fully available to someone else. I could only do so to the extent that it would work for me and Nan. I had heard people talk about 'friends with benefits', but it seemed all the women my age on the dating apps were seeking a full and committed relationship.

Eventually, after much left and right swiping over multiple dating apps, I met Emily. The first occasion was in a bar in the CBD, quite near where she lives. It was around 9pm, and I went there after settling Nan in bed for the evening.

Emily is significantly younger than me but was happy to see an older man. She is Malaysian and has been in Australia about eighteen months. She was seeking Australian residency or citizenship. I told her I couldn't help with that. She had other options and ideas about how to achieve that anyway. She told me there was another guy she saw as well, but it was only very occasional. That bothered me but I didn't think too hard about it at the time. I guess the 'no strings attached' bit meant I shouldn't question any of that.

I told Emily of my situation with Nanette. She was sceptical about it. Why would a man with a sick wife do this? It seemed by this stage completely logical to me. I explained the nature of my life as it was by then. I told her that this might go on for a long time, but I didn't want a new partner. She accepted this, and we were both prepared to go ahead.

We went to her apartment and became lovers. It was what I needed. We talked a lot and I liked her. She made me some food and we sat at her kitchen table talking and eating late at night. I instantly felt a bond with her. Perhaps all I needed was to experience intimacy again. But it was more than the sex. It was the conversation. Getting to know each other. A close female friend.

She wanted to know more about Nanette. I explained her condition and our history in a lot more detail. She was saddened by what had happened. She told me more about her life. She was the fifth of six children. She had been raised by a woman she called her 'nanny' because the parents had too many children and too much going on to manage. I told her that I often called my wife 'Nanny'.

Emily was here on a student visa, studying business. She was also working on her English to pass the stringent language requirement necessary for residency. She hadn't made a lot of friends here. She worked as a masseuse and a beauty technician, but there were limitations on the number of hours she could work each week.

I initially saw Emily every four or five days. We met at her place in the evening after I had been with Nan all day. Despite our age difference, we became closer, and we met in other circumstances too: breakfast before I went to Nan, late night movies, I even took her to her first AFL football game. It was a night match and she enjoyed it a lot. I noticed how polite and friendly she was to the people around us in the crowd. Not exactly football behaviour, but it was interesting to see her in another context.

We maintained frequent contact via text and met more often. It soon became nearly every evening after I left the nursing home. Occasionally, I would stay over at her place and then go to the nursing home the next morning, but I was uncomfortable about that. She was only in the CBD, four kilometres away from my place, but I was anxious being further away from Nan should there be any overnight emergency.

Nan had several hospital admissions over late 2016 and early 2017, and Emily would regularly check in on how we both were while I sat in the emergency room with Nan. It's easy to assume the worst motivations in a situation like this, but I didn't ever see anything but goodwill extended from Emily towards Nan.

We had a problem a few months into our relationship when I discovered there was another man I hadn't known about. I became enraged and walked out on her. She begged for forgiveness and after I left she wrote me some nice texts thanking me for our time together and apologising.

I caved in after a short period. I contemplated finding someone else, but I had a good connection with Emily, she lived relatively close to my place, and it was easier to take her back. I was also feeling very sad about not seeing her. She agreed to end things with the other guy and only see me.

After this I noticed she was developing stronger feelings. She admitted she was falling in love with me and somewhat callously, I told her not to, reminding her that I was with Nan and that my relationship with her would go nowhere longer term. In theory we had a 'no strings attached' agreement but the reality is that emotions and connections don't take much notice of contractual dealings, and rightly or wrongly, we were in a relationship. She was my girlfriend. Again, it changed nothing about my feelings for Nanette or the time I spent with her. Nan remained the priority. Nan was still the only woman I loved.

* * *

The sleep doctor referred Nan for a sleep study after seeing the videos. Private hospital insurance means we are able to have it done promptly. It would have been better if we'd had to wait. Or in fact, better still if it had never been done.

Nan is wired for the study with nodes attached to multiple points on her head and scalp, torso and legs, and a pulse sensor on her finger, which she keeps wiggling and playing with until we transfer it to her immobilised left side.

The study confirms she has sleep apnoea and it is occurring so frequently she is getting no REM sleep at all. No wonder she is tired every morning. It is the apnoea that is messing her sleep up now, not the amantadine.

The sleep doctor advises we could try CPAP but cautions that if the apnoea is central (driven from her brain) rather than obstructive (because of her airways collapsing), then CPAP will do nothing to help.

'Do you think she slept like this before the stroke?' he asks.

'I don't remember her waking like this, but she did snore a lot and quite loudly,' I tell him.

He sends us on our way with a referral for CPAP and the advice to initially try the unit on a low-pressure setting. When the technician arrives to set it up, he insists that the unit be set to automatic mode so that it finds the right pressure setting for Nan. I look back on that now and wonder why I didn't force him to follow the doctor's instructions, but that's hindsight talking.

I put Nan on CPAP a few times while she is napping in the afternoons, or early evenings after she goes to bed and before I leave for the night. She seems to be OK with it, so it is time to try her on it overnight.

It is a Saturday evening, and I place the headpiece and straps over Nan's head and the oxygen mask over her mouth and set the machine running. Nan seems comfortable and I wait until she drops off to sleep. I am still video recording her at night. I let the afternoon nurse know that I have left the unit on her and ask her to keep an eye on Nan, and if there are any problems, then just remove it. It wasn't enough. I should have stayed with her or arranged for someone else to stay with her. I should have been firmer in my instructions to the nurse. The facility should have done a better job monitoring her, but I knew they couldn't be relied upon. It just should have been OK.

I go into the city and see Emily for a few hours. I tell her about

Nan and CPAP and that I hope it will deliver better sleep for her. I even speculate that her memory and cognition might improve if she can get quality sleep each evening. I am feeling very hopeful and quite upbeat that maybe I have solved an important issue for Nan. Emily listens attentively then tells me she has been studying English again and has an exam approaching, so we spend some time looking over that. I go home to my place at around 11pm.

When I arrive at the nursing home the following morning, I find Nan still asleep and the CPAP mask and tube on the chest of drawers next to her bed. I am a little disappointed that it had been taken off. Something must have gone wrong. Maybe Nan became uncomfortable with it.

I wake Nan and call in the carers to put her on the toilet and then shower her. She is falling back to sleep while on the toilet, so it seems the CPAP hasn't delivered her more energy.

After her shower, and back in the wheelchair, she looks very pale. I realise that she is passing out and I can't wake her. I grab my phone and ring the nurses' number. Maureen is the nurse on duty, and I ask her to come quickly.

'Maureen, I think Nan has passed out. I can't wake her,' I tell her when she arrives.

Maureen can't wake Nan either, so she begins taking her blood pressure and checking her oxygen level. Her blood pressure is low which is unusual for Nan, and her oxygen saturation has dropped beneath ninety per cent which is why she's passed out. Maureen goes to get some oxygen and when she returns, puts the mask on Nan's face and turns the tank on. After a minute or so on oxygen, Nan starts to wake again.

'I had her on CPAP last night Maureen. Did anyone report anything about it?'

'I only know they took it off her, nothing more,' she replies. 'David, I think we had better send her into hospital,' Maureen decides, and she begins arranging an ambulance to come.

I stay with Nan while waiting for the ambulance and gradually her colour improves. She is now either awake or dozing and I check that I can wake her. I then begin downloading the video to my laptop and reviewing the previous night's events.

In the early hours of the morning, Nan is awake and seemingly alert. She is moving her head around. When I slow the video to actual speed, I can see she is distressed. She is calling out and her face is red. Her sound is more of a moan or a cry than any words. No one is coming to her. Every now and then she puts her hand to the mask, but she doesn't know how to take it off. It is clear that the mask and CPAP are the source of her distress.

This goes on for what seems like an eternity. She is foaming at the mouth. I find it awful to watch. Thirty or forty minutes elapse of this. I have to fast-forward the video because I can't bear to keep watching it. Eventually, a carer comes into the room. I am hopeful this will be the point where the mask will be removed.

'Are you OK Nan?' she asks.

Nan nods. Her usual nod. Like there isn't a single thing wrong. Like she doesn't want to create a fuss for anyone. She doesn't indicate to the carer she has a problem. *Oh no* I'm thinking to myself as I'm watching.

The carer seems to hesitate a bit and looks further at Nan. She doesn't take the mask off despite my urging her to as I look on, powerless. It is frustrating and horrible to watch. She then turns the light off again and leaves the room. I fast-forward further through the video.

Nan struggles some more, and eventually, another carer comes back and takes the mask off and leaves the light on for Nan. Nan just lays there in bed, seemingly comfortable enough until Maureen arrives later to give her morning medication. To Maureen, Nan would have looked just the way she always did on weekend mornings when she came in.

I shut the video off and seeing Nan is settled, go to tell Maureen what I have found.

The ambulance arrives soon after and I report it to them as well. They put Nan on the stretcher, keeping her on oxygen the whole time and take us into The Alfred. They run the usual battery of tests: brain scan, blood tests and chest X-ray, but once again they find nothing new to report.

I am sure something has changed because Nan is unresponsive. I can't get her to follow any command despite my urging. She is awake and looks OK, but she is not responding.

A respiratory registrar comes to check on Nan and I tell him what has happened. I have the CPAP machine with me, and he checks it over.

'CPAP really shouldn't cause a problem like this,' he says. He is a helpful guy in his early thirties, and he spends quite some time talking with me and testing the machine, which to him looks to be OK.

Nan remains unresponsive all of Sunday and Monday. I am less alarmed than usual given her brain scan confirmed no change, but when Tuesday comes and she looks brighter and begins responding, I am relieved.

The hospital tries her on CPAP under nurse supervision, but only for a few hours at a time. It doesn't create any new problem.

They discharge Nan and once back at the nursing home, we resume our normal lives. I am feeding her and taking her out. I'm not really prepared to run CPAP again. It had to be the cause of the problem.

I ring the technician and tell him what happened and that I don't want the machine any longer. He understands this had been serious and says he will come by and pick it up. He never does, and I still have an unused CPAP machine in my garage four years later. I make a few more attempts to call them but can never get them to respond. Their loss. No, in truth it is my loss.

A week later, I am again yanked from a deep sleep at around 1.30am. This time, it is the nursing home. An African nurse calmly tells me that Nan has had a huge vomit. She says she has rung Angela who told her to admit Nan to hospital. She has already called the ambulance.

I thank her for ringing me, get dressed and race to the nursing home. When I arrive, it is clear Nan is very unwell. Her eyes are red, and she isn't responsive. She is barely conscious. Some of the remnants of the vomit are still around her in the folds of the bed sheets and her pyjamas.

When the ambulance arrives, we load her in and drive the short distance to The Alfred once again.

Over the next few hours, Nan vomits several more times. The hospital take her for another brain scan. As it approaches dawn, a young female registrar comes to talk with me. She brings me the kind of news I have been dreading and hoping against for almost three years.

'David, I'm sorry to tell you that Nan has suffered a new bleed in her brain. It's in a part of her brain called the cerebellum,' she says.

'Shit. What does that mean? Is it bad?' I ask in a panic. I can tell from the way she's looking at me so apologetically that it is.

'The cerebellum is quite a small part of the brain, but it's important and damage there can impact your balance and equilibrium, fine motor movements, and even other autonomic functions like swallowing and speech.'

I go back to be with Nanny. She is lapsing in and out of consciousness. She still seems to be responsive when she wakes, so I take that as a positive. The hospital will send a neurosurgeon to tell me what, if anything, can be done. I expect they will wash their hands of her and tell me game over. I ring Jill once it is light to tell her the bad news. I text my siblings. I text Emily and let her know what's happened and that I won't be over for a while.

I feel guilty for trying to address the sleep apnoea. Granted I was not to know and was only trying to help, but I should have left well enough alone. I can add that to the list of other things I should have done, didn't do, wished I had done or wished I hadn't.

I wish I had pushed Nan harder to see a doctor before her stroke. Why didn't I have the clarity of hindsight when she had a headache that made her feel she was having a stroke? Or when I told her of my new working contract, and she said she didn't think we would have very much longer together?

I wish I had insisted she come to Melbourne that Monday it all happened. Our apartment is so close to The Alfred, and I would have been at home with her. I wish that I had been with her when it happened. Well, I'm with her now and always will be. There is no way I would consider divorcing my darling to get on with my life. This IS my life.

ANOTHER BLEED

A large man with a round but familiar face arrives to speak with us. It is Charles, the neurosurgeon who installed Nan's shunt and who I met afterwards at the clinic. I feel a little better that it is someone I have met before and who knows some of the history.

'Hi, it's Charles, isn't it? We've met. I'm David, Nan's husband.'

'Hello David,' he answers looking at us both. Nan is unconscious now, so he addresses his questions to me. 'What do you understand is going on?'

'I know she's had a new bleed. I don't know a lot more than that. I'm wondering what happens next.'

'How is she?'

'She's been vomiting. She has been awake at times. She's still a little responsive. How serious is it, Charles?'

'It is serious. She is deteriorating, and she will die if we don't intervene. What do you want to do? What would Nanette want?' I like the way he pronounced Nan's name. A hint remaining of his educated South African accent. He speaks in a calm, matter of fact way. He doesn't sound anxious. His manner makes me feel calmer as well.

'I really don't know what's right. I don't want her to suffer, but I don't want to lose her. I really don't know what to do.' I am transported back to the experience of St George. It is terrible deciding on another person's life. I don't want to give her up.

Charles spends a few seconds surveying Nan and then asks me to tell him what her life is like now. I talk about life in the nursing home. She is eating. Talking a little bit. She does some art. I am with her every day. Her family visits when they can. We go out, weather permitting, for some air. Sometimes back to our apartment.

Charles then takes a few more seconds and makes a suggestion for me. 'I think we should operate and see if we can get her back to where she was. What do you think about that?'

'I am happy with that,' I reply with much relief.

With the decision made, Charles leaves to make the arrangements and before too long, a porter and a nurse arrive to take Nan for the surgery. She is no longer waking, and I kiss her and tell her I love her. I don't know if I will see her alive again.

I ring Jill to tell her what is happening. I sense she is surprised that they are operating. Concerned even. I tell her the neurosurgeon had suggested it when he heard what Nan's life was like and I accepted it. She is quiet on the other end, and I feel she probably doesn't think it is the right decision. I don't want to let Nan go but if I was told to, I would. The neurosurgeon must have heard enough in my description of our lives together to think surgery is justified. I didn't gild the lily. I can't know and no one can know what this means for Nan.

Jill told Joan what was going on, so Joan is waiting anxiously for further updates. Joan is blind, and later, when Jill rings her to advise the surgery is done, she forgets herself and races to the phone, catches herself on a desk and falls over, breaking her hip. She is eighty-seven. Joan can't get up to hang up the phone, leaving the line open. All that on top of the distressing news about Nan. Jill tries to contact Bruce or a neighbour and after doing that, she and Frank set out the next day to return to Albury to support Joan.

Things between Joan and me are much better now. More than a year before this, she decided I was doing a good job and from then on, she became supportive and pleasant again. It dawned on her that I had fought very hard for Nan, wasn't ever going to stop, and that as her carer constantly by her side, I knew her condition and her needs better than any doctor, nurse, or anyone else. She rings regularly now, and I put her on speaker phone to talk to Nan.

The surgery addresses the bleed, and Nan comes through it. She is admitted to the neurosurgery ward afterwards, where we were after the shunt was installed. Over the next few days, the vomiting remains a problem. She can't tolerate being moved into or out of bed, or even being turned while they change her pad. It isn't every time she is moved, but there are vomits each day. Her balance and equilibrium are affected by the cerebellum bleed. This is deeply troubling, and I ask a registrar whether this will settle down. He 'thinks it should over time', whatever that means. In the meantime, they are loading Nan with all sorts of anti-nausea drugs to try and manage the vomiting.

The outlook for Nan is grim, and within days, I think I have made the wrong decision. It's not only the vomiting, but she also seems to have lost her speech. We don't even try and give her anything to eat. She is fully dependent on the PEG feed again.

I am fearful for her quality of life. It won't be good if she feels sick all the time. It's a lot to bear. How can I know? Quality of life is a subjective value reduced by every setback. It's an equation: 'Quality of life now' equals 'quality of life previously' less decrements due to stokes and illness. Anyone could assign different values to the variables for themselves or any other person. Then there are the offsets which act as counterbalances. 'Quality of life now' is offset by the variables 'how much I love her' and 'the pain of loss'. These two are powerful variables that have the potential to outweigh the other. I must be careful of them.

On the Saturday morning four days after the bleed, I arrive to find Nan wearing an oxygen mask. A young female doctor advises me they are struggling to maintain her oxygen level. They are monitoring her and while we are talking, it suddenly plummets, down below eighty per cent.

The doctor thinks Nan has suffered another bleed. It seems this is the end. I won't ask for more surgery and I don't think they would offer it now. It is so upsetting that I start crying in the public area of the ward. I never cry in public, but I can't help myself. Nanny didn't deserve this. I don't deserve this. I shouldn't have tried to address the fucking sleep apnoea. I don't know for certain that it's connected, but it seems mighty coincidental.

They send Nan for another brain scan to check for a new bleed. The porter arrives and the nurse transfers her to portable oxygen tanks so they can keep oxygenating her throughout the process. The porter pushes and the nurse and I flank and form an escort for Nan as we roll her through the hospital corridors for her scan.

They won't let me into the radiology department. I don't care about the exposure. I just want to be with her. Sometimes staff are more forgiving on this front but not today. After about fifteen minutes, they return, and I can see Nan is looking better than when she went in. She is awake and more with it.

Back in the ward, her oxygen is checked again, and it's closer to where it should be. There was no new stroke, and they think that she had a mucus plug or something blocking her airways. It must have dislodged when they moved her for the scan.

The rest of that day I spend getting over the first part of the day. I'm sitting by Nan's side holding her hand and kissing her. She wakes every now and again and is looking brighter. She looks comfortable. I'm glad to still have her. Nothing else in life matters.

* * *

It's a fortnight before Nan stabilises enough that the team thinks she can be discharged. They've been wonderful. A highly resourced ward. It's not the 1:1 nursing ratio of intensive care, but there are some rooms where it is 1:2. When there is a problem, a lot of people arrive quickly. Just like at Caulfield. They are all competent. The registrars are training to be neurosurgeons. The nurses are handpicked and trained to deal with patients suffering neurological conditions.

I continued a good rapport with Carl, the very kind, six-and-a-half feet tall, bespectacled British nursing manager I met last time we were there. He would regularly come in and have a chat and check how we were doing. Finally, we are all comfortable that Nan can leave the hospital for the nursing home, and she is discharged.

The very next morning, back in the nursing home, the vomiting starts again. Not once, but multiple times. Whenever she is moved and even when she is not. I decide quickly that I want her back in hospital and the ambulance is called. This time we are processed through emergency as usual and admitted to the general medical ward after a kindly doctor of Malaysian descent reviews Nan.

When Nan is ill, it is difficult to fully convey the relief once she is in the hands of The Alfred. Suddenly I don't feel as alone in caring for her. There are great nurses and people in the nursing home, and Patricia is a wonderful and kind doctor who is always there for us, but they are all stretched too thin and it is definitely not a hospital environment. The management like to point this out. 'We are not a hospital,' they would say as they washed their hands of care.

'You certainly aren't,' I think and sometimes say back to them.

In the general medical ward, Nan is under the care of a Middle-Eastern registrar named Adem. Adem is dark, shortish, roundish, with a receding hairline and glasses. Given he is approaching the end of his registrar training, he must be nearly forty years old.

I see Adem or the Malaysian consultant who admitted Nan most days, but the situation remains the same. Nan is still vomiting regularly. Less so than before, but too frequently. They are prescribing different medications to try and control it.

One doctor suggests that she/we may have to live with the vomiting. Easy for them to say. It's dangerous for someone like Nan who can't move herself. She could asphyxiate should she be in the wrong position at night. No one might find her for hours.

A senior nurse who has provided a lot of community support to Nan recommends we consult the palliative care team and get them involved. I recoil at the thought.

'Palliative care? That's giving up. I don't want to do that,' I say to Stacey.

'David, palliative care do more than just manage end of life. They are experts at managing difficult symptoms that no one else can get on top of,' Stacey responds.

I say I'll think about it but after a few more days of the same and feeling increasingly that I made the wrong decision agreeing to Nan's surgery, I find myself on the palliative care floor of The Alfred, looking for help. I knock on the door and upon entry, meet a British consultant named Rohan. I explain Nan's situation to him, and he promises to pay Nan a visit and have a longer chat. I am clear I'm not ready to let her go and want to know if they can help with her symptoms.

They arrive in Nan's room a day or two later: Rohan, a female registrar, and a male chief nurse in his fifties. After an initial discussion, Rohan wants to look over Nan's medical chart. The chart has grown considerably over time. There are several medications aimed at preventing urinary tract infections, now another four to combat the vomiting, two to manage the PEG and digestion, and another three for keeping her bowel regular and formed. There is also the neurostimulant amantadine, Keppra to prevent seizures and some precautionary Panadol. By the time drugs had been started and stopped, the medical chart extends over four or five pages.

Rohan wants me to review the meds with him. He explains that medications can interfere with each other and that some might be negating the effect of others. One by one, he wants a justification for each of the meds. He takes a ruthless approach, drawing a line through all the meds aimed at warding off UTIs.

'There is no evidence than any of that stuff works,' he says, as he crosses them all out from future administration. 'Keppra?' he asks.

'She's had big seizures. That needs to stay on,' I reply in defence.

'Amantadine?'

'Please keep that. She will become unresponsive without it, Rohan,' I implore and then explain some history.

When it comes to the anti-nausea approach, Rohan recommends removal of all the current drugs and replacement with one: Maxolon delivered twenty-four hours a day through a syringe driver. He prescribes Maxolon at a level above what is normally used. When Nan is settled, he will wind it back.

Once finished, Rohan has reduced Nan's list of medications from a four-page chart to one-and-a-half pages. I am impressed by his decisiveness and willingness to come at it from another angle. The rulebook has gone out the window. This is medical pragmatism at its best. Nan must be made comfortable. This isn't about hastening an end to her life. This is about hastening away her distress and discomfort and improving her quality of life.

After they leave, I sit with Nan with my mouth agape. We'd been visited by superheroes. They didn't wear capes, but they should have. I didn't know this is what palliative care was about, but I am so happy to have them involved.

The syringe driver is brought in. The nurse inserts a needle under the skin in Nan's arm. It is connected to a Maxolon-loaded syringe which is then placed into a case housing an electronic pushing mechanism. It pushes the syringe at an imperceptibly slow speed, delivering the drug over twenty-four hours.

Within a day or so of its application, Nan has stopped vomiting. It is an enormous relief. When Rohan and the team visit again, I am very grateful. A few days later, the Maxolon is reduced to a safer dosage. After that, the vomiting returns, so it is a case of trying to find a workable but not excessive level.

After only a day or two of no vomits, Adem tells me Nan will be discharged.

'What?' I fire back. 'It's only a day since she last vomited. She's not stable. She can't go back to the nursing home yet. It's not safe.'

'David, she's had another four weeks. She's had her time here. I've got bureaucrats all over me about it.'

I doubt if he had this over again, he would say what he said there. I think he was panicked. He is a good person, and he had looked after Nan, but I saw red.

'Adem, you send whoever these people are in to talk to me directly, and I will sort that problem out. Let's see whether they have the courage to face people in this circumstance. They can have the conversation. I will relish the opportunity. She's not leaving. She is far too unwell, and you know it mate.'

I wasn't budging on it and Adem sensibly let it go. He returns next day with Paul, a very senior professor I met on one of Nan's previous Alfred admissions. After initial pleasantries, Paul asks that I accompany him to talk privately in an office. I feel like I am a naughty schoolboy summoned to see the principal.

Paul is mid-sixties with long grey hair, a child of the early fifties who would have come of age around the time of the summer of love. He looks a bit like a hippy. But, like Richard the neurologist or Charles the neurosurgeon, he has years of experience in dealing with difficult situations and people under duress. He knows not to make ultimatums. It is better to negotiate and to discuss. Let people feel heard. Get them on side and make a deal. However, he has some points he wants to make as well.

'David, I know the background here and I know Nanette and therefore you have had a very rough time. What are you looking for?'

'Well, she had surgery to try and repair the cerebellum bleed.

There has been a lot of vomiting and it's unsafe to send her back to the nursing home.' I lament about life and the quality of care there and that it would mean my own challenge would be even harder.

'How do you think we can help?' Paul responds.

'I want to see if she can recover and stabilise from the surgery. I want another four weeks in hospital here. If she can't, then it's a matter of managing her through palliative care to end of life.' I can't believe those words have left my lips. Managing the end of Nan's life.

'I can probably sort that out,' Paul responds, and I immediately feel like I've had a victory. Then he has a message for me. One that no one has yet delivered so effectively or even courageously.

'David, you've fought as big a battle as I, or probably anyone here has ever seen, but you've lost. Nanette is going to die.' He says that last statement more slowly and very clearly. He leaves a pause for it to sink in and then he says it again.

'David, she is going to die.'

I'd heard it the first time and it felt like the blow of a powerful left uppercut. The second time is the follow up right cross. Cassius is back. I am numbed and shocked and can't say much. Staggering, waiting for the killer blow. He is leaving time to make sure I've heard it and absorbed it. I have.

'No one has said that to me. Are you sure?' I eventually ask him.

'Yes. In fact, I suspect she's only hanging on because she thinks you can't do without her.'

Hell. This is painful to hear despite being numbed by shock. Two-thirds of the knockout complete, I am still reeling. There is no possible response to this news. There is no argument I can mount in defence to get us back on track, to keep us in the fight.

'Can people actually do that Paul? Delay their own passing? Have a say in when it occurs?' I need confirmation this is true. I am talking with a very senior scientific person, but this for me is a leap into the mystical world.

'Yes, we believe so. We see examples like this quite often.'

Cause to pause. Makes me think. Is Nan still only here for me? Still unselfishly putting me first like she has always done? Even now, despite what she has gone through and is going through? Am I being weak and selfish? Clutching to her and refusing to let her go because I can't live without her? Has that been the case since all this started? Am I making her suffer? Fuck.

I know I am fearful of losing her, but surely, she must desire to stay too. Is she actively thinking this and deciding, or just feeling it? Just feeling the overwhelming drag of my desperation pulling her towards me like a child not wanting to be separated from its mother. If that is the case, she hasn't been able to turn her back on me and just leave. She must want to stay.

I had asked her one day in the nursing home. Actually, demanded a response. I was feeding her lunch and she wouldn't eat. I was impatient given all the effort over weeks and months it had taken to get her eating again. I knew she enjoyed the food because she had told me. I was ever fearful of her going backwards on this or any step forward.

'Come on Nan, you need to eat your lunch.'

She took the mouthful and didn't swallow, leaving it dangerously in her mouth and I needed to fish it out. 'You've got to eat. You can't leave food in your mouth. Do you want to die?' I angrily said to her.

'No,' she said, panicked, and she shook her head fearfully. I felt like shit. How could I have got angry with her and said that?

It told me she wanted to live, but things were different then. She was stable and she was comfortable. She was eating and she wasn't vomiting from vertigo like she has been this last month.

Paul and I talk more about life in the nursing home. We have otherwise concluded. He will work on a longer hospital stay for Nan and I will work on giving up my darling. I'm not sure I can be good to my word, but I know I don't want her suffering like this. As we finish our meeting, he again tells me Nan 'is going to die'. The final knockout blow for me. Paul wins that bout. Not a points decision.

Nan stayed in The Alfred for another few weeks and between the regular medical team and the palliative care team and the syringe driver, her vomiting settles down again. Paul dropped in to see us quite regularly in addition to Adem, and when it was time to leave, I thanked him and asked him how long he thought Nan would have.

'I think a matter of weeks, or maybe a low number of months,' he responded solemnly.

* * *

The cerebellum bleed occurred on 17 May 2017. It was 11 July before Nan was discharged back to the nursing home, a week before her fifty-seventh birthday. By then they had stabilised the vomiting.

I maintained regular daily contact by text and phone with Emily but hardly visited her at all during Nan's hospitalisation or the following weeks. I explained to Emily that they didn't think Nan had long. Emily understood the challenges and that I needed to be with Nan. The days were long again, and I didn't have much energy or headspace for conversation anyway.

I have several photos of Nan and me from those weeks, both in the hospital and the nursing home. In most of them, she looks surprisingly alert and well. In one of them, she is in bed reaching out to Max, a beautiful black Labrador that one of the staff at the nursing home brought to work and loaned us for a few hours. Nan only has eyes for Max in the photo. Max is busy looking at me as I photographed the pair of them.

Nan is stabilising and building her strength again, but the cerebellum bleed has taken a terrible additional toll on her. She can no longer speak. I can only elicit from her an almost imperceptible head nod or shake if I ask questions necessitating a yes or no answer. She can no longer swallow and therefore eating even the pureed meals has stopped. She is totally reliant on the PEG again. The nausea is managed by the syringe driver. She can't properly control a pen or a pencil now. The doctors had said that fine motor movements were also managed in the cerebellum. The emergency doctor was correct when she said the cerebellum is a small but significant part of the brain.

There is a new and insidious challenge as well. Nan's lost swallowing means a regular build-up of secretions in her mouth and throat. We swallow many times every hour to digest our secretions. We do it unconsciously. Now Nan isn't swallowing, they are accumulating in her mouth, and I can hear them gurgling in her throat when she breathes. I need to suction her quite regularly and I have rented a machine to use in her room.

The secretions are better treated with medication to dry Nan out. We tried a couple of different meds but the one that works best is glycopyrrolate. It is very expensive, costing hundreds per week. It isn't covered on the PBS for this purpose. Fortunately, we can afford it, but I feel sorry for those needing drugs like this who can't.

With the vomiting settling and a medical solution for secretions, we seem to reach a strange, new period of stability. It is possible to shower and toilet Nan again each morning. I can take her outside for walks, with the syringe driver tucked into a Dan Murphy's bag slung from the back of the wheelchair. The Maxolon is working well as none of those movements now cause her to vomit.

Val starts coming again for some limited physiotherapy sessions. Nan is now more passive in those sessions than she was. Val works mainly on her immobilised left-hand side. It is good to have Val back again with her sunny personality and undoubted rapport with Nan. The rapport is still there, although Nan can no longer express herself through speech.

Nan still understands what she is being asked and can respond albeit within the confines of now massive physical constraints. She knows who I am and can point to various people or objects around her when asked. We sit in the room together and hold hands. She reaches out while I am next to her and strokes my neck and hairline. It's very soothing and relaxing for me. It's what she can do. She does this for long periods while I fall asleep in the chair next to her. She is as drawn to the touching as I am to being touched.

* * *

Like she always has, Nan exceeds expectations. This time, it's Paul's estimate of how long she would survive. Christmas 2017 is approaching, and she is quite stable. It is seven months since the new stroke.

I have some assistance now from the newly-formed National Disability Insurance Scheme. I contacted them when Nan was in hospital and then heard nothing for a few months. In September, my phone rang, and a nice young guy told me he was coming to see us. He listened to our plight and immediately arranged funding for some carers to help me out.

Through the NDIS, I found Tecie and Rachel, two lovely Filipina nurses who moved here in pursuit of their Australian nursing qualifications and residency visas. They come twice a week each and stay with Nan for a few hours while I take a break. Often, I just go home for a rest or to play piano. Sometimes I visit Emily. I am not brave enough to venture further away from Nan.

When I return from my break, I might find Tecie holding Nan's hand and them watching TV together, or Rachel massaging her shoulders, both unaware that I am back and observing their kindness. They take Nan for a walk or sing to her or talk with her or just be there. If they have any doubts or concerns, they are quick to ring me and let me know. It's given me a great boost to have such help from two very good young women.

After discharge from The Alfred, Nan was placed under a community palliative care team, and a doctor there encouraged me to investigate Botox injections into her mouth to dry up the secretions. She didn't need the saliva any longer because she wasn't eating. Another application for Botox!

Patricia referred Nan to a rehab consultant for review and consideration of Botox injections. It meant a forty-minute ride by wheelchair taxi for Nan and me to get to his office. We had regularly taken taxis to and from Caulfield hospital for rehab consults in the time before the cerebellum bleed, but I was now very anxious about straying too far from home given the dramas of 2017.

In the first appointment with the consultant, he prescribed an eyedrop to be dispensed under Nan's tongue. The eyedrop was sometimes effective in drying up secretions. I had to be extremely careful not to overdose her. After a few applications though, it was clear that it didn't work. We continued to rely on glycopyrrolate and had to wait almost another month for the next appointment.

When we returned and reported that the eyedrop hadn't worked, the consultant agreed to inject, and he organised the Botox. Within seconds he injected Nan in either side of her jaw and said he was done. He was very proficient. We then took the long ride back to the nursing home. I was relieved to have Nan 'home' again.

Sadly, the Botox didn't work either. I could still hear the gurgling in Nan's throat. There was no pooling of saliva in her mouth. When I talked to doctors, I learned that secretions come from our stomach as well. The body is constantly secreting and absorbing fluids like a giant car wash sponge. The Botox injections were never going to solve the problem and glycopyrrolate is the only solution.

Nan always loved Christmas, and Christmas 2017 would be our third since she became unwell. I was concerned that this might prove to be our last. I had had enough of celebrating alone in hospital or the nursing home, so I arranged for Joan, Jill and Frank, and Bruce and Joanne to visit Nan at the nursing home a week before. I booked a meeting room and arranged catering from The Alfred. A three-course meal was delivered for us. Nan couldn't eat or talk but she could sit among her family for a Christmas celebration, experience the conversation around her and interact in her way. The family brought gifts. Joan sat next to Nan and held her hand. Joan remarked that Nan knew everyone and what was going on, even if she was unable to speak. I loved seeing her with her family in a Christmas celebration again.

I think Nan had regained quality of life then. What are the most important things to most people? Love and health. Perhaps health that even if compromised, is stable enough to enjoy and experience love. Nan enjoying some medical stability and a proper Christmas celebration again for the first time in three years. Her affected short-term memory means she lives in the moment. I am sure that for her, the bad moments like vomiting with movement and secretions issues were forgotten about then. She is with her husband, her mother and her family and it is Christmas. The mood is happy; this is a good moment. At that time, it is a good life.

A year before that, Caulfield hospital invited me back to address their executive management team about our experience at the hospital. I talked about Nan before and after the strokes. I had around thirty minutes. When it came to an end, the CEO asked me what the one message was I wanted to leave them with.

'You cannot determine whether an individual has quality of life. You don't know the person and it depends on what really mattered to them, what sort of person they were and what sort of person they are now.'

Every time Nan was re-admitted to hospital, a junior doctor would ask me whether there was an advanced care plan in place for Nan. In other words, a clear statement of when she should or should not be given medical treatment. I always responded with a no and that I did not want one created. She should be treated, and I should always be contacted. If the time comes to let her go, I felt I would know, and I didn't want anyone else making that decision.

I am sure some medical staff with a five-minute exposure to Nan didn't value her life. They viewed what she didn't have, not what she still had, and they didn't know her.

Only a month before Christmas that year, I was sickened by the euthanasia debate in the Victorian State Parliament. As we watched the TV, I sat holding Nan's hand, appalled by the macabre spectacle of politicians queueing for their turn to sob on camera about their stories of personal tragedy and woe.

I understand that there are cases where people want to make their own choice to die, and I don't resent or reject that. It is very different when it comes to deciding for someone who cannot make their own decisions or speak for themselves. It is a slippery slope. Medical people, mostly ignorant of Nan's life outside of a hospital bed, didn't value it to the same degree they would if she were well. As I said to the executive team at Caulfield, they don't know. I fear the future now that euthanasia is legal.

As 2017 came to an end, Emily and I ended our relationship. It was too difficult. She needed more than I could give, and I needed and wanted to focus only on Nan. Emily remains a friend and still rings me now, years later, to say hello and see how I am doing. She has been in a relationship with another man for some time. I still thank Emily to this day. I couldn't have got through 2016 and 2017 without her.

PASSING

I'm looking back at photos from December and January of that 2017–2018 summer. There's one of Nan with Rachel in a craft class. Rachel is standing at Nan's side and leaning over the tray on Nan's lap. She is helping Nan cut shapes for a collage they are making. Both are completely focused on what they are doing, unaware of me taking the snap. Nan's hair is wet and combed to the side. She's just had a shower. Her mouth is partly open and shaped in an 'O'. She was unable to speak by then and I think had lost more control of her face to the cerebellum bleed eight months earlier.

I flick through subsequent and unremarkable photos from the time and then land on one of Nan in her chair looking straight ahead at the camera. She's wearing a long, striped dress made of stretchy material, an easy one for the carers to dress her in. The syringe driver is sitting on her lap. The PEG tube disappears down the top of her dress. I was feeding her during the day by then instead of at night when I wasn't there. Her left arm is in the splint she wore to keep her hand open and manage the spasticity.

The skin on her face looks so youthful and has a healthy pink glow. Not a wrinkle to be seen despite her fifty-seven years and despite the illness of the last three. Her hair, now cut short and let grey, is swept back. It's been recently cut and well-shaped. It also looks thick and healthy.

Her face is in two parts rather than a whole. The lower half is inactive. Her mouth is slumped down at both ends and her chin dimpled because her mouth is in that pose.

Her eyes though. She seems to be looking at me accusingly. Judging me perhaps? My conscience goes to Emily, but it couldn't be that. Of course, I never mentioned her to Nan. Is Nan looking at me that way not because I'd kept a girlfriend, but because I'd kept her? Perhaps she didn't want her photo taken, but she cooperatively looked at me and the camera when I asked her to. She looks quite healthy, but she doesn't look content. I can't know now whether she was or not, just have to rely on my judgement at the time.

There are two more photos of her from the following month. One with a small female hand on her shoulder. Tecie sent it to me to tell me Nan had vomited. Nan's face is red, her eyes focused on the camera and her mouth closed. She looks a little shocked.

The other photo is by me. Her mouth is back in the 'O' shape and her eyes look tired and worn. Her skin and hair still look great.

The next photo of Nan from March 2018 is very different. She's in hospital again. There was yet another vomit. Tecie rang me because she was with Nan, and I was home having a break. Poor Tecie seemed to be getting the bad luck. I went straight over.

Nan was clearly very unwell, so we called the ambulance and to my dismay, they took us to Royal Melbourne Hospital, not to The Alfred where the emergency department was already overflowing with patients and ambos.

'She's had a new cerebellum bleed,' said the lead of three doctors.

'God, not again,' I responded as my face and body went into a cringe.

'Yes, it's the other side this time though,' he added.

'I guess we won't treat,' I said, falling into a deep depression. She had stabilised again. It depends on the definition of stable though. There was no CPAP or other intervention or anything else new or special to blame for this bleed.

'One other thing,' said the doctor. 'Has anyone ever said anything about cerebral amyloid angiopathy in relation to Nanette?'

'No, what's that?'

'It's a condition where you keep having bleeds.'

He kept describing it in more detail but by this time I wasn't listening. I could google it later if I needed to. I just chose to take my position sitting with Nan, waiting for what I presumed was inevitable.

'No one has ever said anything about that. The assumption was that she had undiagnosed high blood pressure.'

Nan stayed awake, unlike when she had the other cerebellum bleed. She was still holding my hand, still reaching out to me. Still raising her eyebrows when I spoke to her. Still capable of a little nod or shake. But the photos show her head thrown back, her brow furrowed and her eyes and face wearing a pained expression. There is no denying it.

Only a day later, she looked a little better and the day after that, she looked even better again. After a few days, the hospital wanted to discharge her. I asked that she stay in their care for the weekend, and they agreed.

The secretions were worse though. That's what the photos don't show. Photos weren't 'live' and didn't have audio then. I can hear the secretions now with every breath she was taking. She was receiving the glycopyrrolate, but it wasn't working as well. I was sitting in the small two-bed room in the hospital, and I started freaking out. I couldn't fix it, no matter what I did. The gurgling continued. It was mid-afternoon and I needed to get out. I went for a walk, and I rang Joan.

'I think all hope is lost, Joan. I don't think I can handle it anymore,' I admitted. I was feeling totally powerless. Totally overwhelmed. I think I just needed those words out. To experience the relief of saying them and then the guilt of admitting them out loud. I kept walking and talking.

'Oh David, you can't give up now,' Joan said.

'I won't. It's just very hard. I'm going to lose her. I love her more than life itself and I'm going to lose her.'

'Yes. That's life I suppose. There's not much we can do about it.'

It was like I had been to confession and confessed my sin. A sin of weakness like all sins are. Once confessed, I was absolved and went off again with a new tank of fuel. Of course, I went back to Nan after confession and smothered her with kisses and with love. That was my penance, but it was gratefully accepted.

We were discharged to the nursing home, and I became concerned about Nan at night when I wasn't there. I couldn't rely on the facility. It was no criticism of the individual nurses. There were two hundred residents, and they had a lot to do.

I contacted the agency that supplied Tecie and Rachel and asked whether the girls could be available overnight instead. They had other engagements, so two other nurses were sent to me, and I paid for them to sit with Nan for a few nights.

There had to be a better solution and I decided to ring Patricia, give her the update, and ask her what to do. She suggested we contact palliative care at Cabrini Health, which was a small facility nearby.

I spoke with a compassionate doctor from there and once he understood what was happening, he offered Nan a ten-day stay to see if they could get on top of the secretions again. I was very relieved. It meant Nan would be back in hospital care twenty-four hours a day.

* * *

Cabrini Palliative is a beautiful place. It is small and quiet. Only twenty-two beds, it exudes calm. The interior décor is stylish. There is dark wood panelling everywhere, the floors are carpeted and there is a library and open fireplace in the common area for patients and visitors. Patients' rooms are spacious and comfortable.

The care is outstanding. Palliative care doctors and registered nurses. No doubts on the capability or availability of those looking after Nan.

Occasionally I glimpse other patients. Obviously, they are dealing with tough, often end-of-life circumstances. Mostly cancer patients it seems. Next door to our room is a woman in her fifties. Occasionally I see her outside of her room in a wheelchair. Her family is there all the time. Husband, daughters. We nod to each other. One morning, the daughters leave the room. They are distressed and distracted. No one is nodding today. Then the husband. It is all over for them. The mother didn't look that bad when I saw her only a day or two before.

Nan is under the care of two female doctors. Jane is a registrar in her thirties. I like her. She's kind and personable. The consultant is very lovely too. I see less of her. Just a check-in every few days, but Jane is doing most of the running.

They decide to temporarily lift the level of glycopyrrolate to combat the secretions. They try putting it into the syringe driver to deliver it continuously. They are successful with the steps taken and Nan is soon doing better again. The secretions have eased. She's looking a lot more comfortable, and I know she is in excellent hands.

This is the kind of care I wish she had had the whole time. Here or the capability of Caulfield, but this is a much nicer place. It's like a health retreat for the terminally ill. Nan's life would have been better if she had had this level of care, and mine would have been easier as well.

Patrick arrives from Sydney to visit Nan and me at Cabrini. Between Nan's improved wellness, Patrick's company, and the vibe of Cabrini, I am feeling more relaxed. I don't want her to leave here and return to the nursing home. We have a couple of meals out and Pat spends plenty of time with Nan again.

After Patrick leaves, it's Easter. I find Nan to be the most responsive I've seen her in a long time. Her responses are speedy, her eyes are bright and sharp. She is very tuned in. Each time I ask her to do something, she completes it and then is eagerly awaiting the next request. Not only that, but she just looks so well.

My initial reaction is the high-quality care at Cabrini has given her an incredible lift in her wellbeing. But I can't quite believe that. She's too sharp. As I reflect on it, she is more like she was when she was on a much higher dose of amantadine some years ago. I wonder if the dosages of Keppra and amantadine have been mixed up, but when I ask, the nurse is certain she didn't.

We have a visit on Easter Sunday from Natasha, the head of palliative care. I instantly warm to her. She is so engaging to talk to. She spends forty minutes with us and it's Easter. Tecie is there. She and Rachel still wanted to come and help look after Nan. What a pair of sweethearts they are. Suddenly, Natasha, seeing Nan and I holding hands together, addresses Tecie.

'Look at this Tecie, this is love. This is real love. People want everything in life, but this is what love is about.' Tecie is looking at us. I start to tear up at the focus. It's love alright. No doubt about that. I love this one for sure.

'Oh, look at David,' says Tecie, smiling and stirring me a little. She had thought on first meeting me that I was a bit stern. Now she probably thinks I'm a sook. I'm embarrassed and wipe away a couple of tears and regain my composure.

Later that day we have a visit from Nan's brother Bruce and his wife Jo. They find Nan in good shape considering she's in a palliative care hospital.

We had agreed to go to a concert together. I said it depended on how Nan was but booked a ticket for me anyway. Quality care at Cabrini enabled me to make a choice like that.

We see Robert Plant of Led Zeppelin perform with his band. I've loved Zeppelin since my teen years, and they were a band I wished I had seen and haven't. This is the closest I would likely get to it. The show is amazing. Plant is in good voice despite pushing seventy.

* * *

Nan is discharged back to the nursing home just after Easter. Cabrini reported that she had gone well at night on the new medication regime, so I don't need to organise special night care. I ask that the night shift nurses keep an eye on her. Things seem more stable once again, but I'm wondering how long that will be the case.

I manage to organise a neurology clinic attendance with Richard to discuss what has happened. I don't take Nan this time. I ask him about the cerebral amyloid angiopathy the doctors reported at Royal Melbourne. Richard looks for the latest scans, but they aren't to be found. He finds one from a year before.

'Actually, look at this,' he says, turning his screen towards me. 'See all those little red dots,' as he points to what look like pen marks on the screen.

'Yes?'

'They are microbleeds,' Richard responds.

'Does that mean she has this condition?'

'It's possible,' he says.

It doesn't seem that he can be conclusive, and I'm later told that an autopsy is needed to diagnose it properly, but it would make sense to me that this might have been what was happening all this time.

Each one of those microbleeds could explain the days I found Nan totally wiped out. Not drastically changed or anything but looking very unwell. They might explain the occasional vomits she had before the cerebellum bleeds. They might explain the generally downward trajectory she seemed to have been on since she left Caulfield, or even since St George for that matter, where I witnessed her play back a memory from the day before. One of them might even explain that day in 2012, two years before the big stroke when she was so ill at our home in Albury.

She was vomiting and vomiting. She couldn't get out of bed she felt so sick. I was taking buckets to her. Jumped up, country-town doctors wouldn't make home visits and Nan wouldn't let me ring an ambulance. I wish that I had. They likely would have brain scanned her and maybe found something if there was something to find. Maybe put her on blood pressure medication. Maybe taken steps that avoided the big hit that was coming. Maybe let us off the hook. Maybe.

* * *

Nan seems stable again and life returns to our idea of normal; two fifty-somethings spending their lives in a nursing home. It sounds worse than it is. We are still together. At least I still have her. Tecie and Rachel continue coming to give me breaks. I play some music at home when I can with my friends Tom and Laura. I even attend a couple of gigs.

I have several psychological appointments with Caren. I began seeing her eighteen months earlier. Over that time, I was mostly letting off steam. Venting about the nursing home. Stressed about Nan.

When things were stable, Caren would encourage me to live a little, to take care of myself. That was hard for me to do. When they weren't, she had to be a wailing wall, an outlet for my stress, grief, trauma, fear. All those things. She knew there was no point in suggesting living a little then. I wouldn't do it.

I even have some landscape gardeners in to renovate the front courtyard at my apartment. They quoted on the work some time before Nan suffered the most recent bleed. It is only now that they can do the job.

A few weeks of calm before the storm. A storm that any weather forecaster would have been able to predict was coming but couldn't be accurate on when. Rather than heed such a warning, I deliberately put my head in the sand. Continued to dress in summer clothes and not take an umbrella you might say. Expecting something isn't knowing it, especially when you don't want to know it. In the meantime, I should enjoy what was left of the good weather. It was May after all. Sunny days, no rain to be seen.

The rain comes soon enough. There is a storm cloud building in the form of a large, pus-filled sore on Nan's arm. It's from the syringe driver needles and is the diameter of a tennis ball. Nan is looking unwell again, so I ask for her to be admitted to The Alfred. All is fine until the treating doctor learns that Nan is under palliative care. He evicts us. I am furious and make a complaint to the hospital some days later. What did it matter that she was under palliative care? She needed help and she is a member of the public and should therefore be treated in a public hospital.

I contact Cabrini and they accept her back again. Better to be there anyway and I am pleased she is under the same people as before. I show Jane the pus-filled sore, and she starts Nan on a course of antibiotics for an infection that turns out to be septicaemia.

I also discuss feeding with Jane. I tell her it is so hard to get food into Nan now without her vomiting. I'm worried we will be starving her to death.

'Doesn't that place her at greater risk of organ failure and blindness and a whole host of other issues?' I ask.

'We need very little food to just exist like she is doing. She is not going to starve to death. Don't worry about that. That's not an issue. It's a case of feeding her a little so that she isn't feeling hungry,' Jane responds.

I'm reminded of a discussion with Rohan at The Alfred where he asked me whether I thought Nan would get hungry if we stopped feeding her. I resisted it, assuming it meant giving up, but it was probably aimed at reducing the vomiting. That was a year ago now and I wasn't ready to lose her. I'm not ready to lose her now either. I never will be, but it's coming.

We have several visitors. My sister Michelle and her husband Bernard, who I spoke to that day of the first stroke, were travelling in regional

Victoria and made the trip to Melbourne. Tam and Cherilyn drop in as well. They haven't seen Nan during the illness, but they have kept in good contact with me, and I've been to dinner with them several times. They are a little overwhelmed at the change in Nan from the youthful and happy, dark-haired beauty that they last saw some years back.

Patricia, Nan's doctor from the nursing home, also visits. She is shocked by the change in Nan, and it's only been six or eight weeks since she last saw her. I am with Nan all the time, so I haven't noticed the changes as they've happened. I'm surprised to hear Patricia say this in fact, but when I look back on the photos now, I see what she meant. Nan's head is thrown back, her mouth open, her cheeks are drawn and there is a pained expression on her face. All these are little shocks along the way, harbingers of what is coming.

And then it comes. Sunday morning, my phone rings and it's a nurse at Cabrini. She tells me that Nan is not well this morning. She asks me whether I will be in. Of course, I will. I'm always there.

I arrive within thirty minutes, and they are in the process of getting Nan up into her chair or for a shower. She looks so unwell that we all agree she should go back to bed. Her eyes are bloodshot, and she looks sick. She is only just conscious. I am very unnerved by the sight of her.

They return her to bed and make her comfortable and she quickly falls into a deep sleep or is unconscious. I let her rest for a while and then see if I can wake her. I cannot, so clearly, she is unconscious, not asleep. I decide to leave her be.

The consultant doctor arrives and when we discuss it, she thinks Nan has had some event, most probably another stroke. We can only wait and see what happens now.

I ring Jill and put her on notice once again that Nan has taken another step backwards. Perhaps I should have said forwards to a new destination. Pick your euphemism.

I wait and wait. I'm becoming convinced that she has had a stroke. They come out of nowhere. She can seem comfortable and settled and then bang. But she is dealing with a lot now. I think her brain is like a damaged dam wall, structurally weakened by previous events and now giving way completely. She has fought back so many times, I still think she will. She has been indestructible. She's even defied Paul's estimation and lived another year.

It's not until 4pm, seven hours since I got there that she suddenly wakes. Those big blue eyes are on display. They shine like the brightest gemstones, windows to her beautiful soul. She looks at me and raises her eyebrows in a kind of hello that you do when you wake in the morning next to your bed mate. I reach over and kiss her and give my usual acts of devotion to her. She looks very rested from being unconscious so long. I ring Jill and tell her Nan is back again.

Jill and Frank arrive the next day to visit. Nan is in the chair and looking OK-ish. The consultant doctor and Jane arrive for a review. I had previously thought that Nan was responsive since she woke, but try as I might, I can't get her to do anything now. No thumbs up, no pointing, no tongue pokes, no nod or shake. Nothing. I feel like a charlatan exposed.

It seems she has taken another hit from whatever happened on the Sunday. She still does seem attentive to what we are saying, but she's not moving at all. I'm sure she is totally paralysed now. Jill and Frank stay for the day and then head home to Warrnambool.

Left alone with my now unresponsive and immobilised Nanny, I know Paul's prophecy is about to be realised. It's significantly later than he thought. That's down to her amazing strength and will, and perhaps also to our love for each other. I'm not sure that she's hanging on just because she thinks I can't be without her. I think she's hanging on because she wants to stay with me too. I think she has a fierce will to live and to love.

I'm going to lose her though. I know it. I can't use the 'D' word. I never can say it about Nan. I feel myself plunging into a deep despair.

The despair mutates like a COVID-19 variant into panic. I'm freaking out. I need to talk to someone, but I can't let anyone see me this weak. I reach out to Caren. A professional. She already knows me inside out and we've talked about everything.

'Caren, I'm going to lose her. I know it. I can't handle it. I've done everything I can but it's not enough. I can't live without her. I love her,' I blurt out. There are no tears, but there is plenty of exasperation, panic, and despair. Caren can hear it and in turn, I hear her sigh.

'David, you've known this is coming. For some time.'

'Knowing, expecting yeah, but not perhaps believing it. She kept stabilising. It always gave me hope. Always gave me the belief that she would beat anything.'

'No one can beat everything. She's been through an enormous amount.'

'I can't be without her. I can't lose her.'

'You will adjust. You will need to rebuild your life. It will take time, but you will get there.'

'I don't want to adjust and rebuild. I want Nan,' is my petulant but truthful response.

I go silent while Caren tries to help me accept it and relax. We speak for maybe twenty minutes while she talks me down. She manages to do that. It's the talking and being heard and expressing terrible sentiments that build up inside. Expressing them like we do with a poisonous boil or like Nan's septicaemic abdominal sore.

* * *

'It's started David,' the nurse says to me. 'Feel her feet and her hands. Her extremities are getting cold.' I put my hand under the sheets and feel for myself. She is right, they are cold. I didn't know that was how 'it' started. Nan lays unconscious on the bed under her oxygen mask, turned to her right side.

'I want to stay the night please,' I add. They had offered that I could.

'I'll get the sofa bed organised for you.'

'Thanks.'

The nurse leaves the room to go about her other tasks and I'm there with Nanny. She's been unconscious for three days now. I haven't seen her with her eyes open since Friday. The doctors told me that pneumonia has set in, and they upped the morphine dose again the last few days. They come in each day and listen to her chest.

There's my darling. My little angel. The love of my life, my wife, best friend, and soul mate. She's at the end. I know it's time now. She's been unresponsive for a week and a half since I'm sure she had a new stroke. We didn't send her off for a scan to check this time. There was no point. It's clear to me she has lost all function. Movement, responsiveness, consciousness are all gone. I said I would know when the time would be, and I know it's now. I don't want it to be, but my precious darling has been through enough.

'We are keeping her now, David. We aren't sending her back to the nursing home,' the consultant tells me, to allay my fears on that front. It is both good news and of course bad news. There is only one reason you are not leaving a palliative care unit.

Nan's been sick with septicaemia and the antibiotics are not working. There is another pus-filled sore on her abdomen and two now on her arms. Jane squeezed an enormous amount of pus out of her abdominal sore a few days back.

'I love you Nanny,' I tell her as I sit to her right and hold her hand. My other hand is on her head and stroking her forehead and shoulders. She remains motionless. I tell her I love her countless times during the evening. It's a repeated prayer of devotion. Hail Mary's said ten times in a decade. I wonder if she can hear. I hope she is having a near-death experience and can. I thank her for our lives together and wish that I could go with her, or she could stay with me. I wish she was well again.

There is nothing to do but wait now. The nurse returns with the foldout bed, and I help her make it up. I have an overnight bag with me in case I decided to stay. I change into my pyjamas and go to Nan, tell her I love her again and then get into the foldout bed next to hers.

There is enough light in the room to see Nan and I turn to my side and look at her. I don't really want to go to sleep. I feel I should be awake for her last remaining hours or minutes or however long we have. Am I like the biblical apostles in the garden of Gethsemane? Sleeping on the job?

It's almost the complete opposite. I sleep fitfully, waking every hour and checking on her. I get out of bed each time and walk around to see if she is still breathing. I stroke her and tell her I love her and then get back into bed and try and sleep for another hour.

When I wake just before 6am, I notice Nan's torso is making a regular but unusual and small movement. It seems her brain and lungs have stopped breathing, but no one has told her body yet and it limps on valiantly. I know it is the very end. As I watch, even that movement stops, and I know she's gone.

I get out of the bed and check. I speak to her and tell her I love her once more. It doesn't matter that she's gone and I'm saying that. I've been saying it ever since.

I wait a few minutes with her. I can't believe I'm alone without her for the first time in thirty-five years. She's here but she's not. The next and final step downwards in the taking of her by strokes. Memories are flooding back already. I'm missing her already. I'm missing both my Nans, pre-stroke and post-stroke.

I decide to buzz the nurses to tell them, and one arrives. I inform her and she tells me she will be back with another nurse to help her. As I sit there waiting, I notice Nan's eyes are open. She looks like she is in a daze, staring at something in the distance. She looks different. Like someone else. She doesn't look like Nan anymore.

When the two nurses return, they ask for some time with Nan. I'm not sure what they want to do exactly, but I leave the room and sit out in the lounge room near the fire. Several of the other nurses come over and express their condolences and I thank them for both that and their outstanding care while we have been here. Someone brings me a Coke. It's early for that, not even 7am yet, but I'm tired from the night and it will give me a boost.

When it's 7am, I ring Jill to let her know what's happened and she expresses her sympathy and tells me she will inform Joan. I can't talk to her and don't want to talk to anyone else. I just want to be alone with my thoughts. I'd like to be back in the room with Nan. I compose a text to advise siblings and key friends.

The nurses are finished with Nan, and I can return to the room. I notice they have closed her eyes and wrapped a towel around her throat, I guess so her mouth doesn't drop open while I'm there. Nan's passing is more final now that her eyes are closed. It does seem like she is gone.

I need to wait a while to sign a death certificate and Jane brings it to me and offers her condolences. I contact a funeral director who will come and collect her and then I decide it's time to leave. I kiss Nan goodbye and tell her I love her and leave for home.

The greatest person of my life has left me. I feel alone in every way. Much love Nanny.

PART
THREE

AFTERWARDS

I am now in my second life. I didn't want it. Although I knew it was coming, I wasn't ready for it. I was too busy wrapping up the first one.

It's now August 2021, more than three years since I lost Nan, and almost seven years to the day since her stroke. Soon, I will have had as long without her as I had with her during her illness. How can that be? Time hasn't passed more quickly because I was having fun.

After the funeral was over, I was incredibly fatigued. It stayed with me for weeks. It was as deep as any jetlag I have experienced. I had been sleeping badly for a long time, but each night I fell into a deep sleep that was difficult to wake from. Even when the first light realisation that Nan was gone rose as regularly as the sun, I struggled to wake from the stupor.

'I think you have been running on fear and adrenaline for four years. Now it's over, you are realising how exhausted you are,' Caren observed at our first session after the funeral. Well, that was part of it, but not all of it; my mind and body realising there was nothing more I could do now and finally relenting. Giving in. It was over. As Paul said, I had fought a battle, but I had lost.

As much as anything, it was the sadness. Sadness was a drain down which energy, life, purpose and meaning disappeared. Sadness for losing her, but just as great was the sadness for her own loss. She was too young to go. She should have had so much more life to live. Too good, too talented, too kind. The world doesn't need less Nanettes, it needs more of them.

I am starting over, trying to build a life again from scratch. I have financial security and I have family and friends, but none of that is enough. I am trying to piece it together. Trying to find a new path.

My second life so far looks nothing like my first. I had good jobs in a successful corporate career. Then when Nanette became ill, I looked after her. It was stressful, but more meaningful than any paid work. I tried a couple of contract jobs in 2019 after Nan passed. They were short term government roles. Twenty days each. At the end of each, I had been well-paid, but the work had been pointless.

I had a great wife for three decades. After a while, loneliness and the absence of a close companion got the better of me. I dated and had some girlfriends but nothing that lasted anything more than a few months. I met a lot of other women in between those short relationships, each of us tyre kicking the other to pressure test and see if we had enough grip. Some of the 'no go's' would accurately conclude I wasn't ready. Sometimes I would tell them that if it wasn't obvious.

I had to learn to feed myself. Nan had been the cook. I started initially with Lite 'n' Easy deliveries. It is well named. The food was certainly easy and there is choice. Delivered weekly and microwaved into life when I wanted it. But it was too light for me. The meals left me feeling hungry, and I would load up on unhealthy options like chocolate or biscuits to supplement them.

Eventually with the help of my elder sister Christine, I started to become more self-sufficient, adding a few items to my virtually non-existent repertoire. Bacon and eggs, some roasts with vegetables where I followed the prescription Nan gave me ('If ever anything happens to me,' she had foretold), home-made pizzas, then some pasta dishes with prosciutto or chicken. I bought a large pan that would enable me to combine meat and vegetables into curries, stir-fries, or dishes with rice.

Before Nan's illness, I was never much of a drinker at all, but after she died, I drank more. Self-medicating. Evenings I felt the absence and the pain the most. A gin and tonic at 5pm every day. I realise now it was probably three standard drinks on its own. I poured to what looked like the right quantity. Then sometimes a little bit more. There would be multiple wines with dinner and afterwards while watching TV. It helped. I needed to be numbed.

Two months after Nan passed, I was worked up as I ate my lunch. I mustn't have chewed enough, and part of the food got stuck in my oesophagus. I went to the toilet and used the two-finger method to try and vomit it up. Multiple vomits, but it was still stuck. It was extremely uncomfortable and unpleasant and felt like my chest was going to explode.

After a couple of hours of vomiting, and even jumping up and down, I walked across Fawkner Park to the Alfred Emergency department. Every now and then I needed to stop and puke, first checking that nobody was watching. When I got to the hospital, I spoke to admissions then told the woman I needed to go and vomit.

It was only four months since I had been in this very department when Nan was the patient. The sights and sounds were too familiar and evoked painful memories of her just to remind me she was gone. I didn't need any reminders.

This time, it was me who was having a medical problem. I'd been Nanette's carer for four years, but I had no one. Nanette wasn't there when I needed her like she had been in the past. I didn't want to ask a neighbour or friends for help. My niece Elodie would have been at work. This is the sort of thing that your partner does for you. Or your kids if you have them. I thought it was way too tragic to impose on anyone else.

When I was eventually examined by a young doctor, I told her what had happened with Nan. I knew I was more prone to this problem when under stress. She asked me several pertinent questions.

'Do you drink?' she asked in a matter-of-fact way.

'Yes.'

'How many standard drinks per day?'

'I guess about half a dozen at the moment,' I replied, knowing it was more than I used to drink, but not thinking it was that excessive.

'Oh,' she responded a little surprised. 'We will monitor how you go overnight. See if you experience any withdrawal.' She looked me right in the eyes as she made that point.

'What? Surely, it's not that much? My dad drank twice that for decades. I've only been drinking more these last few months.' Well, I guess it could have been longer.

'It is quite a lot, and you know that red wine contributes to this kind of problem.'

'Yes …'

After seven or eight hours, I knew the food bolus had cleared itself. I had nothing more to throw up other than stomach juices. They kept me in overnight and thought it was best to conduct a procedure the next day to ensure the bolus was gone. The hospital was busy, and I slept on a short bed in an upright position in emergency. My legs dangled over the end causing me a lot of discomfort in my calves the next day.

They gave me a general anaesthetic and checked it out. They confirmed when I woke that it had cleared. I was taken back to a ward to recover and be observed until it was time to leave. Once in the ward, I got talking to the nurse who was looking after me.

'Have you got someone to pick you up?' she asked.

'Actually, no I haven't. I only live across Fawkner Park. I'm recently widowed and I don't have any kids.'

'How did you get here when you came in?'

'I walked over.' After a pause I added, 'I really don't want to involve anyone else.'

'I'm supposed to ensure that someone collects you, or you get a taxi home. But you seem to be a sensible man. You do what you think.'

'Thanks, I will.'

When discharged, I hobbled back across Fawkner Park to my apartment. My calves were aching. I was tired from not much sleep and a general anaesthetic, but none of these were as acutely painful as the sadness of feeling bitterly alone. Being July, it was cold and damp. Even the weather was inhospitable. When I got home, I poured a stiff gin.

I don't want to give the impression that nobody cared, and nobody provided support. The reality is I had a lot of support from those around me. My siblings, Jill and Frank, Patrick, John and Jenny, Peewee, Ian and Barbara, Andrew and Ingrid, Tam and Cherilyn and plenty of others. Unfortunately, those closest to me were physically remote, and siblings and close friends have their own lives and own families to attend to. You don't spend every day with them. You might see or talk to them weekly, but they aren't at home with you in the evenings.

What was missing was an immediate family. It had been Nan and me and no children. That equation was OK while things were fine in life, but there was a lack of redundancy in the event of the passing of one of the partners. It would fail even something as unfeeling as a corporate security test. Single points of failure. Where is the fallback? It's a high stakes gamble to rely heavily and almost exclusively on one other and Nan won that bet by being first to go. I lost it.

The support slowed down after a few months. The phone wasn't ringing or pinging as often, and people were visiting less too. Caren thought it was quite normal.

'You're at the three-month mark,' she pointed out. 'That's what happens. Support dries up at around this time and it's no doubt earlier than you're ready for it. People move on. You won't want to hear this, but you will need to think about how to rebuild your life. I know it's actually a little early to think about that, because you're in the middle of heavy grief, but it's something to tuck away in your mind.'

I winced. I hated the thought of a life without Nanette and rebuilding anything without her. It felt disloyal, like I would be moving on and forgetting her. I didn't of course.

I did a pretty good job of keeping myself busy in those early days. I tried to have something to do each day. Even if it was mundane like getting my car serviced. Something that made me get out and interact. I planned some trips away to see Jill and Frank in Warrnambool and Patrick and Steve, and John and Jenny in Sydney.

Music became a new purpose. A stand-in partner. A life raft with a pilot that happened along at the right moment when lost in heavy seas. Something I loved doing and wanted to do again after Nan passed. It wasn't like the first fifteen months of her illness where I couldn't bring myself to play. This time, I wanted to play. I needed to play.

The engagement of my mind and my body working in concert. The cool, smooth feel of the keys beneath my fingertips. The instant feedback of sound upon their depress. The varying harmonic possibilities of major, minor, or dominant. The happy marriage of consonance and dissonance working in tandem. Too much of one is boring. Too much of the other is unpleasant. This was my church to turn to. My solace.

The pilot of the life raft was Lana, my classical piano teacher. I had been taking lessons from her for almost two years when Nan passed. I wanted to improve my technique. I wanted some structure around my playing. Something to aim at. I wanted to be able to play Bach. My technique was poor, my hands old and my progress slow when I started. Our lessons had to stop when Nan had medical setbacks. They would restart when stability returned.

I rang Lana and asked to restart lessons only three weeks after Nan's passing. We met at her place at my regular Friday afternoon timeslot. I climbed the three flights of stairs to her apartment, and she greeted me with a hug.

'I am so sorry for your loss David. I know how much Nanette meant to you,' she said. 'I was surprised when you wanted to come back so soon, but Michael (Lana's husband) predicted you would.'

Lana the life raft pilot was there with a map to find a way out when I arrived. The map was the Australian Music Examinations Board syllabus.

'David, I think we should work towards an exam this year. I recommend you aim for the Certificate of Performance. There are no scales and arpeggios and I know you don't like the technical work. It's a recital exam. Around thirty minutes of playing.'

I instantly liked the idea. I hadn't been playing, so there wasn't much we could do that day. We started discussing repertoire to work on. Having taught all the grades to a lot of students, Lana knew the pros and cons of the various pieces and their suitability for various students.

It gave me structure and purpose. I had a lot to do to be ready. We had about six months. Lana, an ex-concert pianist who had studied in Moscow and the U.S., had high standards, an enormous amount to impart and an impeccable record when her students sat exams. She was just what I needed.

I would attend my weekly lesson with Lana on Fridays and work for hours each day trying to get my Mozart sonata, Moscheles etude, Scriabin studies and Bach prelude ready. As the exam approached, I lifted my load to three to four hours per day practise.

Soon after we started, Lana told me of a forthcoming all-Bach piano concert at the Melbourne Recital Centre. She knew I loved Bach and I told her I would go along. The pianist was Kristian, a friend of Lana's. I was amazed at the complexity of what he played.

As I watched and listened, I reflected that classical piano performances are like bullfights. A fight to the death. The matador walks into the ring to take on a 400 kilogram, nine-feet long behemoth in front of an audience that wants to see the beast slain by its master. This beast can deliver brute power but beauty, delicacy, sophistication and emotion as well. It can't be slain. It can only be accommodated. It can be played to the limits of human endurance and capability. When the matador is exhausted it will still be there, ready to fight again, perhaps only in need of a tune up or other basic maintenance. Any misstep by the matador will result in a goring by press and public. High stakes game.

Halfway through the performance, Kristian took a break and addressed the audience. He thanked us for coming and talked about his program. He then acknowledged that a student of Lana's who had been through a lot was in the audience. He said he hoped that the concert would help in the healing and offered that I come and say hello afterwards. I did that. I was deeply touched by this event.

As the exams approached, Lana arranged that I have a couple of lessons with Kristian, who came to my apartment each time. He was very kind and very helpful. He had an amazing ability to instantly see new solutions to musical problems. *Genius level problem solving* I thought.

Somehow, Lana and Kristian managed to drag an old guy with 'old hands' over the line and I passed the exam. I didn't set the world on fire, but it was very meaningful to me. I know it improved my technique and musical appreciation. Mostly though, it gave me a way through that very difficult first six months.

Around that time, I also auditioned and was accepted into Monash University to study jazz piano, thanks to the help of a nice young guy Lana had recommended. Nick is based in New York City and our weekly lessons were conducted online. He put me in touch with a bassist and drummer who came to my place for some rehearsals and accompanied me for the audition.

I tried working and through my mate Tam, landed the two short government consulting roles. In the first there was a laughable series of exits from the CEO, my manager's manager, and then my manager himself within two weeks of my arrival. It left me with no sponsors nor recipients for the work I was doing. When they all disappeared, I witnessed a risible quest for power by several contractors. It was a team without direction, without leadership and without certainty. Most ridiculous was seeing the contractors think that leadership should be by committee of the entire team.

In the second contract, I was dealing with an arrogant and difficult board of directors. There were too many of them for a department of this size, and none of them had any real corporate IT knowledge or experience, yet they scrambled all over me at the first presentation to tell me that they wanted a stand-alone IT facility – no dependence on other departments and the ability to make all their own strategic decisions.

This was an idiotic position, motivated by hubris and bitterness. I tried to tell them but was shouted down. Fortunately, the contract only lasted a month, and I found a way through it that satisfied them and preserved some of my own dignity. In the end they didn't have the funding to do anything anyway.

I didn't get the same arguments at the next meeting, but by then, their shit had fed my shit and my bowel was out of control. The timing also coincided with Nan's first anniversary. Of course, that contributed. I was going eight times a day. I couldn't eat anything without needing to rush to the toilet within minutes. This went on for months.

I had recently had a colonoscopy when this started so I went back to the gastroenterologist. He decided to conduct a sigmoidoscopy (like a colonoscopy but they don't go up as far) to take another look. Again, I didn't want to ask anyone else to come along, so I elected to have it done without anaesthetic. He told me that it was very manageable and that in the U.K., colonoscopies were often done this way.

Easy for him to say. Between the nurse giving me an enema and him shoving what felt like both arms and a fire hose up my arse, I decided once and for all that I did not have a penchant for anal intimacy. The procedure didn't find any cause and my problem was therefore lumped into that broad category of irritable bowel syndrome or IBS.

By mid-2019, I decided I'd had enough of work for the time being. Those contract experiences left me feeling as violated as the sigmoidoscopy. I had been through enough. Why would I want to subject myself to unpleasant situations if I didn't need to? These and another contract experience in Melbourne some time earlier made me wonder about the level of capability here. And the level of arrogance. I retreated to the sanctity and serenity of my apartment and my piano, and the reassurance of proximity to my own toilet where I spent many hours of devotion.

* * *

In July 2019, my mother became very ill and in September she died. She had a chronic lung condition and kept contracting pneumonia. She was in her ninetieth year, and she had had enough, resisting any further treatment.

She was a kind and compassionate person. She was tolerant and accepting, but not a pushover. Calm, but could anger and be formidable. Strong and resilient yet could be emotional. Very good and very human. Self-sacrificing, she was well-qualified for motherhood, and was a good mother.

I delivered the eulogy at Mum's funeral. I was sad to lose her, but she'd had a good, long life. This is how things are supposed to be. It was impossible to not draw the comparison with losing Nan at only fifty-seven. The truth is the greatest sadness I felt at that time was for Nan. It had never left me, and Mum's passing ignited it again.

After this, I set myself an objective to play a jazz piano trio gig. I worked up enough standards and located a good jazz drummer and jazz bassist to play with. We played in December at the Arcadia Hotel near where I live. Jill and Frank, my sisters Christine and Michelle, my niece Elodie, my cousin Brendan, and several friends from Melbourne all turned up to watch. It was a sympathetic audience.

We did two sets. About fifteen jazz standards with solos from each of us, and it went well. Once calm and comfortable, I enjoyed the experience, floating on top of a powerful and proficient rhythm section. Improvisatory freedom within a framework of harmony and structure. It was a very uplifting thing to do, and I took a while to come down afterwards. The high lasted for a few days.

The experience gave me more confidence and enthusiasm about starting the Monash music degree. It was now or never, and I was out of ideas for any better alternatives for 2020. I decided to enrol part time. Classes were to start in March.

In January, my friends John and Jenny decided to come to the Australian Open. John had played a lot of his adult life. I wasn't a tennis fan, but they bought me a ticket to accompany them to a men's open quarter final. It was Rafael Nadal v Dominic Thiem.

My impression of tennis was that it was played by spoilt brats who were overpaid and behaved badly. I found the sport boring to watch on TV. Too repetitive. The same people always won. I went along in good humour though, thinking it would probably be better to watch live.

My whole view of the game was changed that night. I had no idea how hard they hit the ball. It was so athletic. The shots played were amazing and they fought for the win like any sport at the elite level; like their lives depended on it. Another fight to the death.

John hadn't seen tennis at this level live either and we looked across at one another after breathtaking rallies or unbelievable shots and shook our heads in amazement.

Thiem prevailed in four sets, and we filed out of Rod Laver Arena at close to midnight feeling both elated and exhausted, as though we had played and won!

'It was a slugfest!' John exclaimed merrily as we walked home.

'One of the best live sporting events I have ever witnessed in my life!' I replied. We continued talking about it enthusiastically as we made our way home.

I reflect on fights to the death. People throwing their absolute all at a cause. Leaving nothing to chance. No stone unturned. Playing as though their own lives really were dependent on the outcome. It's hyperbole to think that concert pianists or all elite sportspeople are actually in a fight to the death. There is certainly a lot riding for them on what they do. Why were these situations so appealing to me? I then realised that's what it was like looking after Nanette.

It had been a fight to the death. Not in the usual way. Not against each other at all. With each other. A fight to avoid death and keep life, but a fight until the death of one of us, nonetheless. Nothing else really mattered.

When I woke up the next morning after that thrilling tennis experience, I decided to take tennis lessons. There were courts near my home and I thought it might be fun to try, an opportunity to meet people and good exercise. I began lessons soon after, around the time I began my classes at Monash, March 2020.

The day of my first music class on campus, I drove to Clayton, telling myself not to worry about being forty years older than the other students. When I arrived, I felt very self-conscious. On orientation day, I had been twice mistaken for an academic and had to explain that I was one of the students.

At the end of that one day, the threat of COVID-19 had become too much for governments and institutions to bear, and it was decided that all classes would be delivered online. This wasn't a great outcome for jazz education, which is very much about the experience of playing with others.

My phone rang one Saturday evening at the start of the semester. On the other end I heard a gentle, female voice who introduced herself as Vashti. Vashti had been assigned as my piano teacher for the first semester at Monash. I was impressed that she rang, and that we talked for thirty minutes about where my playing was at and what goals I hoped to achieve musically. She didn't talk about herself at all. I immediately liked her.

When our lessons started, they were conducted via Zoom sessions due to COVID-19. It worked well with a one-on-one piano lesson. A few lessons in, we settled into an easy comfort with each other and began talking about music we had heard or how we were going with COVID-19.

When the first lockdown ended, I invited Vashti over for my lesson and dinner. When we met in person, we talked for four hours. We listened to music, each of us taking turns to select tracks. Vashti is a deep listener. She would hear things I wouldn't notice. She likes percussion. I like basslines. The next time together, it was six hours. We were united by our deep love of music, but our friendship evolved beyond that.

Our conversations extended well beyond music to cover our families, our backgrounds, past relationships, current politics and of course, COVID-19 and lockdowns. Vashti was interested in what happened with Nan and the length and happiness of our relationship.

Our discussions often ventured into the search for meaning, beliefs, spiritualism and what happens after this. She told me that she sometimes visits a psychic. I was always an arch sceptic, but this, coming from a person of Vashti's undoubted intelligence and integrity, made me think. I wondered if I could have contact with Nan. Anything that made me feel she was out there somewhere waiting for me. What if and why not try? My interest was pricked, and I was more open to any possibility like this.

SEARCHING

There'd been enough tragedy in Joan's life before Nan became ill. Joan and her husband Bob had four children. Nan was the youngest, but not the first to pass. Stephanie was the eldest child and she and her husband Rob were killed in a car accident in 2003. Jill and Bruce remain.

Joan suffers from Retinitis Pigmentosa: a progressive eye condition that left her legally blind. R.P. is passed on genetically, and Bruce has the condition as well.

Bob died of a heart attack in 1999. Between 1999 and 2014, Nan became Joan's primary carer. The relationship was more than that. They were very close. Joan confessed to me that losing Nanette was even harder than the loss of her husband Bob.

Nan checked on Joan three times a day, either in person or by phone. Morning, lunch, and evening, before bed. Nan took her to medical appointments and out for amusement, did her grocery shopping for her, and even picked up her cigarettes and alcohol. In later years, she made food for her as well. Nan was always thinking of how she could help, how she could make Joan's life better.

Nan and Joan operated two retail businesses together in the 1980s and 1990s. They ran those shops side-by-side for years. After Bob died, Nan began using his workshop for her art. She would spend hours there working and talking with Joan.

When I was asked to move overseas for my job, Nan wouldn't go without Joan and Joan wouldn't go. Nan believed she may not have much longer with Joan and that we should maximise our time together with the ones we love. It was Nan that didn't have much longer. Nan made the right decision, but I think for the wrong reason. I thought we should take the opportunities presented, but I'm glad Nan didn't become ill in another country. In the end, it was the right reason and right outcome for her, and that is what matters.

Soon after Nan passed, Joan and I began talking regularly by phone. Before long it was three times a week. Most days we talked for thirty minutes or more. The rest of the world had moved more quickly to a post-Nan life, but Joan and I weren't ready. We kept her alive talking mostly about her. Remembering what she was like, remembering times with her.

We asked how the other was going, and our answers would be the same. There was a huge hole in both of our lives. Our favourite person was gone. The conversations were often repetitive and probably would have bored someone not so enthusiastic about the subject matter, but we weren't bored. We didn't want to let her go.

It was a poker game of fanaticism. Joan would talk of Nanette's intelligence. I would see that bid telling of her huge vocabulary. I would say how kind and caring she was, Joan would say she seemed intuitive about people's needs. Joan described Nan as sometimes tough and not allowing her to get away with things, I would agree she could be stubborn. Each of us would tell a favourite anecdote. All this was keeping Nan as real and as vivid in our minds as we possibly could. We didn't want to give her up. We wanted to keep her. I knew with Joan there was no limit to how much I could talk about Nan. I knew with others there was a limit and I exceeded it. Our relationship was completely mended. We were both lost and very alone without Nan. We were truly united in our grief.

In June 2019, more than a year after Nan passed, Jill found Joan collapsed at her home in Warrnambool. Jill lives across the street and called an ambulance.

The hospital did the usual assortment of tests and discovered Joan had a heart condition, but more significantly, she had suffered multiple small strokes. Vascular dementia was diagnosed. The strokes had occurred over years and no doubt had been affecting her behaviour. The hospital found her difficult to manage and a decision was made to medicate her.

The many conversations I had with Joan after Nan's passing helped us both deal with the loss of Nan. As did my many counselling sessions with Caren.

* * *

I've often experienced anxiety in my adult life. It hasn't been crippling, but it has been a nuisance. Working myself into a lather, losing large amounts of sleep. Much of it related to work and the anticipation of things that never happened. On reflection a lot of it was trivial, but I obsessed and amplified the importance of it. Worry and anxiety are like that. They engulf you and they don't seem trivial when you are dealing with them, only in retrospect.

The experience of caring for and worrying about Nan compacted another lifetime of anxiety into those four years. At least my anxiety there was well-placed. It really was life and death stuff. I don't begrudge any personal toll I took for her. She was the person I loved the most and she could no longer decide for herself. I would do anything for her. Loved the very bones of her.

It was tricky; I didn't know Nan's mind unless I probed, and I couldn't always get there then. She wouldn't volunteer that something was wrong. Richard said the first stroke damaged that part of her brain responsible for initiation. I had to read the signs and then question her to narrow things down. When I went home in the evenings, I had to entrust her to whatever care facility she was in and hope for the best. The phone only rang a few times at night, and that was terrifying, but the worry of something going wrong always lingered.

I've been seeing Caren for psychological counselling sessions for over four years now. Our focus has varied with the stages of Nan. When I first went, I was Nan's carer. Then I lost her. Now Caren helps me along the way in search of my second life.

Recently, I've seen Caren more frequently. Fortnightly in fact. I like her. She's my age, a long-term Melburnian, and of Jewish descent which gives her a natural pedigree for this stuff. Perhaps that's also why she has a good sense of humour. She's helped me through the hardest times of my life. She knows when to support and when to disagree. We have argued and we've laughed. The best source of our laughs is often my dating, but there was a memorable day when she tried to coach me through mindfulness.

'Imagine your consciousness as a big blue sky and your thoughts like passing clouds,' she suggested with good intention.

'Puffy clouds?' I asked sarcastically and with a smile.

She looked at me and saw all hope was lost. 'Sorry, I just remembered you don't do twee!'

Caren is not judgemental, I have complete trust in her confidentiality, and she 'welcomes profanity', I guess as an assistant to venting. It's just as well.

Her office is a kilometre from my home, and today I walked there for my session. She works in a clinic located in an old building, along with several other practitioners including psychologists and psychiatrists.

I was getting over a cold. I decided to grab a drink of water while I waited for Caren, and as I headed to the tap, I was overcome with an urge to cough. It came out of nowhere. As I exploded into my cough, a tall, bespectacled man emerged from an office right in front of me and recoiled in horror as though I was plague-ridden.

'It's OK. It's just a cold. I was COVID-19 tested last week,' I explained to him. By this time, he was walking down the stairs to get as far away as he could, peering at me in disgust as though I was a leper. A bad-mannered leper at that.

'It only takes four hours to contract COVID-19,' he cautioned me, carefully emphasising each syllable with his hands for effect.

Oh, for fuck's sake, I thought. There were zero cases in the state at the time.

Caren was by this stage standing at her door watching and I shook my head and rolled my eyes as I walked into her room.

'What was that all about?' she asked.

As I recounted what happened, I extended vigorous two finger signs in his direction after he had gone.

'That's Jerome. He's a psychiatrist here,' she responded.

'Maybe I could give him a consult. Jerome, get on the couch. Now, get over yourself and get on with it. Shit …' I shook my head in disbelief.

Caren stifled a laugh, not wanting to be too amused at the expense of her colleague.

'He's a nice man,' she said.

'He's a little paranoid. I hope he checks that at the door when his patients come in.' Turning to business, Caren asked me how I was.

'I want to review where I am now against when I first came to see you and then against how I was when Nan passed. I wonder whether I'm doing any better. Life just seems so fucking empty. I have tried new things each year. I haven't found my new purpose. In the past, I knew what the next few years looked like, and there was a sense of stability or continuity. I don't feel that now.'

'David, this was always going to be the issue for you. You've had your whole life stripped away from you. You had a good career and that went and you had a great wife and now she is gone too. You have to rebuild. You must keep trying things. Some things will work for you and others won't. Look at tennis. You enjoy that. That's a new thing. You need to get into a social comp. What have you done about mentoring work?'

'I've been interviewed and reference-checked, and I'm about to be trained.'

'Good. You need to keep working at it. What about playing golf or joining a men's club?'

'I'd rather be dead,' I responded. 'I don't like golf and I can't think of anything worse than being in some men's club listening to a group of blowhards bragging about themselves. Nothing is of interest, Caren. I can't get started. Anyway, I mostly prefer the company of women now. I'm sure it's from losing Nan. So, how have I made progress? In many ways, things seem just as hard now as years ago. I know it's not the same. I'm not dealing with the terror, or the extreme grief, although the grief is still there. But I don't feel I'm progressing.'

'That's not true. You have made progress. You've got music. You are trying to write. You have tennis. It's a pity in a way that you don't need a job, David. It's also not that long. You were together for so long. It's just three years since you lost her.'

'You say I have to rebuild my life and friends. But I think that's just plugging gaps. It's not a solution. I still feel a void without Nanette. It's such a huge hole. I don't think friends and acquaintances can plug that. Your partner is the one constant. The one who is always there for you. The one who has your back. You can be at home doing your own things. It doesn't matter. They are there.'

'I know that is true and I understand that. Nanette was a one-stop-shop for you. You are not ready for a relationship yet. You are needy, and you are anxious, and you are using dating and women to fill this void in your life. You need to be more self-sufficient before you are ready for a proper relationship. You keep getting involved with women that aren't right for you. You find someone that ticks some of your boxes and then you are all in.'

'What was I like when I first came to you? It might be helpful to reflect on that.'

'You were highly anxious. You were depressed. You couldn't focus on anything else but your care of Nanette. You were very controlling. You were always "on". Never resting. You were video recording her at night. You were fighting so hard. I remember you were angry. You were furious with the nursing home. You were quite a prickly customer to deal with. You don't suffer fools.'

'What about after she passed. What was I like then?'

Caren slowed it down, hesitating over each word as it came to her. 'You were … Sad … Empty … Lonely … Tired … You were still angry. You were lost and bereft. You'd not only lost Nanette, but you'd also lost your purpose as well.'

'What about now as a comparison?'

'I think you are in an addictive phase. You are struggling with and addicted to not being alone. You are obsessively chasing women and company to mask the pain and loneliness.'

'Caren, I've had almost seven years living alone.'

'But you still had Nanette. You weren't really alone. You haven't had that long. I don't think you have accepted the loss yet. You were with her so long. It's hard in your fifties. It was a terrible shock, and the trauma and grief were prolonged because it went on for four years. However, you are making progress. You have got your humour back. In fact, I think you always kept that to some degree. You are more open to making friends and having new experiences. You are looking for connection and meaning in your life now.'

I paused, taking all that in. 'I'm going to see a psychic with a friend of mine,' I blurted out, expecting her to laugh in response.

'You?' Caren asked with a broad grin, knowing how sceptical I was.

'Yes, me. I am open to it. I am missing Nanette so much. I've just read this book about people close to death and others around them getting some sense or idea of it. What if she's out there? I want to try it. Plenty of people do. I would just like some hope.'

It's Caren's turn to be sceptical. She raises an eyebrow and can't help smiling. She knows me too well.

'Well, it will be an experience. We will have a nice day out together. Let's see what happens,' I say before she can say anything.

I pick Vashti up from her flat around 9am. As she climbs into my car, we look at each other with some nervous anticipation.

'Are you ready for this?' she asks in her happy voice. She's smiling and surveying me. We both feel like we are doing something a bit illicit, a bit on the edge. I would never have contemplated anything like this before.

'Yes I am. I don't know what will happen. I'm a little nervous about it.'

'I hope you don't get too overwhelmed by it, Dave.'

'Yeah, me too. But I guess if something like that happens that will be a good thing. I'd love it if I had some sense of Nan. Some contact with her. That would blow my mind and give me hope.'

'For sure.'

We are driving down to Mornington to meet up with Sheila, a psychic. She's the mother of one of Vashti's friends. As we drive, we compare our latest dating disasters and plans.

We make our way down the peninsula, following the beach road and after an hour or so, pull up at a 1970s brown brick home at the end of a cul-de-sac. Vashti goes in first. She's having a Reiki session. I'm not sure what that is exactly. Some kind of energy transference. She tells me to come back in ninety minutes, so I head off for the town centre to buy a few things and kill time. When I'm back, I'm too early and lay my driver's seat back and have a sleep. Eventually my phone pings and it's Vashti telling me to come in.

When I enter the house, I meet Sheila, who looks like a normal enough woman in her sixties, and Vashti is sitting on one of the lounge chairs, sipping some tea. Vash looks like she has been unconscious since I saw her. Like her mind has been completely blown. She is smiling and looking very relaxed.

'How was it? You look like you've had a big sleep,' I ask and tell her.

'It was incredible Dave,' says Vash.

It's my turn, and Vash leaves the room to have a rest elsewhere in the house. Sheila starts with some basic Reiki. She tells me to sit in a chair, close my eyes and breathe deeply. She walks around behind me and places her hands at various parts of my back, arms and head and is taking very deep breaths. When she exhales, she is blowing out the air. She starts singing. It's a little unnerving, but at least she is tuneful. After ten minutes or so, the Reiki part is over, and Sheila directs me to sit in a more comfortable lounge chair for our psychic consult.

'I will qualify with the two things I know about you David. You've lost your wife and you're writing a book,' Sheila says in her British accent. 'I did feel the energy of a beautiful lady beside you, and she was showing me you have been very lonely. She's giving me a feeling that she blesses whatever is to come for you and wants you to know she stands beside you. What was her name?'

'Nanette,' I respond a bit nervously.

'OK,' says Sheila and straight away 'is there a Josephine or Josie somewhere around you?'

We pause. I can't think of anyone. 'Could be someone still around you now. I feel she has a grandmotherly presence. A strong and direct person.'

'Joan?' I respond. 'That's my mother-in-law's name. She's still alive but getting near the end.'

'OK. I have the feeling that Nanette is spending an equal time with you and with Joan now.'

We talk about Joan getting older and needing greater physical help. She then calls the spirits back. She needs to do that. She asks me if I've come from a corporate background with problem solving and I've changed my focus. I tell her I have. She feels I'm trying to find my true purpose now, perhaps a bit over corporate stuff and feeling a bit tired. I tell her that's all true too. Sheila says it's given me financial security and choice. So far, she's right on the money.

Nan's telling her I need to make my home more of my own. We talk a bit about technology. I tell her I worked in IT but I'm over it. Sheila says the spirits are encouraging me towards nature. I'm like an elephant and nothing gets in my way, or I mow it down. Sometimes I get stuck and go around and around on things. I should use nature as a tool to clear these problems. She asks me about a connection with water. I answer that I'm swimming more now. In the bay.

Sheila talks about my connection with Vashti. Sheila senses we are like family members. We probably have a past life connection. We look out for each other. I tell her we had an instant connection. I tell Sheila I sometimes wonder if Nanette sent Vashti to be just the right friend at just the right time. There are similarities between the two of them I say. They aren't the same, but they are alike. Both Cancerians.

Strangely, Sheila starts talking about my lower back. Yes, I've had issues there I say, even just getting out of the car earlier. Try yoga, maybe Qi Gong, I don't think you love a gym she says. I don't.

'I get the feeling you are searching. That's what I get from the spirits.' I really am but of course I would be. That's what life is completely about now. 'Nanette comes around you in your sleep. Quite often you will wake up with thoughts around you. She gives you answers for questions and new inspiration.'

I tell her I do wake like that. Wake thinking of her. Then I feel sad I've lost her. Sheila says I haven't lost her though. I've lost her physically. She is still around me. Nanette tells her she had a wonderful life with me. She has no regrets. Nanette is waiting for me. She is happy for me to go forward in my life and gain new experiences. That will give us more to talk about when we are reunited.

Sheila says the spirits are encouraging me to travel. When I say I'm not keen, she encourages me to try some experiences different to the ones I've had. Off the beaten track, perhaps. I will know where they are. I might find a companion who wants to travel with me. I tell her there isn't anyone, but I would be open to it. We can't travel anyway because of COVID-19.

She starts talking about what I'm like in relationships. I'm conservative. I keep to myself. My friends are good friends and family is important. Nanette is telling her that I'm still waking up from a bad dream. *I wish it was a bad dream*, I'm thinking. And that I woke, and she is here. But she's not. It wasn't a dream. It happened.

Sheila is clairaudient, and the spirits interrupt her to say I should start my day with a cold press juicer. To get my vitamins. Probably because I'm not eating well enough. Our immune systems are compromised when grieving. Am I planning a cooking class? Not really, I say. She's encouraging me to try that. A good way to meet people as well.

Sheila hands it over to me and asks if I want to cover anything else. Will I have another permanent partner? The spirits are telling her I started too soon. It didn't serve me well nor did it serve the others. I made a few friendships through this. I have Nanette's blessing, but they are showing Sheila it is going to be a while before there is someone I can give my whole attention to or think seriously about. It's too early. I'm missing mostly the friendship part of the relationship she says.

Sheila tells me there has been a time I lost myself. I talk about being Nan's carer and not thinking there was much purpose after losing her. I don't think life can be as good again. What does Sheila think? She says it can be. She tells me to keep dating and having nice times. It's an awakening. There can be time for living. Life may not be as happy as with Nanette, but it can still be good.

By this time, an hour has gone by, and we have come to an end. We call Vashti in from the back room. She emerges looking a little anxious, no doubt wondering how it went. I give her a smile and tell her it was great.

When Vash and I walk out, we hug, and she wants to know what happened.

'It was really interesting. There was a lot of stuff that Sheila said that felt absolutely right. Honestly though, I didn't feel Nan's presence. I don't know what I should have expected, but that's what I was really hoping for. To have some direct feeling or sense that she was there in the room with me. I just wanted to really feel her again. Feel that she is still there Vash.'

I'm not disappointed as we make our way back up to Melbourne. I was hopeful of a direct connection but not really expecting it. I had a nice conversation with Sheila. I thought she was a very intuitive and insightful person. There were moments in the discussion where she said things that were perhaps just what I wanted to hear. Other moments where I perhaps drew a connection, but she was very close to the mark. There were even a couple of things that she said which I didn't connect with at the time, but that with more time I could see may have had meaning.

I've just done a health retreat for instance. We had daily Qi Gong sessions. I'd never heard of Qi Gong before. I found myself recently contemplating buying a house. Is that what she meant by Nan telling her to make my place more my own now?

All my life I would have been sceptical and chosen to see these as purely coincidences. But I know I'm searching. I know I constantly wonder whether Nan is out there somewhere waiting for me. I'd love to know that. To genuinely feel that. To have some connection, feeling or experience.

* * *

Three women here; Joan, Caren, and Vashti. All good women, all significant in the path out of grief to a new normal. Spirits of Nanette past, present and future. Joan, her mother, and Jill, her sister. Living connections to the Nanette I had and have now lost. They are the closest remaining beings to her, but not quite her. The sense of recognition of someone from a distance, then realisation it's not them once they approach. At very least, stability; the physical resemblances and reminders that Nanette was here, and still lives on through our shared memories and understandings of her.

Vashti, and Lisa, Anh, Lana and others. New female friends. Open doors to the future. All of them reminders of what I like in people and specifically in women. Nan; my best ever friend. Vashti et al; like her but not her. Warm, smart, soft, close, kind, fun, conversational, artistic, dependent and dependable. None of them her, but all good. All worthwhile. Multiple providers of female friendship rather than my one-stop-shop. Nan a permanent mainstay. Some will be permanent, others will pass with time. Elements of her but not her.

Caren, the bridge in the present from the past to the future. A roadmap. Mentor. Confidante, a wailing wall. Psychologist and professional, not family or friend. Tough when I need it, supportive when I need it, fun when I need it. Less expensive than a wife!

All of these to fill the void left by a great woman.

LOVE IS EVERLASTING

In February 2021, Premier Daniel Andrews called another immediate COVID-19 lockdown, this time for the state of Victoria. Living alone and through Melbourne's prolonged lockdown of 2020, I feared lockdowns more than I feared contracting COVID-19. Three months on since the great lockdown of 2020 ended, Victorians were just regaining confidence and had begun living again, but not for long.

As I made my way home by tram and foot through the CBD late that afternoon, I descended into a seething internalised rage and then a deep funk about more time locked down. I had a great week planned. John and Jenny were to visit, and we had booked tickets to the Australian Open Men's quarter final. It was a week to look forward to. But greater than the anger, was the fear of isolation and the possibility of extension to our confinement. They kept moving the goalposts last time.

Something of a false alarm, this lockdown concluded within the five days scheduled. Long enough to blow my plans though, and it made me determined to get out of the state of Victoria. I decided to drive to Canberra and Sydney to visit my sisters and friends Patrick, John, and Peewee. If another lockdown was called while I was away, I would keep travelling until the dust settled again.

Driving gave me flexibility and meant I could visit Nan at her grave in Albury. I also decided to return to Kogarah and St George Public Hospital while in Sydney.

I know I had a pilgrimage in mind. Finding ways to be back with Nan again, physically, and emotionally. Visit her at the cemetery in our hometown, go back to Sydney and key friends there, and to St George where we lived out that frightening and exhilarating two months almost seven years earlier in 2014.

I also contemplated catching up with Bernard, an ageing Catholic priest I had known since my youth. He'd lived in Sydney for over twenty years and had visited us at St George when Nan was still unconscious.

* * *

I'm more anxious as I pull up and park the car in the Albury cemetery. I felt that anxiety every morning I arrived at the nursing home, wondering how I would find her. Nothing more can go wrong for her now though. I'm still anxious, but anxious to be with her. Anxious to feel the calming wave of physical proximity wash over me like it usually does when I visit.

I get out of the car and remember I've left my phone in the glove box. As I lean across to retrieve it, Nan's sunglasses fall out. She had left them there. Such a natural place for them to be and a natural thing to happen in normal times. A personal item. They were her prescription. Her choice in fashion. They fell lightly to the car floor but heavily on me. She's not putting them on again. A telling blow to the guts as I am about to visit her grave. They've fallen out before like this with the same emotional impact and I've put them back each time to where she had left them. Another surprise awaiting me sometime in the future when I've forgotten about them again.

As I approach the grave there is a man attending to another one nearby. He hands me secateurs and offers to get me some water for the flowers I've brought for her. That's kind but I don't want him around when I'm visiting. I unwrap my flowers and fill the pot with water. Nan's grave is now fully grassed over, two and a half years since she passed. I do my usual poor job of flower arranging trying to make them sit nicely.

For privacy, I sit on the park bench ten metres away. As I look down the hill and over the cemetery, I see the building that houses the crematorium and the chapel where we had the short service the day we buried her. The day Joan called 'the saddest day of her life'. For me it was one of several.

Which one was the worst? That one? The day she died? The day of the first stroke? The day of the last one? The day I visited the funeral parlour and saw her for a few seconds with the casket open, then urged the funeral director back to close it again? All have a claim.

Eventually I begin to ease into the meditative state. Slowing, relaxing, becoming more still and memories flooding into my mind and my sight. My shoulders drop. My anxiety always seems to slip away when I am back here close to Nan again. I see her beautiful, youthful complexion. Her smiling face. I hear her voice and her laugh. I'm with her again.

I'm reliving a Christmas at Mum and Dad's. We are there with my siblings and their families. Uncle Fred and Auntie Biddy are there too. Nan is happy and everyone loves her. It's probably twenty-five years ago. I think of the awful possibility that I could yet have that long to live without her. It's too long. I don't want to be without her another minute, let alone years.

'I hope I go first,' we would say to each other, meaning neither of us wanted to be left without the other.

I walk back to the graveside. It's still hard to believe she is down there somewhere. It will probably never seem real. I feel like someone picked my pocket. It's happened, my wallet is gone. I'm amazed they got away with it and I didn't know it was happening. Almost three years on and I'm still shocked. Still dumbfounded. Still in disbelief.

I start to wonder what physical state she is in now. How long does decomposition take? I want to be in there with her, under a blanket of dirt to keep us warm and away from everything and everyone else.

I gradually return to my reverie and wonder where Nan is now.

'Were you in the room that day with the psychic Nanny?' I ask out loud.

I don't know. I feel closer to her here. The sun is shining and it's a beautiful day. Birds are chirping. Some cockatoos start to make a raucous din. I look up at the tree-covered hills around the cemetery. Nan used to ride her horses through there. A fitting place for her to be. No, she should be with me. She should be alive. It was way too early to lose her.

I remember them lowering Nan's casket down. They used manual ropes because there wasn't an automated system available that day. A momentary panic for me as one end seems too much lower than the other and I fear the casket will slip and fall. It's righted and then placed. We throw flower petals in. The others move away, and I crouch at the graveside for a last look in. I throw my funeral booklet for the service of the next day in with her.

I continue talking to her under my breath. I'm saying the same things I always do. Telling her I love her. I miss her so much. I think of her all the time. Life can't be as good as it was. I wish we had been in Melbourne when the stroke happened. I wish she had gone to the doctor more often, had her blood pressure checked and been on medication that might have averted all this. But maybe she'd had that condition where she suffered regular bleeds. Maybe nothing would have mattered.

I wish I was still looking after her. Wish I still had her, admittedly with more stability. Wish I hadn't asked for that sleep study to be done. Wish we hadn't had the shunt put in. Those things took her backwards, not forwards.

Caren keeps telling me I need to rebuild my life. Put more things in it. She says I was too dependent on Nan. She on me too. Now I'm completely lost without her. I'm not interested in anything much. Not even playing music now. Well, I guess tennis has been a positive addition. Maybe counselling or mentoring will be a worthwhile thing to do.

I turn my thoughts to being in Albury. I think about bumping into Nan's friends recently or having dinner with Patrick and Sandra and Cathy. I feel I have nothing to talk about. I feel the absence of my partner. My better half. I feel like a satellite out on my lonesome when I'm with couples. I'm sure my loss is acutely and glaringly obvious when people see me.

'I can't live here now Nanny. It's too quiet. It's eerie to be back in this town without you. I have been in every street and every place with you, multiple times. Wherever I go here I can't stop thinking about you and about the loss. I can't handle it here. I will never return here to live. I'll come here to be with you when I die.'

I know I will visit again on my way back from Sydney.

* * *

Local street and property signs show I'm in the suburb of Kogarah again. The railway line is to my left and I have entered a shopping area which must be the town centre. I notice a sign for parking and turn left and into an underground carpark.

After paying for a few hours, I find the lift and ascend a few floors to ground level. I exit the building and find myself in a town square. It feels kind of familiar. I look around and notice I'm standing in front of the library. The Clive James Library and Service Centre. I'm instantly taken back to my birthday in 2014. I had a massage nearby and then killed some time in the library during a hospital rest period. One of those days when my hotel was suburbs away and I needed a break. I found a quiet chair in the library and slept. Just like a homeless man. I was itinerant and with Nan unconscious and on the brink, effectively homeless.

The library helps me get my bearings. I know to turn around to find the street I walked many times to the back of the hospital. Across the road is a Greek Orthodox Church. One Saturday on my way to Nan there was a large wedding group exiting the church. They were happy. I wasn't.

I'm on Belgrave Street and decide to turn left to find the railway station. There is a pub to my immediate left. The Dank Tavern. Patrick and I ate in there the last night before Nan and I left for Melbourne.

At the end of Belgrave Street, I turn right and see the train station. Above that is the Woolworths where I would buy essentials. Back then, I ate lunch and dinner in cafés but needed stuff for breakfast and toiletries. I remember the feeling of utter chaos and a near anxiety attack every time I went into the supermarket. Too much noise, too many people. A normal activity and normal experience but normalisation wasn't possible against the terror and trauma I was feeling. I decide not to relive that experience and round the block to pass the police station and then cut back into Belgrave Street.

I want to find the café where I ate a lot of meals and the kindly owner consoled me on that terrible first day. The layout of the suburb is exactly as I remembered it. I can see the back of the hospital looming ahead as I make my way up Belgrave towards the café.

The café is gone. In its place is an Asian food shop called Golden Chopstick. It's hard to believe it's not there and I walk past the shop and back again to double-check. To my regret, it is gone. I had hoped to find the owner and say hello and talk to him. Next door was a sandwich shop. It is still there. I guess more profitable, but they were certainly less hospitable when I bought food there.

Disappointed, I make my way towards the back of the hospital.

There are COVID-19 vaccination signs up at the back, so I don't enter. I walk along the side to the front entrance. As I do so, I am transported back to the sadness of 2014. I walked that route many times on my way to Nan, and the fear, sadness and foreboding are back with me.

When I round the corner at the front, I see Bezzina House. I look immediately up at the hospital, looking for the window that was Nan's room in the neurosurgery department. The room from which I could look out and see Kogarah Bay and Cronulla.

I crossed the road to Bezzina House and walked tentatively to the front door. I paused for a moment and then knocked. I wondered if Natalie would be there, and I could say hello. No one answered. I knocked again but no luck. As I walk away, the security gate is open and I can see down the balcony and the rooms, one of which I stayed in. Again, it looks exactly as I recall.

I walk back to the hospital front entrance, wondering if COVID-19 means I won't be allowed in. There is no restriction other than the need to check-in and I enter. The hospital has had a major revamp but structurally its essence is the same. Reception has moved to the left. It looks more professional.

I know I'm looking for her again. Or ways to feel I am with her again. Here in this place almost seven years before, I experienced the most traumatic period of my life, but I still had her then. There was still hope. Then she seemed to recover and there was even greater cause for hope.

There don't seem to be any restrictions on movement in the hospital, so I take a lift to the first floor to find the intensive and critical care units. It's all changed. The waiting room is there but it's now a reception for an early pregnancy assessment service. Ironic that its purpose is now oriented to the other end of the spectrum of life. From a place where lives involuntarily ended or came close to it, to a place where lives have just begun. Perhaps a way to psychologically freshen up, although intensive care can and did bring good outcomes and I'm sure early pregnancy assessments often bring sadness and decisions to be made.

We don't know what we want until we are faced with decisions. Decisions force us to be clear on what we want even if we don't want to have to make them. Even if we hadn't thought fully about the need to make them. But one thing we do know is that we want the freedom to choose.

Unlike in 2014, the doors which were then the entrance to intensive care are now wide open. It's not intensive care anymore. I look inside and down a corridor but decide not to enter. It doesn't look as I remember the entrance area, and I don't feel it's right to go in.

I take the elevator back to the ground floor and find out where intensive care is now. It's in a large newly-expanded area of the hospital but I don't want to go there. That's not where it all happened. It happened on the first floor, where I was. I am a religious pilgrim visiting the holy sites. This place is holy to me. This place and the people in it saved Nanette's life and gave us almost four more years together. They gave Nan a second life. It was short, it wasn't perfect, but there was love and we were together for longer than we otherwise might have been.

I've seen enough of the hospital and of Kogarah generally, so I walk down Belgrave again towards my car. In doing so, I stumble on the Italian restaurant where I went that evening Nan responded more fully. I was an apostle spreading the good news to the junior doctors dining there. Then to Stuart the neurosurgery registrar when he walked past. He returned later to confirm Nan's responsiveness. That was a happy place then.

The restaurant is called Amici. The pizza oven is there in a brick wall on the corner. The dining space is an area shared with other food shops along the corridor to the side of the Kogarah town square. It's just after lunch time on a Thursday in Kogarah. The place is not busy like it was that Saturday evening. In fact, it's quiet.

By now, I have retraced my steps and visited the sacred sites of

2014. Kogarah seems smaller than I recall it. The distances shorter. Probably everything just seemed harder then, carrying the weight of trauma with me. The place looks the same but on the closer scrutiny of this visit there has been change. Time has changed it. Some, but not all of it.

Life and people have moved on. It's six and a half years, so of course things have moved on. People I remembered from the time may not even be alive now. I wanted everything to be preserved as I remembered it. I wanted the café to be there. I wanted intensive care to be there and the people like Rania and Colleen to be there. I wanted Andrew and Raju to be there too. I wanted everyone focused on bringing Nan back to me. Most of all, I wanted Nan to be there. I want her to be here now.

* * *

Bernard became parish priest at my local Catholic church sometime during my teen years. He remained there until I was in my late thirties, when he decided to move away. I suspect no longer able to tolerate the arch conservatism of the church and the diocese that Albury belonged to. He was a standout among the priests that floated in and out of Albury. He was a late vocation, educated in Boston and highly intelligent. The others by comparison were often dopey misfits, steeped in fundamentalist ideas after their time in the backwater of Wagga seminary.

When my father died in 2006, I was able to contact Bernard and asked him to come to Albury to celebrate the funeral. He flew down from Sydney to do that. When Nan became ill in 2014, I made contact again, even though Nan wasn't Catholic.

Bernard came then to St George Hospital to visit Nan and me. Nan was still unconscious at the time. Bernard anointed her and said a few prayers and then we went to lunch in the café at the back of St George.

I maintained occasional contact with him from then on and spoke to him when things looked very grim in 2017, and then again after Nan passed a year later in 2018. I was hopeful that he might celebrate Nan's funeral too, but he declined, citing age at that time. We had a nice discussion all the same.

I spoke to Bernard again when my mum passed away in 2019 as well but didn't attempt to persuade him back to Albury for the funeral. He was by then eighty-eight years old and winding back his commitments.

Each time I called him, we had long discussions and he encouraged me to call him for lunch should I make it to Sydney again. So, with my trip to Sydney planned, I decided to phone him to see if we could meet for that lunch.

Bernard wasn't available to meet. We got talking though, and I told him I was still trying to find my way in life, almost three years after losing Nan.

'You had a wonderful marriage, David,' he said. 'You did absolutely everything possible for her.'

'She was a great person, Bernard. I was very lucky to have her and then very unlucky to lose her,' I responded.

'Do you still feel her David?' Bernard asked.

'I don't know Bernard. I know I still love her. I know I always will. I know I'd still be looking after her if I could.'

Afterwards, I wondered what he really meant by that. Do people experience some strong ghost or spirit-like presence of a deceased loved one? Did he know of occasions where people had been in contact with them? Was I missing out on something? I was contemplating calling to ask but didn't get around to it before I left for my trip.

So, when Bernard phoned to say he could meet after all, I was keen to talk further. We agreed on lunch at the City Tattersalls Club in Sydney, and he made a booking.

'Bernard, what did you mean when you asked me whether I still feel Nanette?' I asked him soon after we had ordered our meals and completed the initial small talk.

'Well,' he said. 'Do you still think about Nan a lot?'

'All the time,' I responded.

'Do you ride emotional highs and lows when you think of times with her and times without?'

'Absolutely I do.'

'Do you talk to her David?'

'Actually Bernard, I do all the time. I often tell her I miss her, or I love her, or I might say something to her like 'What am I going to do now, Nanny?''

'Well, I suppose that feels like you are praying to her, does it?'

'Yes, yes it does. I mean I don't want to sound disrespectful to your faith or God or anything but that's exactly what it's like. It's like she's my little god or a saint or something and I'm talking to her.'

Bernard sat back with a half-smile at this point and opened his palms and gave a kind of shrug.

'David,' he said. 'That just shows, love is everlasting. There has to be something in that.'

BANG. No one had been able to put it quite so well for me before. I knew I would always love Nan. I feel it now and whenever I think of her. I feel her physically. No wonder people always bring the heart into it because that's where I feel it. Deep in the centre left of my chest and into my gut as well. I had always thought that what I felt was just sadness, longing, and loss.

It's not necessary that I have some apparition, a dream, feel her touch or hear her voice. But my body has a reaction to the thought of her. A physical one. Loss and longing are part of it, but there is a genuine physical reaction. Bernard is right. I do still feel her. It's the love. I am still bonded to her. Her impact to me and on me is there and will always be there. I love her still and love is everlasting.

I remember how I felt that day on the train station at Arncliffe. Nan was comatose in intensive care. The situation looked hopeless. I contemplated whether there was any point in continuing to live. I felt like half of me was gone, half of me carved out. Hollowed. Was I replicating how Nan would feel after the stroke? They always talked about left side neglect or loss. Or was I feeling she was gone? Was she gone then and later came back again? I felt her then too, or I felt the absence of her.

The discussion with Bernard was a profound encounter for me. It is OK to keep talking to Nanny. I need to. Our bond and link will always be there, and I can pray to her in my way like she is my own patron saint: Saint Nan. I don't pray to ask for stuff. I pray to talk to her, to not let go of her. To maintain my everlasting love for her. To maintain contact with her wherever she is on her cosmic journey. To keep her with me always. It's not something I have to force myself to do. I just do it.

It's easier to pray to her than to God in fact. God is an abstract notion. Nan was a human being like we all are. Nan was here. I married her, hugged her, made love to her, laughed with her, talked, consoled, argued with, slept next to, woke next to, learned from, taught, cared for and was cared for by her.

Most importantly, I loved her to her very core. I wanted to be completely consumed and internalised by her. To become one of her own vital organs. I became her voice and her brain when she lost the ability to speak for herself and take key decisions for herself. I became hers. Another of her faculties. Completely at her disposal. Completely for her purpose.

I feel her for sure. That feeling deep in my chest and gut when I think of her must be like what an amputee feels when they lose a limb. They still feel the limb. I still feel Nan even though she has been amputated from me. I think she feels the same way. Wherever she is. Hopefully she will pull me towards her like a planet pulls its inhabitants with gravity. Pull me to you Nanny. Any time from now is fine.

People would say time to move on, but there is no time when it's right to move on. You can't move on. That's not to say there can't or won't be new or future loves or likes or experiences. But I don't have to move on.

I feel her in another way when I visit her graveside. It's another holy site for me. I pray to her there. The anxiety I constantly carry seems to dissipate. It's where her physical remains were laid. It's where I will one day be too. We will be together at least in that way. I feel a deepening calm as anxiousness strips away from me. I talk to her and remember her. Images float into my mind of times and memories past. That's feeling her too.

I think it's why I don't sleep well. The anxiety because she's not there next to me. I'm feeling that physical separation. Separation anxiety. Perhaps I would sleep better at her graveside. Some people sleep with an article of clothing of their lost one, so they have something to touch, feel and smell.

After Nan died in 2018, Cabrini Hospital offered me a referral to a prominent psychiatrist. I will call him James. He was described to me as a world class authority on grief and loss. I was already seeing Caren but thought it wouldn't hurt to get another perspective.

He was in his sixties, bespectacled and fair-haired but with a touch of ginger. I found him warm and welcoming. He had obviously done some homework before we met and congratulated me on the rare achievement of a long marriage.

He asked a lot of questions about how I was then spending my time, a month or two after her passing. He asked me about my background and sleeping and what had gone on. We talked a bit about our marriage. I noticed him watching me closely as I spoke.

'You will be OK,' he suddenly announced maybe thirty minutes into our discussion. I think he had been appraising whether I was a risk to myself.

'James, I keep talking to her. Keep wanting to tell her I love her and trying to keep her close. What do you think of that? Is that nuts?'

'That's not mad!' he responded adamantly.

As we talked further, and given we were in a Catholic institution, I developed an inkling about James.

'Are you Catholic James?' I asked.

'Yes I am.'

'Are you a practising Catholic?' I probed.

'Somewhat,' he said.

I liked that answer: somewhat. I don't go to church and haven't since my dad died. I have been much happier since I made the decision not to. It had nothing to do with the many issues around child sexual abuse. It predated that. It was a complete loss of faith in God and afterlife. It was also a rejection of the notion that people on earth know the mind of God and the arrogant right to judge accordingly.

I believe religions have something to offer. Community, ethical principles, spiritual comfort, and hope. But they can't offer certainty. They can't offer absolutes or another 'ab' word: absolution. They don't therefore have the right to dictate what is right and wrong. Things are always greyer than that. Well, they can't offer me those things. They might be able to give them to others.

'Do you believe in an afterlife James?' I asked him. 'You're a scientific guy and most people in your situation don't. Given I've lost Nanette, I'd like your view. I wonder if I can ever be with Nan again.'

He paused for a moment, looked down and then up, moved his head from side to side. Then responded a little tentatively.

'I believe that some reunion of minds or spirits somewhere in the universe is a possibility.'

BANG. He had his own conclusion. His own hope and he gave me hope. A scientific guy who still had faith or hope. He wasn't pushing a certainty. We just can't be certain.

'I hope that's at least the case,' I responded. 'In fact, I can't quite call myself a believer. I've been in every position on this stuff. A believer, an atheist, an agnostic and now I consider myself just a hoper. I hope that one day I can be with Nanette again. I don't think life can ever be as good without her.'

When I played that view to Caren, she would interject that I don't know that life can't be as good. 'You might meet someone where you are just as happy. That you love just as much. You don't know what's in front of you.'

'I doubt that. I doubt that life can be as good. I'm open to it and it would be nice, but I think I was very blessed with the woman I had. I doubt there is anyone as perfect for me as Nanette was.'

Caren is not so quick to make that point any more. I think she sees that the size of the relationship and the size of the loss may not be repeatable or replaceable. She knows me and knows I won't take just anyone. Even if I am lonely.

'Well, you have to remember you had a very long time with Nanette. Any other relationship or friendship that you start now has been just the tiniest period by comparison.'

After leaving Sydney, I return to Canberra to see my sisters again. I also teed up lunch with Peewee. I was keen to talk with him about my discussion with Bernard. Peewee is a very spiritual person and has a deep faith. He's the most assured of an afterlife and God of anyone I have spoken to in my adult life.

'I'm certain of it. I know you will be together again,' he once said to me. He's an intelligent and reflective man. He is no fool. It's nice to have someone that still gives you hope in a world full of people quick to announce their atheism like some kind of trophy to their intelligence.

When we meet for lunch at Federal Golf Club in Canberra, I update him on my latest dating tragedies and talk about this modern-day penchant for the declaration of atheism.

'Pete, it's all ego. It's people bigging themselves up declaring they are atheistic. They are trying to say how intelligent they are. Next time someone wants to knock being a believer and proudly declares their atheism, ask them to give you the scientific explanation of the origins of the universe and human life. Firstly, they won't be able to, and secondly there are leaps of faith in any scientific explanation still. Ask them to explain consciousness. Ask them to explain the brain. When they talk about the marvel of medical science and science generally, tell them you know someone who has seen this stuff up close and remains quite underwhelmed.'

I realise I'm getting a bit worked up and carried away. I return to tell him of my discussion with Bernard about praying to Nan and that love is everlasting.

'Dave, I'm really glad that you've been able to maintain that relationship with Bernie and that he's been able to give you such a spiritual boost.'

I then tell him I can't really believe but I can hope.

'Well Dave,' says Peewee. 'The bible says it's faith, hope and love.'

BANG. Another moment. Well said, Pete. I hereby canonise you in advance as Saint Peewee in my new Church of Nan. I won't go as far as saying I have the faith bit, but definitely the hope and definitely the love. Bernard gave me the right to keep praying, and the reminder that love is everlasting. James, the hope of a spiritual reunion somewhere in the universe. That's scientific enough for me.

We had miracles. Nan becoming conscious again after so long in a coma. Then when she began responding. When she talked. When she wrote. When she drew or coloured with crayons and pencils. When she laughed, perhaps the most beautiful miracle of all to witness. When she gave hospital staff the three variants of her own 'royal wave'. When she stuck her middle finger up at Lucy. When she began eating again and enjoying her food. When she held my hand or stroked my neck. When she stabilised again after a cerebellum bleed and survived another year, despite losing her speech and ability to swallow. When she sat surrounded by her family, holding her mother's hand for Christmas lunch that final time at the nursing home in 2017. Miracles aplenty. Tragedy as well, but so many miracles and what a privilege to have had her for a 'Second Life'.

Prayers are offered hourly to my deity. I pray to her first thing in the morning and last thing at night. Not everyone needs to honour her this frequently. Prayers can be offered in whatever format one desires. It might be to remember her or talk to her. We are a very informal institution this early in our life. This church may not remain for thousands or even hundreds of years. It will most likely lapse with my own passing, but who knows? It might catch on.

My home will remain a shrine to Nanette. Perhaps I should also name it St Peter's after our first saint (Peewee) too. Or St Peewee's Basilica instead. That has a ring to it that I like. Yes, it is loaded with my own collection of relics, and it will remain that way. Nan's artworks will continue to adorn the walls. The other art, furniture, rugs, and many ornaments that she lovingly accumulated will also stay. They are all holy relics now.

Dogs, cats, horses, in fact all animals can be church members and saints as well. She loved them as much as humans. Hester I can safely assume, is a saint who rightfully and faithfully takes her place at Nan's right-hand side, looking at each other when it is well before time to go to bed. Nan's big bay horse Sam would not qualify behaviourally as a saint in many of our known religions, but I'm sure Nan will manage a justification for him too.

I ask people I meet to tolerate my religion. I won't force it on anyone else. Everyone can have their own beliefs and their very own 'Nan' to whom they pray. But I ask that people respect my right to maintain my beliefs. I am now a committed Nanian.

I can have relationships with women. They will have to accept my religion. It doesn't mean I can't love them too. Just like a parent loves multiple children, I can love multiple women. The point is, there will always be another woman: Nan. I would be polyamorous with my love. Always in a love triangle. I ask you to accept and not judge.

My concept of heaven or an afterlife is to be reunited in mind and spirit with Nan somewhere in the cosmos. We will be free to spend our time doing the things we loved. Just being together, riding horses, walking our dogs on the beach, listening to music where we take turns to choose. Without the physical constraint of bodies, our existence can be timeless. There will be no illness and no sadness.

We will take communion by somehow imbibing the sumptuous feasts that Nan will lovingly prepare. Her cooking by that time will have graduated from restaurant grade into and beyond the cosmos where Michelin Stars are awarded and abound.

I will keep talking to her. I will always feel her. Our love is everlasting. I know she is waiting for me. We will be together again.

27 August 2021, seven years on.

THE AUTHOR

David Hoysted was born in Albury, NSW. When David at age 22 was diagnosed with testicular cancer, his then girlfriend, Nanette Parker was constantly at his side. After marrying, they had no children but always maintained a menagerie of pets, including horses, dogs and cats. Both David and Nan pursued creative interests; Nan was a visual artist and David a keen amateur musician, playing both piano and guitar. In 2020, David enrolled in a Bachelor Of Music at Monash University majoring in Jazz Piano. David had a successful career in IT, including twenty years with the Mars Corporation where he rose to the senior-most IT position in Asia–Pacific. When Nan became ill in 2014, David became her carer until her passing in 2018. David currently resides in South Yarra, Melbourne.

David, Nan and Hester, December, 2013. Eight months before Nan's stroke.